"It will inspire readers everywhere to remain sober until they've finished." —Michael Lewis, author of *Liar's Poker* and *The New New Thing*

"Deep down, all guys are searching for the Perfect Beer Joint. Ken Wells was a late starter but he has grasped the principles: a pint to procrastinate; don't drink to forget—drink to remember; drink to digress. *Travels with Barley* is a keen elucidation of beer and the passions that surround it, and Wells digresses with real flair." —Michael Jackson, the "Beer Hunter"

"Wells belongs in the beer guy's hall of fame." —*The Montreal Gazette*

"A compelling, sprightly sociological description of what Wells dubs the 'River of Beer.'" —*The Baltimore Sun*

"Thoreau said, 'The tavern will compare favorably with the church.' Following this premise rather closely . . . Wells searches for his preferred house of worship: the 'Perfect Beer Joint.' Along the way, Wells encounters quirky characters, and the pages he devotes to describing brewers, bar proprietors, bartenders, and plain ol' beer drinkers prove he's more interested in beer people (84 million Americans drink beer) than the industry itself. Wells's storytelling abilities complement his journalist's eye for stats and facts, making this a humorous, lively, and informational tour." —*Publishers Weekly*

"Ken Wells is the engaging Everyman of beer . . . but his quest to find the Perfect Beer Joint delivers more than beer: *Travels with Barley* is a perceptive and affectionate essay on everyday American culture through the lens of a beer glass." —Julie Johnson Bradford, *All About Beer*

continued . . .

"Wells writes with wit."
—St. Louis Post-Dispatch

"Wells has a nice touch, and he brings gentle humor and innate friendliness to his quest...His travels make for an enjoyable and interesting trip."
—The Miami Herald

"This account of journeys through the soft beer belly of America exudes that expansive happiness that springs from a guy who is truly enjoying his bottle of brew."
—Kirkus Reviews

"Wells is a literate and entertaining guide."
—South Florida Sun-Sentinel

"Finally, a beer book that doesn't labor over beer styles and mind-numbing tasting notes. Wells has written a witty, informative, easy-to-read book."
—Gregg Glaser, Yankee Brew News

"A witty, informative narrative."
—New Orleans Times-Picayune

"Interesting stuff."
—The Idaho Statesman

"A subversive and terribly well-written book about beer culture in America...This is the kind of responsible, believable book craft beer needs as an introduction to the mainstream drinking public. Everyone should go out and buy a copy for their unenlightened beer brethren."
—Lew Bryson, Ale Street News

Travels with Barley

Barley

The Quest for the Perfect Beer Joint

KEN WELLS

BERKLEY BOOKS, NEW YORK

THE BERKLEY PUBLISHING GROUP
Published by the Penguin Group
Penguin Group (USA) Inc.
375 Hudson Street, New York, New York 10014, USA
Penguin Group (Canada), 90 Eglinton Avenue East, Suite 700, Toronto, Ontario M4P 2Y3, Canada
(a division of Pearson Penguin Canada Inc.)
Penguin Books Ltd., 80 Strand, London WC2R 0RL, England
Penguin Group Ireland, 25 St. Stephen's Green, Dublin 2, Ireland (a division of Penguin Books Ltd.)
Penguin Group (Australia), 250 Camberwell Road, Camberwell, Victoria 3124, Australia
(a division of Pearson Australia Group Pty. Ltd.)
Penguin Books India Pvt. Ltd., 11 Community Centre, Panchsheel Park, New Delhi—110 017, India
Penguin Group (NZ), 67 Apollo Drive, Rosedale, North Shore 0632, New Zealand
(a division of Pearson New Zealand Ltd.)
Penguin Books (South Africa) (Pty.) Ltd., 24 Sturdee Avenue, Rosebank, Johannesburg 2196,
South Africa

Penguin Books Ltd., Registered Offices: 80 Strand, London WC2R 0RL, England

The publisher does not have any control over and does not assume responsibility for author or
third-party websites or their content.

Published by arrangement with Free Press, a division of Simon & Schuster, Inc.

PRINTING HISTORY
Wall Street Journal Books hardcover edition / October 2004
Berkley trade paperback edition / April 2008

Library of Congress Cataloging-in-Publication Data

Wells, Ken.
    Travels with barley : the quest for the perfect beer joint / Ken Wells.
        p. cm.
    Originally published: New York, Free Press, c2004.
    Other title information on prev. ed.: A journey through beer culture in America.
    Includes bibliographical references and index.
    ISBN 978-0-425-21953-9 (alk. paper)
    1. Beer—United States.   2. Breweries—United States—History.   3. Bars (Drinking
establishments)—United States.   4. Beer industry—United States—History.   I. Title.

TP577.W44 2008
641.2'30973—dc22

                                                                                            2007041590

PRINTED IN THE UNITED STATES OF AMERICA

10   9   8   7   6   5   4   3   2   1

For Al Delahaye, mentor, benevolent drill sergeant, and friend, whose imparted wisdom about reporting, writing, and life continues to serve me well; and for Ray Dill, now retired, and the late John B. Gordon, fine men and stalwarts of scrappy community journalism, who first opened the door to my life's work.

Contents

Beer is proof that God loves us and wants us to be happy.
—Benjamin Franklin

Foreword

Beer is, unofficially, the national adult beverage of the United States of America. There are more beer drinkers in this country than there are wine drinkers or liquor drinkers...and that is a beautiful thing. Okay, I own a brewery, so I might be a little biased. But I think you'll agree with me after you read this book—after you read this story told *by* Ken Wells but really *through* the incredible people he encounters on his journey down the River of Beer.

You won't soon forget the colorful cast of characters in this book. People like Joe Gilchrist, who presides over the insanity that is the annual Mullet Toss at his timeless roadhouse, the Bama. Or Jimmy Paige, the Grand Wazoo of the Dixie Cup Homebrewing competition. Or Michael Jackson, the world's foremost beer expert, who reminds Ken, "The more macho the bar, the wimpier the beer." What makes these stories so special is the way Ken brings us right into the thick of them. Ken doesn't just watch the mullet toss, he busts out his stopwatch and times the jaw-dropping pace of hundreds of beers being served per hour. He doesn't just attend the Dixie Cup, but sits down elbow to elbow with seasoned judges to rate some great and some not-so-great homemade beers. Throughout his journey he shows that the love of American beer culture is inseparable from the love of American beer people.

But during his quixotic quest for the Perfect Beer Joint, Ken never loses sight of the fact that there is no such thing as the world's "best" beer. All beer is good. It's just that different beers taste better to different people. American beer is as colorful, diverse, and varied as the American populace itself. Ken applies that open-minded enthusiasm to all aspects of American beer culture that he encounters—from the most technical to the most folksy—with candor, intelligence, and chutzpah. When you read this book, you feel like you're listening to a story told by an old friend whom you've met at your local pub, eager to share his latest epic adventure over a few frosty pints. It's a story as deeply embedded in American culture as the Mississippi River itself.

Some of you might not realize that we came close to losing the color, diversity, and distinction of our beer culture. In the decades leading up to Prohibition, nearly every town in America had at least one local brewery. The experience of the local beer culture was woven into the fabric of the townspeople's daily lives, and these small breweries produced beers that reflected the ethnic and social character of the townspeople. But by the time Prohibition ended, there were fewer than 100 breweries left in this nation. Those that survived and thrived in this new era did so by growing into regional and national powerhouses. They relied on economies of scale and focused on the production of very light, less-flavorful lager beers that appealed to a wider market. But in the seventies, eighties, and nineties a bunch of pioneers, whom you will meet in this book—folks like Fritz Maytag of the Anchor Brewery and Jim Koch of Boston Beer Company—brought the excitement of diversity and experimentation back into American beer culture.

America is now in the midst of a craft brewing renaissance. Today, people want to know where their beer came from. They want to connect to the people who make it and sell it and drink it—they are looking for a transaction on a more human scale. Small is the new big. For instance, my own company, Dogfish Head Craft Brewery in coastal Delaware, opened thirteen years ago with the same mission that we have today: Off-centered ales for off-centered people. We have always made beers that are winelike in alcohol content and complexity, using nontraditional ingredients like raisins, chicory, and peaches. When we started, not many people knew or cared about our exotic beers, so we really struggled; but we stuck to our guns and brewed the kind of beer we wanted to drink. Our little company is now one of the fastest-growing breweries in the country, thanks to consumers trading up and demanding more from their beer.

Now, happy days are here again. Today there are over 1,300 commercial breweries in the United States. Every sizable town has a brewery that reflects the local color and character of the townspeople. In fact, the average American lives within 10 miles of a local brewery (just for comparison's sake, the average American lives over 100 miles away from the closest distillery or winery). Remember, whereas wine-making either succeeds or fails at the whim of Mother Nature—the ground, the climate, the harvest—beer making is a decidedly human endeavor. People make the beer. People drink the beer. As modern brewers, we all have nearly equal access to the world's highest quality ingredients; it's what we do with them that makes our beverages special. And as modern beer drinkers, we all have nearly equal access to the world's best beers. Take a trip to your local beer store and notice the proliferation of different styles and brands. Go ahead...cheat on your go-to beer. Broaden your horizons, and you'll be amazed and surprised by the quality, distinction, and diversity of the brews out there, regardless of your socio-economic background or geographic location.

I offer you this as a closing thought: Generally, beer drinkers fall into one of three categories. Beer Folk account for the vast majority of beer drinkers, who drink it because they like it, simple as that. Then there are the Beer Snobs, people who learn a lot about beer only to lord their wisdom over those who aren't as knowledgeable. Luckily, they make up the smallest contingent. Lastly, there are the Beer Geeks, those of us who are obsessed with beer—maniacal about trying more beers, learning more about beer, and turning our friends on to our newfound beer experiences. I think it's safe to say that Ken Wells began his journey as Beer Folk but ended it as Beer Geek. It's amazing how much he learns about beer between the covers of this book, and it's amazing how adeptly and respectfully he translates this knowledge to the reader. I got to know Ken as he wrote this book and spent some time with me and my coworkers at Dogfish Head. We've become good friends. Over the course of hundreds of e-mails, many visits, a few late nights, and more than a few shared pints, I bore witness to his transformation from Beer Folk to Beer Geek. It has been a most beautiful transformation, and he is now as much of a hophead as I am.

Be careful. Reading this book and seeking out the wide range of beers and beer joints described within may turn you into a Beer Geek, too.

—Sam Calagione, owner, Dogfish Head Craft Brewery, and author of *Brewing Up a Business*, *Extreme Brewing*, and *Beer or Wine?*

Helpful Clues About Brews

Beer.   The beverage admired by both Ben Franklin and Norm at Cheers; pizza's amiable companion; the bestselling adult drink in America (and the world). It is typically made with malt (germinated, dried barley), hops, water, and yeast. Unless it's Extreme Beer*—then it could be made with almost anything.

And bear in mind as you travel down the River of Beer that the River divides into two major beer channels:

Ale.   The world's oldest beer style, loved by pharaoh and Pilgrim alike; the beer of Shakespeare and the British pub; the beer that arrived here on the *Mayflower* in 1620 but was largely chased from the American beerscape two centuries later by the beer juggernaut known as lager. Derisive (and ignorant) American drinkers often put down ale as "that warm British beer," but ale—meant to be served at cellar temperatures—has undergone a makeover, notably at the hands of American and new-wave British craft brewers who will even serve it to you slightly

---

* For a definition of Extreme Beer, please refer to the glossary of beer terms at the end of this book.

chilled. Technically, ale is brewed from top-fermenting yeast that work best at warm temperatures; it is characterized by an earthy, fruity flavor and a wide color spectrum. Well-known modern examples: Sierra Nevada Pale Ale and Bass Ale.

Lager.   The clear, golden beer that, thanks mostly to the Czechs and Germans, conquered the world and nowadays accounts for 95 percent of all beer consumption worldwide; the beer synonymous (in America) with the beach, the ballpark, and the frat party. Lager is brewed cold from yeast that ferments near the bottom of fermentation tanks; it gobbles up more fermentable sugars than does ale yeast, producing a taste that most palates discern as crisper, cleaner, and drier than ale's. Pilsner Urquell was the world's first clear, golden lager. Well-known modern examples: Budweiser, Corona, and Miller Lite.

Travels with Barley

Introduction
Why Beer, Why Me?

They who drink beer will think beer.
—Washington Irving

I was eleven years old, sitting on the front porch steps next to my father on a summer's day, when I took my first sip of beer, Pa holding the can for me so I wouldn't get carried away. Maybe he knew something. It was a Falstaff and it was warm. We lived in a hot, sweltering place in Louisiana's Cajun Delta way below New Orleans. A cold thing cracked open didn't stay cold long down there.

I didn't care. I took a big swig anyway.

Pa drank Falstaff because, cold, it wasn't all that bad, and because it was cheap, and mostly because Falstaff sponsored the Major League Baseball Game of the Week every Saturday afternoon on television. I was one of six brothers, and all old enough to talk were rabid baseball fans. We'd just gotten our first TV, a piece of heavy dark furniture with big, yellow-trimmed plastic knobs and a tiny screen in the middle. Out where we lived in the country, the reception was iffy. But if somebody went outside and twisted the antenna in just the right direction toward the station in New Orleans while somebody inside watched and yelled when the picture came into focus, we could catch a mildly snowy black-and-white broadcast of the game.

Pee Wee Reese and Dizzy Dean did the play-by-play. We liked them both, but Dizzy Dean was particularly important because (a) he would sing "The Wabash Cannon Ball," one of my dad's favorite songs, during the Seventh Inning Stretch, and (b) my grandfather Wells had briefly played semipro ball against a young Dizzy and his brother Paul back in Arkansas, where my dad, grandfather, and the Deans all were from.

Pa's way of thinking was that Falstaff wasn't just sponsoring the ball game—it was helping out Arkansas folk that we practically knew. (This is how Arkansas people thought, and I couldn't see anything wrong with it.) Pa would now and then go for a Pabst Blue Ribbon and, when he had a little extra money, Miller High Life in a bottle. But he was loyal to Falstaff till the competition and the money men eventually drove the company into the ground.

At first, I didn't know quite what to think about my swig of beer—mostly it startled me. In retrospect, I'm sure the jolt I felt was actually the foamy, mildly bitter pop of hops in the back of my mouth. But beer vapors ran up my nose and my ears turned red and my scalp tingled and chills ran down my spine. What little I knew of sin, this seemed like it.

Though I didn't become a regular beer drinker until I entered college, I've been a Beer Guy at heart ever since that moment—that's kind of how it is with Beer People. To this day, in fact, most of my friends are Beer People, too.

Now, I admit there is a question as to what exactly a Beer Person is and stands for, and it was one of the questions that got me pondering when a *Wall Street Journal* colleague first suggested that, far beyond writing an article or two, I should look into writing an *entire book* about beer. With a publisher keenly interested, this was something that obviously required deep and unconventional thinking, especially after checking the landscape and finding it already littered with beer books. Most of them are about beer tasting; some are about beer history; some are about the beer industry or beer marketing or beer barons or some aspect thereof. As subjects, all are worthy, as are many of the books that have sprung from them, yet none of these subjects individually interested me as a writer. But it did occur to me that there might be a more eclectic way to look at beer that included elements of all of the above but strove to get inside the passion that I first brushed up against in that beer jolt I got as a kid. For lack of a better term, I proposed a look at beer culture in America, which I saw as inextricably tied up with Beer People.

If you tell people you're writing a book, their first question is usually, "What's it about?" But as I moved around the country in the reporting of this project, running into lots and lots of Beer People of all persuasions, I often got a quick second question: "Why you?"

It took awhile to realize that what the Beer People were really asking was whether I was *one of them*. What were my beer *credentials*? Beer People, I learned, can be something of a fractious lot amongst themselves, but they tend to be protective of the object of their passion with perceived outsiders. So I would tell the Beer Folk about drinking beer at my daddy's knee and that, though I've had my flirtations with single-malt whisky and wine, it's still hard to think of anything (printable here) better than a cold beer on a warm day at the ballpark or the beach. I also had to confess that I came to this book with no more beer knowledge or tasting experience than that of your average enthusiastic amateur but also with few biases, save perhaps a distaste for light beer, though I cast no judgment upon those who drink it. I was not when I began this book, nor am I now, a Beer Snob. I grew up with people who knew of only three categories of bad beer: warm beer, flat beer, and, worst, no beer at all. Beyond that, the salutary effects of cheap beer during the penury of graduate school left me too grateful to mock inoffensive mass market brew, or the taste predilections of the great middle-class beer masses that I so long shared. Face it: a guy who drank 99-cent six-packs of Buckhorn should never get too carried away with himself.

True, I was thrilled to get introduced to a previously unknown universe of European beers when I took my obligatory summer backpacking tour across Europe right out of college in 1971. Later, in the early 1990s, when I served as a roving *Wall Street Journal* correspondent in London, I even came to appreciate that style of beer known as British bitter, figuring any beer that was good enough for Dickens and Samuel Johnson was good enough for me. And having now spent well more than a year totally steeped in beer, which has mandated a fair amount of incidental beer sampling in various parts of the country, I have by necessity and osmosis gained both knowledge and experience.

There are roughly 3,500 brands of beer, domestic and imported, available in the U.S. market, and I'd hazard that I've tried a respectable 15 percent of them. And I'm positive that in a blind tasting I could tell the difference between Dogfish Head's 60 Minute IPA, Smuttynose Portsmouth Lager, and Budweiser, but the appreciation of one doesn't require me to vilify the others. I've learned that all represent a huge if disparate commitment to quality.

What I did bring to this book was a reporter's sensibility and a notion—after copious research—best expressed as a metaphor: that a huge River of Beer runs through America, smack through the heart of American commerce and through the hearts, minds, and passions of the nation's estimated 90 million beer drinkers. If you doubt this, consider that the beer industry, with retail sales of approximately $86 billion a year, is bigger than the music and movie industries, bigger than cell phones, cable television, and mining. Beer's extended contribution to the economy—essentially Beer Nation's gross national product or GNP—is $189 billion. That's larger than the gross state products of twenty-four of the fifty states and the GNPs of scores of countries, including other B-named nations, Belarus, Bolivia, and Bulgaria among them.

But beer in America is more than a business; it is a business inextricably woven into our history. George Washington brewed beer at Mount Vernon before the Revolutionary War and strongly rebuked the Continental Congress during the war for scrimping on beer rations (a quart a day) for his soldiers. Ben Franklin also brewed beer and was said to love it as much as Homer Simpson does.

For generations, beer has also been America's great middle-brow social elixir, an inseparable companion to the sporting and spectator life, the portal to first intoxication, the working-man's Valium, and a leavening staple of the college experience. It is the only adult beverage, if you're perfectly honest, that goes with pizza. It is a business, as my dad's fixation with Falstaff shows, underpinned by a wide streak of loyalty. Such loyalty is often won not simply on taste but often by marketing—not just clever advertising but alliances with sports, and the teams and stars that turn sport into celebrity.

America didn't invent beer, but we have grabbed it, shaken it, homogenized it, refined it, and made it our own. We are home to the world's largest brewing company, Anheuser-Busch Cos.,* and the world's largest single-site brewery, the Adolph Coors Co. plant at Golden, Colorado. The Czechs, Irish, Germans, and Austrians may drink more beer per capita than do we Yanks, but America is still the world's second largest beer market, only recently overtaken by China and its 1.3 billion potential beer swillers. Americans in 2006 (the latest statistics available) consumed 6.46 billion gallons of beer, or 30.3 gallons for every single person of legal drinking age. That's seven times the combined volume of beer's rivals, spirits and wine.

---

* A 2004 merger between Belgian brewing giant Interbrew and Brazil's AmBev knocked Anheuser-Busch from its perch as the world's biggest beer producer by volume, though it is still number one in terms of sales.

And for the past twenty-five years, driven by a sense of innovation last seen in Silicon Valley before the tech bust, we have sprouted a robust and competitive craft brew movement, a loose alliance of so-called microbreweries, brewpubs, and moderate-sized regional brewers dedicated to repopulating America's beer landscape with thousands of new beer choices. Though it pains the European Beer Snobs to hear it, that movement has made America the seat of what Michael Jackson, the noted British beer expert, told me was "the most interesting beer scene in the world."

And lately, some craft brewers, bored with simply trying to make "better beer" than mainstream beer companies, have begun to fly the flag of the Extreme Beer Movement. What else could you call beer brewed from a 2,700-year-old recipe reverse-engineered from dregs sifted from the bottom of drinking vessels in a royal tomb in Turkey? Or beer made not to be "freshness-dated" but made purposely to be put away for a few years in oak or sherry casks, decanted into ornate bottles, and sold as a rival to cognac? Or blended like good Scotch whisky and marketed with a name like Train Wreck O' Flavors?

And what else but Extreme Beer could you call Jim Koch's Millennium Utopias? Koch (pronounced Cook), founder of the Boston Beer Co. and the Samuel Adams label, brought the beer in at a staggering 25.6 percent alcohol by volume (most beer is about 5 percent). The 2007 bottling wasn't just by far the strongest beer of record ever made—it was the equivalent of a moon shot in the beer world.

The Russians haven't launched an alcohol-by-volume race to get beyond the moon, but Sam Calagione, an Extreme Brewer and founder of Dogfish Head Craft Brewery in Delaware, has, his World Wide Stout achieving 23.6 percent ABV.

He's not done. Koch's not, either. Many Beer People are watching this the way baseball fans watched the Dodgers-Yankees rivalry in the 1950s.

That said, one of two beers sold in America is an Anheuser-Busch product—Bud Light recently moving past its brother Budweiser as the number-one-selling beer in the U.S. In fact, about 38 percent of *all* beer sold in America is low-calorie light beer—astonishing for a style that didn't break into the national consciousness until Miller Brewing Co. popularized it beginning in 1975. Anheuser-Busch, Miller (bought by South African Breweries in 2002 and renamed SAB Miller), and Adolph Coors, the Big Three, claim about 80 percent of all U.S. beer sales. Accounting for the rest: once mighty Pabst, now a contract brewer of relic beers, such as Schlitz and Falstaff, with an odd cult following; a few regional standouts like Yuengling Brewery, High Falls Brewing Co., and Latrobe Brewing Co.; a growing raft of craft brewers; and, most notably by volume, imports such as Corona and Heineken.

Our British-born founders may have given us their notions of liberty and democracy, but the earthy ales they brought with them couldn't ultimately hold on here. German immigrants like the Busches, Pabsts, Schlitzes, Hamms, and Millers capitalized on America, the melting pot, preferring its beer somewhat on the light, cold, and frothy side. Lager—the pale, golden, easy-to-drink beer style epitomized here by Budweiser—didn't get to America until the 1840s and didn't take off until the 1870s, aided by scientific advances, notably mechanical refrigeration and pasteurization, that made beer a highly transportable, less perishable commodity. Lager hasn't looked back since.

In truth, the American mainstream taste for pale lager isn't out of kilter with the rest of the world: 95 percent of the beer consumed worldwide is also lager (though much of it fuller-bodied than American mass-produced lager). This divining of the national beer palate, coupled with the invention of beer mass marketing, itself a billion-dollar business these days, has enriched brewing dynasties like the Busches and the Coorses and vast numbers of others up- and downstream—hops and barley growers, distributors, bottle makers, tavern owners, and advertising agencies, to name a few.

Beyond all that has sprouted a fanatical legion of homebrewers, nowadays in unprecedented numbers, who, wired together by the Internet, have turned basements all over America into finely tuned mini-microbreweries and are reinventing the very notion of what beer is or should be.

Thus, we are a beer paradox: a world beer superpower aslosh in a sea of hot-selling, middle-of-the-road lagers pushed by talking frogs, catfighting bar chicks, and Clydesdale horses, while at the margins, craft brewers and ardent hobbyists turn out beers that now rival almost anything the vaunted Germans, Belgians, Czechs, and Brits have to offer. Craft brewers represent much of the creative heart of American beer—yet they have only 5 percent of the beer market by total sales. In between, we make billionaires of the Mexican family that makes Corona, the unparalleled import success story of all time; we make beer that we now put away in cellars for five years, to be aged like fine wine and whisky, and sell it for $35 a bottle; and on the ramparts, where beer passion splashes into pop culture, we marvel at the energy and vision of the Maryland entrepreneur who has dedicated much of his time to one day launching...Beer TV.

Oh, and would it surprise you that beer—good ole American-as-apple-pie beer—so aggressively and adroitly protects its interests in Washington that it is considered by many to be one of America's top ten most powerful lobbying groups?

This paradox, with its built-in tensions and contradictions, its converging and diverging passions, its entrepreneurs and characters, seemed best explored by journey. So that's what I have attempted to do, setting off on both a literal and a figurative voyage on the River of Beer, traveling through the precincts of the beer makers, sellers, drinkers, and thinkers, trying to gain insight into the forces that drive the mighty River onward.

The narrative heart of this book is a car trip I took, following the Mississippi River the length of our mighty beer-drinking country, in a quest to find the mythical Perfect Beer Joint—a quest that I might admit, if pressed, was part pretext to gain a view of America through the prism of a beer glass. Since all great rivers have their tributaries and backwaters, I knew it would be impossible to stop at every port or scenic wayside. So this book in no way attempts to be an atlas of the American beer experience nor, except coincidentally, a pub or brewery guide, but rather a selective (and thus subjective) look at what makes beer in America interesting today.

By way of affording the reader partial insight into my thinking: the state of Big Beer was impossible to avoid; Extreme Beer gave me a compellingly fresh way to look at the maturing craft brew industry. On the other hand, the people who spend their lives collecting beer cans and what is loosely called breweriana certainly reside on the periphery of the beer world. But I decided early on they didn't fit in this book. That said, as soon as I got a whiff of the very notion of beer yeast smuggling and beer yeast rustling, I was hooked. And I concluded that the pivotal role of the Beer Goddess in modern beer retailing has been woefully underexploited in beer literature.

The River of Beer beckons. Here's what I discovered.

1
Anatomy of a Beer Spill

*Do not cease to drink beer, to eat, to intoxicate
thyself, to make love and celebrate the good days.*
—Ancient Egyptian proverb

Perdido Key, Fla.—Paige Lightsey is certainly in a celebratory
mood at the moment and so, it seems, are flocks of male gawk-
ers who have assembled on a beachside boardwalk on a warm
April afternoon. Tall, blond, and trim, Ms. Lightsey has slowly
made her way up the walk in a blue zebra-stripe bikini and bare
feet, carrying a frosty plastic pitcher of Miller Lite. She holds it
out in front of her, like a subway commuter holds a newspaper,
as she squeezes past throngs of other beer-clutching patrons.

A goodly number of them are bikers, one wearing a T-shirt
that says on the back: "If You Can Read This Shirt, the Bitch
Fell Off."

A blond, lithe, well-tanned woman among the Harley crowd
sports a skimpy two-piece bathing suit made from a print that's
also kind of hard to ignore; it's the Confederate flag. When
she reaches, in a highly provocative gesture, to adjust the stars
and bars of her top, a skinny, shirtless guy in baggy swimming
trunks actually stops and salutes (though perhaps not the flag).

The bikers laugh it off.

The thirty-three-year-old Ms. Lightsey, who works for an Atlanta private banking concern, is oblivious to the commotion, though. She's just hoping her pitcher won't be jostled and the contents lost given the time she stood in line to get it. It's a full 64-ounce pitcher with a long clear plastic straw bobbing indolently in the middle; sharing isn't her intention. She settles easily onto the broad weathered upper railing of the boardwalk, raises the pitcher with two hands, and takes a long slow sip on the straw.

"I'm a beer person, and ordering by the pitcher makes it easier," she says, green eyes peering from under the brim of a ball cap. "I don't have to keep going back to stand in line."

She gestures toward a nearby bar—well, one of seventeen beer stations, actually—where the lines portend a ten- to twenty-minute wait. Considering that it's about 80 degrees and growing warmer, waiting itself can be thirsty business, though there are a number of diversions designed to help pass the time. Nearby, a band on a stage at beach level pounds out some straight-ahead twelve-bar blues, while in an open-air bar up a flight of wooden steps, a songstress is running through a Creedence Clearwater Revival number. Beer pennants flap in a light breeze and bar walls are draped with gaudy plastic signs that say things like "No Shoes, No Kilt, No Service—Killian's Beer." Another announces a "Show Your Hein-y Contest" later in the evening sponsored by the Dutch beer maker Heineken. (Sadly, the prize for winning is undisclosed.)

Near one of the beer stations is a stall offering elaborate temporary rub-on tattoos—from cartoonish kittens to Gothic demons that religious people of a certain inclination might call satanic. The tattoos start at five bucks; for a $100 surcharge, they'll put one anywhere you want them to. "Yes, I've done a few butts," says Shelly, one of the faux tattoo artists. "So far, nothing wilder than that yet but, after dark, who knows? You'd be surprised what people have asked us to do."

This is the scene at the Flora-Bama Lounge and Package

Store, a storied beachfront bar straddling the Florida-Alabama line, during an event called the Mullet Toss. For the piscatorially ignorant, a mullet is a foot-long, silvery fish common to this section of the Gulf Coast, known hereabouts as the Redneck Riviera and famous for its azure waters and sugar-sand beaches. Smoked or fried, mullet is considered a local delicacy. This annual congregation of hedonists, in its eighteenth year, ostensibly centers on a contest in which participants, competing in men's and women's divisions by age, see who can toss a one- to two-pound (dead) mullet the farthest. Jimmy Louis, a longtime Flora-Bama musician, first suggested this idea to the bar's principal owner, Joe Gilchrist, after observing a cow-pie-throwing contest during a break in a rodeo out in Oklahoma. Mullet seemed a more savory (not to mention indigenous) option. Gilchrist, a man with a wry sense of humor and a keen sense of commerce, knew a good beer-selling shtick when he heard one, and so the Mullet Toss was born.

It's technically called the Interstate Mullet Toss, since competitors stand in a ten-foot-wide circle in Florida and fling their fish across the state line into Alabama. The throwing field is carved into the beach like an elaborate, squared-off hopscotch arena and staked out with fluttering red plastic tape of a kind that nowadays marks police barricades; there's a white scorer's tent and table; judges running around with tape measures, as though they might be officiating the javelin throw at a high school track meet; and somebody on a cranked-up PA system announcing results. The only rules are that you can't use gloves and you're disqualified if you step out of the throwing circle or throw your mullet out of bounds, thereby putting spectators in danger of being mullet-smacked.

Techniques vary. Some use a discus throw; others sling mullet sidearm style; others spread their mullet's lateral fins and sail them forward like a paper airplane. (Tip: mullet don't fly very well.) The most popular method is to double up the mullet head to tail and throw it overhand like a baseball. This is exactly how

Michael "Woody" Bruhn, a fire-sprinkler installer from Oak Hill, Tennessee, set the Mullet Toss distance record back in 1996 with a throw of 178 feet (the equivalent of flinging a mullet from mid-right-center field in Yankee Stadium to home plate).

Bruhn, who looks like a workingman's version of the actor Woody Harrelson, is a six-time Mullet Toss winner; his distance record is all the more impressive considering the competition over the years has included former National Football League quarterback Kenny "the Snake" Stabler. It's also pretty impressive considering Bruhn's other favorite mullet-tossing strategy, which he explained a few years back in a Mullet Toss quasi-documentary, available on video for $15.99 in the Flora-Bama's gift shop: "Before I throw, I always drink four or five beers, but not so many that I'm drunk."

In fact, virtually all Mullet Toss competitors and virtually all Mullet Toss spectators like Paige Lightsey, a perennial returnee, lubricate this celebration of airborne mullet with copious amounts of brew. For make no mistake about it: mullet tossing is a side-show to the real action here. The Flora-Bama, though hard liquor concoctions like Lethal Mudslides can be had, is one of America's great beer joints. And this is one of America's great weekend beer spills.

On a jam-packed Saturday night during the height of its summer tourist season, the Bama, as regulars call the rambling honky-tonk, will attract about 1,500 people. There are probably 2,000 here now, and the crowd will swell to 3,000 to 4,000 by dark. And this is only Day One of a three-day event that, before it is over, will draw a rolling crowd of about 20,000 paying customers. So it helps that the Bama sits on an acre and a quarter and, in addition to its five indoor bars, has a scrum of outdoor tents, food and drink stands, pavilions, and picnic tables (not to mention for this event, twenty-five portable toilets). All this is anchored by a handsome beach, some of it Bama property, most of it public, that allows the crowd to spill over and spread out. When Gilchrist bought the place twenty-four years ago, putting down $100 of his own money (which, he says, is all he had) plus loans from friends, it wasn't much more than a dilapidated beach shack. Now, after a number of additions and renovations, it looks like a succession of dilapidated beach shacks. The impression—totally desired—is that an architect has designed an ideal summer camp for convivial drunks. The Bama, in fact, was voted one of America's Great Dive Bars for 2002 by *Stuff* magazine (think *Maxim*)—a designation that Gilchrist considers not a slur but a supreme accolade.

As a scribe wending my way through beer culture in America, I've come to the Bama on this fair weekend not to toss mullets nor to toss down beers and revel in a spectacle that feels a lot like spring break for adults. Instead, I'm here hoping to get a close-up look inside the Great American Beer Machine—the confluence of marketing, distributing, and grassroots retailing prowess that helps to keep America's $86-billion-a-year beer business floating high. The Bama, on its slick website, calls itself "the Last Great American Road House"—a boast that would certainly cause verbal fisticuffs in some parts of, say, Texas that have beer joints that share the Bama's zeitgeist and marketing notions and dwarf it in size and sales. Nonetheless, the Bama sits not just on prime beachfront real estate, where the condos next door sell for $500,000 and up; it sits at the crossroads where the American passion for beer serendipitously intersects music and pop culture, the intangibles of place and ambience, and the shrewd and sophisticated entrepreneurial instincts of people like Joe Gilchrist.

Or put another way: the Bama is a case study in how fortunes can still be made along the River of Beer by those who divine the mysteries of mixing location, live music, and regionally tinged diner fare with a studiously cultured iconoclasm. This recipe consistently draws an appealingly mixed and slightly feral crowd: conversant, attractive, beer-chugging women in bikinis like Paige Lightsey; bikers who, because the Bama is the Bama, mostly leave any bad attitudes at the door; blue-collar types and mildly dissipated local characters who come, in part, because they like socializing with (or at least looking at) people like Paige Lightsey, same as they like seeing what the bikers are up to; and a goodly number of the courthouse and banking crowd, having traded three-piece suits for swimsuits, who like the idea of being able to hang out for a while with all of the above in a kind of socially egalitarian demilitarized zone. All of this is anchored by cold beer, zesty live music, and food good enough that it doesn't scare anybody away. The allure probably isn't that different from people who ride roller coasters at theme parks; it's a hint of adventure with just a whiff of danger—without having to worry that anything bad (except maybe a hangover) might actually happen. This recipe hasn't just built a beer joint: it's built an institution with a rabidly loyal following and one also known throughout the South—an institution that, at its heart, happens to also be a well-oiled small business raking in millions of dollars a year.

All pretty much floating on beer.

*   *   *

And none of it particularly accidental.

Joe Gilchrist is an easygoing man with a pleasing Southern drawl traceable to his hometown of Pensacola, Florida. He's one of those sixty-year-olds who could pass for forty-nine in the right sort of light. He has an open, friendly, mirthful face and an air of mischief about him, an air accentuated by the studiously rumpled casual clothes he wears and the baseball caps or skipper's hats that he has a penchant for. One impression is that he's just a mischievous boy that the years have dragged reluctantly into adulthood. He's about six feet tall and of medium build; perhaps befitting a man who owns a wildly successful tavern, which mandates a fair amount of late night beer sampling, he has the makings of a beer paunch, which he tries to hold at bay by reasonably frequent golf games. He lives alone in a modest wood-frame house on a shaded lot on the bay front not ten minutes from the Bama. A couple of cats patrol the porch and a forty-three-foot Gulf Star sailboat, big enough to sleep on but in no measure a yacht, floats tied to a dock out back. His favorite car is a mildly dilapidated 1976 Cadillac convertible. It's a pretty unostentatious life for a guy that everybody figures is a millionaire.

Gilchrist is well read, leaning toward Southern literature, and pretty well traveled (he once thought about trying to clone the Bama after being mesmerized by the beauty of Cape Town, South Africa), and is something of an authority on the American roots music scene. He can wax eloquent on Stephen Foster, the Yankee who penned Southern minstrel standards like "Oh, Susanna" and "Camptown Races" and is considered America's first professional songwriter. He can argue persuasively that Mickey Newbury, probably best known for writing the late 1960s pseudo-psychedelic pop hit "Just Dropped In (To See What Condition My Condition Was In)," is the worthy modern successor to Foster.

Newbury is actually a songwriter of great versatility—Elvis, Waylon Jennings, and Andy Williams have all covered his songs—and enjoys a kind of cult following in that gray area of music between country and pop. He is a personal friend of Gilchrist's, as is the legendary country music songwriter Hank Cochran (who penned, among other songs, "I Fall to Pieces," made famous by Patsy Cline). Indeed, about the time Gilchrist launched his tribute to beer and hedonism (and commerce) with the Mullet Toss, he also started the Frank Brown International Song Writing Festival.

The festival actually began as an end-of-summer-tourist-season party for area musicians who had become Bama staples—bands and troubadours, such as the duo Rusty and Mike, who have played regularly here pretty much since Gilchrist bought the joint. A number of them have cultivated an enthusiastic local following by writing and performing an indigenous take on blues, country, and rock that never seems to quite break out the way, say, Jimmy Buffett's Caribbean-tinged pop did. Gilchrist sought to broaden the exposure of these local artists while casting an ever-wider net for songwriting talents who might be overlooked in the precincts of Nashville or Los Angeles.

What began small is nowadays an eleven-day performance event featuring a wide spectrum of music genres and spread over sixteen venues, including the Bama, usually starting the first Thursday in November. It typically draws about 200 songwriters and features songwriting workshops put on by the likes of Larry Butler, Kenny Rogers's producer and a hit songwriter himself. One result is that Gilchrist and the Bama have earned serious and respected places in American roots music circles. It's also true that the festival attracts thousands of music-loving (and beer-loving) fans to the Bama and other nearby venues at a time when lots of places around here used to roll up the sidewalks and wait for spring. In fact, the whole thing came about because Gilchrist (again) had a knack for listening to the quasi-commercial instincts of his employees. The festival is named in honor of a lovably cantankerous African-American who, well past his ninety-first birthday, was the Bama's night watchman. Mr. Frank, as he was called, died at age ninety-five a few years back. But for years he patrolled the bar after hours with two six-guns slung low on his hips; he never had to use them because people seemed to know Brown wasn't a man to mess with. All he usually had to do to prevent fights was to tell the would-be perpetrators: "Now, you boys don't have to be like that. What would your mommas say?"

Looking around the Bama one incorrigibly slow November night, Brown decided the bar didn't have to be like that (i.e., empty) either. An enthusiastic fan of live music, he came up with the notion that a slow-month festival featuring local songwriters could be fun *and* help pay the bills by attracting crowds. Gilchrist defines the Bama's ethic as "doing well while doing good." This was right up his alley. It also turned out to be a key building block in constructing a legendary beer joint.

If you spend any time with Joe you realize he could talk this stuff—music, songwriting, and songwriters—all day long. He's basically obsessed. He's such a Mickey Newbury fanatic that he convinces me to drop by the Bama's gift shop and buy the complete Mickey Newbury seven-CD collection, with the promise that if I don't like every single song he'll send me my money back. (He doesn't tell me it's $110, plus tax.)

Gilchrist can also discourse on a variety of other subjects—history, art, politics, and sports—with the ease and practiced manner of the high school history teacher he used to be back in Pensacola forty-five minutes away. He quit teaching because it just seemed too passive for a man of his inclinations; he wanted to be in on the action somehow. For a while he thought the action might be in selling booze wholesale, so he signed on with the Lewis Bear Co., an old-line beer and liquor distributor owned for generations by the family of a Pensacola high school chum, Lewis Bear Jr. Gilchrist, by his own reckoning, just wasn't very good at jaw-jawing on the phone or cold-calling on bar owners or the managers of package stores set in their liquor- and beer-buying ways. So his liquor-selling tenure ended abruptly when "they kind of fired me," he recalls. Still, he worked at it long enough to become charmed and familiar with the bar business. Well, true, he had some previous experience. "Having spent much of my misspent youth hanging out in various and sundry barrooms," he says, "owning a bar seemed a natural fit."

And twenty-four years later, guess what? The Lewis Bear Co. sells about seven million cases of Budweiser and other Anheuser-Busch products a year, and the Flora-Bama is its biggest bar account—astonishing since there are beachfront beer joints in nearby Pensacola and Panama City that dwarf the Bama in size. Gilchrist tells that story (which the Lewis Bear people confirm) with the same kind of understated relish that Bill Gates probably feels when he gets to mention that he never finished college.

Gilchrist's employees will tell you that beyond his business savvy and gift of gab, his other notable trait is a wry, sometimes anarchic sense of humor. One example: rumors that the Bama is for sale sweep the beaches from time to time, a legacy perhaps of the fact that the bar originally sat on four sandy acres until Gilchrist and partners a few years ago sold off a goodly chunk on the Alabama side to a developer. A high-rise condo called the Phoenix 10 and its parking garage now cast long afternoon shadows on the Bama, and Gilchrist still catches some flak from regulars who liked the joint shadow-free. (His real regret, Gilchrist says, is that under pressure from some of his early investors, "we sold the property too soon.")

The episode left some of the faithful worried about Gilchrist's long-term commitment, since practically nobody believes the bar would be the same without him. A couple of years ago, with sales rumors more rampant than ever, he shocked everybody by announcing that he *had* sold the place to a syndicate of Montana rodeo cowboys. He called a press conference to introduce the new owners. A press mob showed up, as did some deeply concerned beer drinkers, as did one of the cowboy buyers dressed in full cowboy kit. Plans for a radically revised Bama were unfurled and given out, and it was only when the press folk flipped the plans over did they see "April Fool's!" scrawled on the back.

Well, it *was* April 1.

The joke backfired somewhat when it was later discovered that the rent-a-cowboy Gilchrist had used turned out to be wanted by the law in another state; Joe hadn't thought his prop, who had become a recent Bama patron, needed a background check. Still, Gilchrist's role as a kind of Merry Prankster serves him well as a saloon-keeper; this was just another brick in the Bama's wall of lore.

I caught up with Gilchrist for the first time on an exploratory trip to the Flora-Bama two weeks before the eighteenth annual Mullet Toss. He'd warned me that he'd be kind of hard-pressed to sit still very long during what he called the "insanity of Mullet Week," where his duties veer between mule skinner and parade marshal. The Toss turns out to be the beer-soaked climax to an eight-day series of events that is equal parts revelry, promotion, and public service. There's the Mullet Man Triathlon (including a Mullet Woman division) the weekend before the Toss; the Mullet Swing Golf Tournament midweek; and in many years, depending on timing, the Mullet Week Easter Egg Hunt. All of these Mullet-badged events attract crowds (more than 500 people race in the triathlon and another 175 or so participate in the golf tournament) and keep the Bama very much in the public eye. Mullet Week, in fact, has become an evergreen for the local and regional press; the Toss, as you might imagine, makes a couple of minutes of pretty good local television.

The events also all have a charity component (duly noted in event literature and on the Bama's Web site). A portion of the golf tournament's $175 entry fee goes to a cancer foundation. The 711 people who will enter the Mullet Toss this year will pay $15 each to enter; the fee gets them an official Mullet Toss T-shirt, but some of it goes each year to area youth groups. Altogether, the Bama gives away about $20,000 a year to various charities, most of it Mullet Week money. Of course, most revelers pay a $5-a-day cover charge to get into the Bama on Toss weekend, and the bar mandates that all who congregate on the beach within proximity—even the public beach—pay the cover charge and buy their beer and booze from the Bama. So, again, doing good clearly doesn't interfere with doing well.

I'd driven to the Bama from New Orleans with a friend named Dell Long, who, as coincidence would have it, had been hired as a publicist by Gilchrist on a couple of Flora-Bama projects. One was a Bama-organized effort, in the months just after 9/11, that made 400 beach-area rental condos, plus free air or train travel, available to the families of New York City firemen and policemen killed in the terror attacks. Gilchrist had also led a group of 100 Panhandle businesspeople and 10 homegrown musicians to Manhattan to spend some money in the wounded city to try to help pump up its economy—and try to entertain them, too. Long, a red-haired steel magnolia in her late fifties, had for years been the publicist for the legendary radio DJ Wolfman Jack and is one of those people who could charm a rabid dog. Gilchrist had hired her to, among other things, organize a tribute party to cops, firemen, and rescue workers; she'd coaxed Manhattan's Waldorf-Astoria hotel into donating a lavish space and letting the Gulf Coasters bring in their home-cooked seafood.

I was down in New Orleans for this book, trying unsuccessfully to get a Budweiser distributor to let me ride through the French Quarter on a beer truck, when I ran into her. When she heard I was interested in the Bama, she told me about her dealings with Gilchrist, including a story about a funny moment that had transpired during the Waldorf soiree. It seems that one of the tag-along Bama musicians, not exactly living up to Waldorf dress codes or table manners, was mistaken for an intruding bum as he pawed shrimp, unencumbered by toothpick or napkin, from a silver platter. He was about to be bounced when Long intervened. Anyway, she volunteered to introduce me to Gilchrist. I accepted—in fact, it was a deal closer.

Face it: there are almost 295,000 licensed "on premise" places in America that serve beer; even after subtracting hotels, restaurants, sports venues, and bowling alleys, that leaves a lot of beer joints. Quite a few hold annual events equivalent to the Mullet Toss. I could go watch one anywhere. But I was leaning toward the Bama precisely because it *wasn't* an obscure dive resisting its popularity like some Mississippi juke joint that only locals could guide you to. It seemed a paradox: a bar that had managed to capture something of that very mystique by assiduously managing its dive-bar image. It was a beer joint that, according to its website, had a special-events coordinator. From the website you could also learn that the Bama had been written up, in the same "you-gotta-check-out-this-crazy-place" way, in a lot of national publications, *Playboy* and *Esquire* among them; it was even featured in John Grisham's evil-law-firm thriller *The Firm*. And I'd not yet met many saloon keepers who hire publicists. In light of all that, the Bama being named one of *Stuff* magazine's greatest

American dive bars seemed about as accidental as Microsoft's becoming a software juggernaut.

I did wonder, though: would it feel like the real deal, or would it feel like a biker bar set in Disney World?

I admit this question was only peripheral to my mission, but I am fond of bars and I like to think I can tell a pure one from a phony. Like Joe Gilchrist, I'd spent a fair amount of my youth exploring them. I'd learned a lot as a cub reporter on my weekly hometown paper back in Houma, Louisiana, by deconstructing school-board stories and cop features with pals over $2 pitchers of Miller Genuine Draft at Curley's Lounge, a dark and dingy downtown hole-in-the-wall. It was run by a crusty (and bald) retired air force sergeant whom everybody called Curley and whose real name nobody ever seemed to know. Curley liked it that way. I was on as good terms with Curley as anybody, but he kicked me out one night for kissing my girlfriend at the dark table way at the back of the bar, even though we were about the only people there. When the next night I asked him why, he told me it was the *way* we were kissing that bugged him, not the kissing itself—implying that I had a lot to learn in the kissing department. From that moment on I knew Curley was a keen observer of the human condition. (I also developed a keen desire, as yet unrequited, to be a bartender one day.)

As a journalist who has traveled widely across the U.S., Europe, Africa, and the Middle East, I have found bars to be perennially reliable oases in strange towns and foreign countries, not just places where you can get a beer and take the sting out of the day but places where you can get the real dope about a place, plus pick up story ideas. We scribes call this Reporting from the Mahogany Ridge. Anyway, I collect bars, metaphorically at least, the way some people collect beer cans, or shampoo bottles from motel rooms. I was plenty curious about the Bama.

I liked the place as soon as I darkened the door. It was a Friday night about 9:00 P.M., and we joined a line of people waiting to pay the $5 cover. Dell Long, being Dell, barged up ahead into the crowd before I could stop her to announce that a journalist writing a beer book was coming through and to convince the door person to waive the cover since Gilchrist was expecting us. I figured it was easier to go along than hold up the line in a discussion about journalistic ethics and why it was necessary for me to pay my own way into the bar. I would just catch the doorman later. This did have the effect, though, of having an attractive woman at the door buttonhole me as I squeezed by to say, "You oughta go interview my husband. He knows everything about beer or at least everything about drinking it. In fact, we're getting divorced over beer."

She laughed when she said it, so I felt I should laugh, too.

The Bama, I would learn, is a bit of a maze, and as we pushed through a small outer bar into the first bar with a bandstand, people were thick as schooling snapper. A group called Jezebel's Chill'n was onstage, playing stuff that sounded like a cross between rockabilly and blues. They were loud, people were clapping and swaying along, and some people were even trying to dance, though, as far as I could tell, there was not an official dance floor (not that that ever stopped a beer-enthused, dance-minded person in any bar I'd been in). I later learned that many of the dancers were elementary school teachers in town on one of those seminar boondoggles—they were certainly dancing like they didn't have school in the morning. Pitchers of beer stood on every table and the beleaguered servers behind the bar, where every stool was taken, were bobbing about and jabbing at beer taps like harried prizefighters. And this room, with maybe a couple of hundred people crammed into it, turned out to be the smallest part of the action.

A few things caught my eye: a sign on the wall that said "Having Sex on the TV Can't Hurt You—Unless You Fall Off"; the fact that a huge number of bras, in various stages of deterioration, were hanging from the raftered ceiling; and that over at a table by the bandstand a couple, oblivious to this sea of happy turmoil, was furiously making out. I knew even if crusty old

Curley were here they wouldn't get thrown out: nobody could get to them.

Someone had sent word to Gilchrist that we had arrived and out of this chaos he appeared, slowly fighting his way through the crowd like a salmon swimming upstream. Long introduced us. We shook hands and exchanged pleasantries and off we went on a Cook's tour of the place. It was so crowded and noisy and Gilchrist was so often stopped by friends and well-wishers that we agreed we'd meet the next day for a proper interview over lunch. Then he was swallowed up by the crowd again.

I wandered around on my own for a bit, satisfying myself that the rest of the Bama would live down to the first of it, and it did, quite nicely. (Somebody, in fact, would later describe the bar as "the kind of place where you wipe your feet on the way out.") Then I decided to go back to our starting point to see if I could get an explanation for those bras. I spied a few other things along the way that warmed me to the joint; one was a vending machine that, besides the usual items like chewing gum, pocket combs, and potato chips, sold guitar strings.

I fought my way back into the room where Jezebel's Chill'n was playing, found a seat at the bar, and ordered a Heineken. During a break in the music, I learned from a bartender that sometime back in the '80s, the time frame no longer being exactly clear, the Bama had experienced, like the mysterious appearance of crop circles, a rash of women prone to ripping off their bras for no particular reason and flinging them at people. Somebody decided that the spoils of this spontaneous sport should be tacked to the ceiling—and, well, here they were. This practice had stopped as mysteriously as it had started, thus explaining the dated and forlorn look of the garments.

When the band finished its set and the bar started to clear out, I wandered over toward the bandstand and bumped into the smooching couple, who, though not smooching anymore, were still sort of pawing each other. They smiled and I smiled and we exchanged pleasantries. They told me they were Steve and Wanda from Birmingham, that they loved the Bama, that they drove over a couple of times a year and were—would you believe it?—*married*. This is about as far as we got: some friends of theirs barged over to grab empty chairs at their table. But before we said good-bye they told me I couldn't possibly leave the Redneck Riviera until I'd heard Rusty and Mike play on this very bandstand.

"And be sure," said Steve, "they play that Wal-Mart song."

"You mean the one about the guy bringing his drawers back to Wal-Mart?" said Wanda.

"Yeah, that one," said Steve. "And the one about the manatee, too."

I slipped out of the bar, promising to try to take their advice.

The next day, Gilchrist and I sat down for a leisurely lunch over platters of fried mullet at a restaurant called the Point that he said had the best mullet around. I had to admit this was the first time I'd ever eaten mullet. Where I grew up in Cajun Louisiana, nobody eats mullet; they are bottom feeders that people use for fish bait. But I did grow up eating alligator, frog legs, fried rattlesnake, snapping turtle, crawfish, squirrel, and raccoon; and once, on assignment in Alaska, I politely nibbled microwaved whale blubber with an Eskimo who had just graduated from Harvard. So mullet wasn't that big of a challenge, and my inaugural mullet was crispy, tender, and good.

I asked Gilchrist, a graduate of Auburn University, if he had an overarching philosophy about life. He smiled and said, "I like beer and money. But beer, like money, is never really yours. You just get to use it till you piss it away."

That's a nice line for the guy who owns one of America's great dive bars, but Gilchrist clearly knows what he's about. Before buying the Bama he'd made a study of successful area beer joints and decided he wanted to transfer "that feeling that comes with a neighborhood bar" to a beach location while avoiding the pitfalls of many beach bars—they simply become tourist traps. He was dedicated at the outset to the prospect that live, original music would be part of the formula (and the Bama has live music 365 days a year). But he was also wary of imposing a "Bama notion" until he had a firm idea of the kind of crowd the Bama might naturally attract. "In large-building construction, a lot of landscape architects will go out and put in the landscaping and walkways before the building is ever done," he said. "But then they find out that people will pretty much walk where they want to anyway. I figured the best approach was to watch where people walk first."

We later talked about the Mullet Toss and I asked him about his greatest concern in putting on an event that big. He said it was "keeping the beer cold."

* * *

Two weeks later, when I arrived for the Toss, it was pretty easy to see what a daunting task that would be. It was mid-Friday morning of Day One and already the parking lots around the Bama were pretty much filled up, there was a tailback a couple miles up and down the highway, and people were streaming into the bar. It was a warm, clear day and would no doubt get warmer—a beer day if I ever saw one. Gilchrist had told me that Mullet Toss beer chores largely landed in the lap of a guy named Body, who, for lack of a better title, was the Bama's beer wrangler, and I should look him up when I got to the bar.

I introduced myself to a woman behind the Bama's package liquor counter named Susan Poston. She knew what I was up to and directed me to an inner storeroom behind the package store. I found Body (pronounced just like the human body) in a cluttered, tight room surveying the Bama's vast reserves of beer and booze. Nobody calls Body anything but Body, and I wouldn't find out for a couple of days that his first name was Edmund. Or that he'd worked his way up into this post after spending a few years as the Bama's janitor, cleaning up the landslide of empty beer cans and bottles after the place closed every night.

I quickly learned four things about Body: on this overwhelmingly white strip of the Gulf Coast, he was one of the few African-Americans around; he was always busy; he ran the bar's beer distribution network with the cool of a college quarterback used to dodging rushing linebackers; and he wasn't a man that anyone would ever accuse of being loquacious. By doggedly following him around all morning and peppering him with questions, I did find out that preparations for the Mullet Toss had begun with a series of meetings starting back in November and that the planning for the event is one part war gaming, but mostly, Body said, "like putting on a county fair without having to worry about the livestock." The Bama normally has about 150 employees, but it hires 50 to 100 extras during the Toss, depending on the weather forecast. Body's main job is to order enough beer in the right proportions (Bud Light, Bud, Miller Lite, Coors Light, Miller, Coors, and a few imports, pretty much in that order) to serve 20,000 people. Then he has to commandeer a clutch of workers and, with hand trucks, move in a perpetual circuit stocking the bar's numerous giant beer coolers. This plan is also dependent upon an unusual logistical arrangement: the Bud, Coors, and Miller people agree to park diesel-operated refrigerated beer trucks on a lot next door to the Bama and keep them there for the entire Toss.

"We just don't have enough coolers on premise to handle the load," said Body, who is thirty-something and built like Tiger Woods.

When I asked other people at the bar what they thought of Body's job, Susan Poston told me, "Body's job is impossible. On the ordering side, you're damned if you do and you're damned if you don't. Imagine being in a position of having somebody say during the middle of Mullet Toss, 'Hey, you just ran out of my beer!' "

I had no idea that a beer wrangler's life was so pressured. I decided I would come back and watch Body in operation during the height of the Toss—late Saturday afternoon and into Saturday night when Gilchrist had told me the crowds could peak at 5,000 or more.

* * *

Saturday was another clear, warm day, and I arrived a bit early because Rusty and Mike were playing on the same bandstand where I'd caught Jezebel's Chill'n on my previous visit. I'd left town then without being able to hear them and I was curious about a duo that wrote songs about the return policy at Wal-Mart. They'd already started by the time I got there and were in the middle of one of the songs that Steve and Wanda had hinted at regarding a manatee. It was actually a song about a hapless barfly who, his judgment blinded by liquor, went home with a woman he was sure was a beautiful mermaid and "woke up with a manatee." The room was packed and everybody laughed every time they sang the chorus.

They then launched into a raunchy though equally hilarious number that sounded like it came straight out of the Bama's bra-tossing period. It is an appeal for certain kinds of women to keep their shirts *on*. The first two lines go:

> *Hey, lady, please don't show them tits*
> *You've done run all the bikers off and you're*
>   *scarin' all the kids*

This song pretty much brought down the house.

It occurred to me that, though I'd never heard of a genre called Trailer Park Rock, this was pretty much what this music was; that Rusty and Mike were performing songs that Jimmy Buffett might have written had he grown up, say, dirt-poor in a storm-damaged double-wide with cars up on blocks in the front yard. Once you cut past the humor, the music seemed to have an appealingly raw honesty that went down well on the Redneck Riviera. In their own way, Rusty and Mike sold a lot of beer.

I'd later learn that of the two, Rusty McHugh, a big-boned, long-haired guy who looks like he could've been the bouncer at Woodstock if Woodstock had not been a love-in, was the songwriter. His sidekick, Mike Fincher, played straight man on guitar and backup vocals—well, straight man, if looking uncannily like one of the stoned-out players in the band ZZ Top could be called straight. When their set ended, I went up to introduce myself and buy one of the CDs they were peddling. Rusty, staying completely in character, said I could steal it if I wanted to, as long as I spelled his name right in the book. (I paid, and promised to spell his name right anyway.)

I went outside into the dazzling late afternoon sun looking for Body, hoping to observe some serious beer wrangling. It was broiler-hot now, and the crowd was a rippling sea of T-shirts, tank tops, and swimsuits, and it was hard to spot a hand that didn't have a beer in it. The aroma of boiled crawfish filled the air—a serious beer association for me. I got in line and after about fifteen minutes snagged a Heineken, then started pushing my way through the mob. I figured a black guy in a sea of white faces would be pretty easy to spot, but it took about half an hour.

I finally caught up with Body pushing a dolly laden with about a dozen cases of Bud into one of the outdoor coolers over by the faux tattoo stand. I stepped into the cooler with him. His face and polo shirt were drenched in sweat and he was consulting with a helper about a crisis: this particular beer cooler, having been opened so many times already, was registering 60 degrees. That's a nice temperature for an air-conditioned room but that's *not* cold enough for mainstream lagers like Bud. (The Bud people, in fact, recommend you drink their beer at 40 degrees F.)

As Body puzzled over how to resolve this, he said he'd already pushed about 600 cases into coolers and expected to reload them with at least 600 or more tonight. He'd been at it since nine this morning; he figured he'd be done at 2:00 A.M. He then unloaded the hand truck in silence, wrestled it outside, and trundled off to reload.

I decided not to follow; I realized a lot of hard work went into beer wrangling but not much drama. Later, I asked Body, after three consecutive eighteen-hour days of this, if he ever dreamed of pushing beer cases around; he said he didn't, mercifully. The one thing he did worry about, though, was catching cold as he moved from the hot sun in and out of the chilly coolers.

I decided to conduct my own little experiment. I went up to one of the outdoor beer stands and punched up the timer on my watch, interested in knowing how quickly the beer was moving. The answer was that over the ten-minute period that I clocked, five bartenders were serving about 3 beers a minute, or about 180 beers (7.5 cases) an hour. A number of the seventeen beer stations were two-person jobs, so clearly not all were doing this brisk of a business. But this was a sobering amount of beer—conservatively, I calculated, at least 100 cases an hour. It was now 5:00 P.M.; if that rate were anywhere close to accurate, Body's 600 cases would be gone by eleven.

Joe Gilchrist was doing his part. Later, out on the Bama's boardwalk, I spied him in a captain's hat, surrounded by a number of young, bikini-wearing admirers and a Bama employee. At first, he seemed in parade-captain mode, but then I heard him in animated discussion about trying to speed up business at a beer stand over to one side of the boardwalk; people didn't seem to know it was there.

The employee suggested the stand could put up a sign offering a special: say, a free fourth beer after a customer had purchased three.

Gilchrist smiled and shook his head. He said, "Well, actually, I'm more interested in selling twenty for the price of twenty-four."

A couple of weeks after the Toss, I e-mailed the Bama hoping to get an exact count of how many beers or equivalents (since a pitcher holds seven 12-ounce glasses) got drunk that weekend. But nobody had that kind of figure (or at least they weren't giving it out). I did, however, get an estimate of Bud products from David Bear, a principal in the Lewis Bear distributorship.

"It was about 2,000 case equivalents," Bear told me on the phone. And with Bud making up about half of all Bama beer sales, the extrapolation is about 4,000 cases altogether.

That's 96,000 beers—if they were bottles laid end to end, a pipeline of beer nine miles long.

I later had lunch with Paige Lightsey when she visited New York on a work assignment. I wondered how she would assess this Toss compared to others she'd attended. She laughed and said, "I can't remember." Then she got serious and said, "I'm very comfortable at the Bama. I work in a very pretentious business, and the Bama is a place where I can decompress and be unpretentious. I'll be back next year."

As for her annual Mullet Toss beer consumption, well, a lady never tells. But Paige did allow that another reason she had such a soft spot for the Bama is that, "I don't have to buy a lot of my own beer."

The only other thing I wondered about the Mullet Toss is what became of the mullet.

The answer is that after the last mullet is tossed, they are fed to the seagulls.

Author's note: Mickey Newbury, Mike Fincher, and Rusty McHugh have all passed away since the reporting of this event. In September 2004, the Bama was seriously damaged by Hurricane Ivan, but rebounded, though in a reduced capacity, for the 2005 Mullet Toss.

2

The Quest Begins

A Pilgrim on the River of Beer

A tavern chair is the throne of human felicity.
—Dr. Samuel Johnson

Stillwater, Minn.—On a fair Saturday in September of 2002, I bumped down through the late summer thermals aboard a Northwestern Airlines 727 and landed in Minneapolis after a two-hour flight from New York. I claimed a rental car, checked into the industrial park hotel I'd booked as part of a last-minute special on Orbitz, and set about plotting my itinerary. I pulled out the Yellow Pages from my bedside table and started looking up bars.

I was going to spend the next two weeks driving the length of the Mississippi River from north to south in search of the Perfect Beer Joint. The Flora-Bama, and its beach-bar/dive-bar niche, was certainly one model, but I was interested in exploring others.

Though I'd already been researching this book for a few months, I dove into this quest with little preparation. First of all, I didn't want to taint my research with anybody else's pre-packaged notions of the Perfect Beer Joint. Second, if my basic thesis was true—that beer is a ubiquitous, even saturated fact of American culture—then little research should be necessary. In principle a person ought to be able to alight in almost any place in America, save the nation's 320 or so dry counties, and find if not a Perfect Beer Joint at least a good one. And surely in the 2,500-odd miles that the Mississippi chugs from Minnesota to the Gulf of Mexico in Louisiana, the odds were good of stumbling upon some place approaching mythical Perfect Beer Joint status.

Of course, I had my reasons for choosing the Mississippi. For starters, it is a storied river, full of lore and color, known to the Old World since 1540 when Hernando De Soto came upon it, though there is no record of him drinking beer along its shores. Mark Twain, a man who *was* known to like his beer, wrote an entire book about his life on the river and most certainly drank beer along its shores. For all I knew, the Perfect Beer Joint might reside in Twain's hometown of Hannibal, Missouri. (Preview: It didn't.)

By contrast, an east–west alternative, following, say, Interstate 80 from Manhattan to San Francisco, didn't seem as interesting. I have a theory about latitudinal homogenization, believing the predilections, tastes, and biases of the urban coasts travel all too easily along the great east–west hypercorridors, spreading a kind of sameness that wouldn't serve my quest. It's probably occurred to you that you could get in a car in, say, Paramus, New Jersey, and drive coast to coast, stopping at the unavoidable shopping malls that crop up every three or four hours. You could visit a Gap or a T.G.I. Friday's in every mall and you could see the same kind of people that you'd left behind...and you could arrive at the Pacific Ocean 3,000 miles later with no feeling that you'd gone anywhere at all. (I'm actually planning to try this one day. But it didn't seem right for my beer quest.)

On the other hand, the vast longitude of the Mississippi, meandering its way through ten states, seemed a lot more prospective. Scenic highways, small towns, a vast range in terrain, demographics, and climate. About 12 million people live in the 125 counties and parishes that border the river. I would begin in Minnesota among folk who, geographically speaking, are practically Canadians and by reputation descended from good beer-drinking Swedes and Germans. I would slide down soon enough into the Great Beer Belly of America, for, by lore at least, Midwesterners are presumed to be the mightiest of U.S. beer drinkers. I would travel through the heartland and land upon the shores of the King of Beers in St. Louis, for though the Budweiser people had shown only wary interest up to this point in talking to me about this book, I could at least visit the huge Anheuser-Busch brewery there as a tourist.

What, I wondered, went on at the beer joint closest to the Bud plant? Would they serve Miller Lite?

Then I would push on down South, where two of my favorite cities, Memphis and New Orleans, beckoned. I was intrigued by the possibility of an Elvis-and-beer connection in Memphis, since a fair amount of beer drinking (among other things) was said to have gone on at Graceland, though there seems to be an enduring mystery about whether Elvis himself was fond of brew. Maybe Graceland would hold some clues.

And I knew, by dint of having grown up near there, that New Orleans harbored perhaps the oldest continuously operating beer joint in the nation. And even if I didn't find the Perfect Beer Joint (and as a man on an expense account, it occurred to me that I shouldn't want to succeed too quickly), what better way to cut to the heart of beer passion and get an intense look at what Beer People were thinking (and drinking)?

Beyond that, the beer joint as an institution, with its vaunted place in beer's sociopolitical and commercial history, surely warranted further exploration. Clearly a New World derivative of the British public house or pub (and in some parts of the country, the

German beer hall), the first licensed beer joint opened in 1634 in colonial Boston. By the time the colonies had worked themselves up into the lather of revolution 140 or so years later, the taverns of the would-be nation were bubbling with sentiment for independence. Benjamin Franklin, Patrick Henry, Samuel Adams (the patriot and brewer for whom Jim Koch at Boston Beer named his brew), James Madison, and Thomas Jefferson were big fans of the early American beer joint; indeed, Jefferson is said to have written some of the Declaration of Independence over pints of ale in Philadelphia's Indian Queen Tavern. Around the same time, in the very same city, military folk plotted how to best structure and equip an outfit to be called the Continental Marines as they drank pints in the Tun Tavern. The organization grew into the U.S. Marine Corps. I've never met a marine, active or retired (including my father), who wasn't universally proud that the Corps was born in a beer joint.

The beer joint also has historically been the main commercial lifeline of America's brewers. Until the concept of mass merchandising, chain supermarkets, and convenience stores swept America after World War II, the beer joint and other on-premise sellers probably accounted for 95 percent of all beer sales. In fact, before the thirteen-year dry spell (1920–1933) known as Prohibition decimated America's brewing industry, the nation's brewers owned or controlled, through often dubious contractual agreements, perhaps 85 percent of the nation's taverns. Many historians have argued that the abuses that grew out of these anticompetitive relationships—free lunches, for example, to entice working men to spend their lunch hour (and pay) at the local beer joint—provided a good deal of the Prohibitionist fodder.

Little more than twenty years ago, beer joints and their brethren (including that newfangled invention, the brewpub, which first cropped up in 1982) were still moving about 75 percent of America's beer. Then the states all began to stiffen drunk driving laws; this and demographic shifts, such as the aging of the population bulge known as the baby boom, set off an astonishing sea change in beer consumption habits. These days, only about 25 percent of all beer is bought and consumed in bars or other on-premise locations, while 75 percent is sold and consumed off premises. Convenience stores, supermarkets, and package liquor stores account for almost 60 percent of off-premise sales, with drugstores and super-centers like Wal-Mart accounting for most of the rest.

That said, the beer joint remains vital to the beer industry because on-premise retailers still represent the single-largest *category* of beer sales, moving about 51.2 million barrels of beer annually—about four million barrels more than its nearest category rival, the convenience store. Moreover, the beer joint is still the industry's great cash cow; it and its allies may account for only 25 percent of all beer by volume, but by dollar amount, they rack up almost half of all annual retail beer sales.

Why? Because beer joints usually charge more for beer than do retail stores, the gross profit margin for the average beer joint is a whopping 82 percent. That works out to almost $30 billion worth of gross profits a year. By comparison, gross profit margins for convenience stores and their ilk average a mere 22 percent.

Now, as to what might constitute the Perfect Beer Joint, I admit this is a highly subjective and possibly even controversial matter. Purists will argue that the Perfect Beer Joint fundamentally has to be about the beer, followed by an ambience conducive to the pleasurable drinking thereof.

This was certainly the answer I got from a newly minted Internet pal by the name of Jimmy Paige. I'd found Jimmy on the Web as I researched the vast universe of homebrew clubs—like-minded people who get together socially to talk about and sample beer they often brew in isolation, with great secrecy and competitive zeal. Jimmy was head of one of the bigger of such clubs, a Houston outfit called the Foam Rangers.

Well, head isn't exactly what Jimmy was. His official title was *Grand Wazoo* of the Foam Rangers, and once his term was over, he would become forever the *Wuz Waz*. It therefore seemed mandatory, before launching my quest to find the Perfect Beer Joint, to get the opinion of the Grand Wazoo as a kind of benchmark to use along the way.

I was halfway expecting a smart-ass answer to my e-mail, but the Grand Wazoo delivered a thoughtful reply: "You may find this definition changes as you encounter different people," he wrote. "Younger crowds will tell you it is the place that has the best drink specials; older, more mature crowds will indicate the ambience. For me it would be the pub where I would always want to go back to for the hardest-to-find beers." He closed with this sober admonition, which I planned to flourish if the accounting department ever got after me for my beer expenses: "If you are like most homebrewers, never be content in saying your quest has been satisfied. We are forever on the prowl, looking for that one perfect place."

"Forever on the prowl..."

I liked that. I liked it a lot.

Michael Jackson, the internationally known British Beer Hunter, seemed the perfect person to whom to pose the Perfect Beer Joint question. When I ran into him during an East Coast brewery tour, he offered a counterintuitive observation. While *his* idea of the Perfect Beer Joint was certainly about the beer, he noted that in his experience, "the more macho the bar, the wimpier the beer." He once made the mistake of postulating this in Australia, which, like America, loves its middle-of-the-road lagers, and was almost run out of the country. But assuming you accept the premise that middle-of-the-road lager is wimpy beer (and some people don't—recall those Miller Lite ads arguing the merits of "great taste/less filling!"), Jackson makes an interesting point. Go, as I have, to any of those big line-dancing, country-music beer joints out in Texas, where every vehicle in the parking lot is a jacked-up Ford 4x4 pickup with a gun rack. Odds are good that about half the guys riding the mechanical bull will be drinking Miller Lite.

Sentiment also can't be overlooked in the configuration of what makes the Perfect Beer Joint. Paige Lightsey, after I met her at the Flora-Bama, went on to become Paige Buckner. She and her new husband, John, carried on a meaningful part of their courtship at the Bama. Though he is a Californian with a farm and vineyard up in Mendocino County, he agreed to buy her a waterfront house about a mile from the Bama as part of the deal because, she told me, "I couldn't live without the beach or the Bama." The Bama is her version of the nearly perfect TV beer joint Cheers.

I admit to a couple of sentimental favorites myself. The place I grew up, Bayou Black, Louisiana, had a sole beer joint, Elmo's Bar and Grocery, which sat in a large clamshell-paved parking lot next door to the bayou Catholic Church. (It opened, not coincidentally, on Sunday right after Mass.) These were the days before almost all beer came from Milwaukee or St. Louis, so Elmo's mainly served regional beers long gone, such as Regal and Jax (and Dixie, which survives).

Bayou Black was a Cajun enclave, and most Cajuns are Catholic, which meant back then that they didn't eat meat on Fridays. So Elmo's marketing strategy was to induce bayou residents to his beer joint on Friday nights by offering free seafood—usually boiled crabs or crawfish that he or some relative had plucked themselves from the nearby bayous or swamps. All you were required to do was buy beer (a quarter a can or bottle) and put quarters in the jukebox (six selections per quarter), which featured mostly Cajun music or its first cousin, swamp pop. (Think the Fats Domino song "Walkin' to New Orleans.") Friday nights were always packed.

My singular memory of Elmo's, though, was the time rumors spread up and down the bayou that Elmo was going to be cooking turtle *sauce piquant* for his next Friday night feast. *Sauce piquant* is essentially a spicy stew of tomato sauce, celery, onion, and cayenne pepper with chicken, rabbit, or turtle at its core. It would take a lot of turtle to feed the hordes that showed up each

Friday. But word came that Elmo had caught a 110-pound alligator snapping turtle—a turtle with a head the size of a cantaloupe, jaws as powerful as a great white shark, and a spiky shell that made it look prehistoric—and was planning to sacrifice it to the common pot. But anyone who wanted to see the turtle before it became supper was welcome to go view it.

I was nineteen then and had gotten my first journalism job, a part-time position writing obituaries and cop briefs for the weekly paper in Houma, about five miles east of where I'd grown up on Bayou Black. When I mentioned this turtle to my editor, I was immediately dispatched with a camera to go take a picture of the beast—monster turtle pictures, I was admonished, were potentially front-page material. I got there and, sure enough, the turtle was hunkered down atop the bar, a crowd of beer drinkers around it. Its massive head was partly retracted, but when Elmo offered it a can of beer—well, prodded the turtle with a can—out came the head and *ker-chunk!*—it bit the can in half, sending beer everywhere.

Elmo's may not have been the Perfect Beer Joint. But as beer-joint moments go, you have to admit that one is pretty special.

Another of my favorite all-time beer joints was the bar tucked into Japan Town Bowl in San Francisco. I worked as a reporter for the *Journal*'s bureau there in the '80s and some of my colleagues and I joined a bowling league because everybody in San Francisco was into fitness back then, and we knew bowling to be on the fun side of the aerobics spectrum. In 1988 I'd even written a page one feature for the paper about how bowling had made it into the Olympics as a demonstration sport that year, so this gave our theory great credibility. (Point of fact: Olympic scientists told me that it takes more pure athletic ability to be a 200 average bowler than it does to become an 80 percent free-throw shooter in basketball.)

The most important thing about bowling, other than aerobics and getting to wear bowling shoes, is coming up with a good name for your team. Since most of us on the team were journalists and thus professional wordsmiths, we arrived at the *Pinheads*, which of course is wonderfully wry, clever, and full of subtext on several different levels. We were quite proud of our name.

Now, as part of our bowling aerobics ritual we would arrive at the alley about a half hour before our match started and head for the bar to limber up. As bars go, it wasn't much to look at. It was small and dark, the tables were crowded together, and the decor was heavy on the Formica and vinyl side, though I recall something vaguely Tiki about the whole thing. It did have cold beer and a jukebox that had both Patsy Cline's "Crazy" and Frank Sinatra's "New York, New York" on it. Given that on most nights, bowling is either raging triumph or utter tragedy, the management of the bar had figured out that those were the only two songs the jukebox really needed. The bar had a convivial waitstaff—well, it had Brenda, a friendly and effervescent thirty-something Southerner who understood the indisputably direct connection between cold bottles of Budweiser, tips, and the length of her denim miniskirts. Our team, being better-than-average customers, became great friends with Brenda later on, whereupon it was revealed that she had several advanced college degrees and was qualified to do both psychoanalysis *and* landscape architecture. But she *liked* working at the bar at Japan Town Bowl, which totally deepened our esteem for the place. The bar also had gloriously greasy cheeseburgers—another plus among the bowlingentsia.

Anyway, you see what I'm getting at. Outsiders might say: Oh, just another dumpy, dark, bowling alley bar. But for me at the time it had a lot of Perfect Beer Joint qualities.

Perhaps best of all, it was a social mixing zone, for the league that bowled just ahead of us was the Gay Bowling League, and the fellows would often come into the bar to do post-match assessments while we were limbering up. They were a good-natured crew, and what I really liked about them is that all of them drank Budweiser, even though the bar did stock some unadvertised Heineken and Kirin way at the back of its cooler. As anybody who has bowled knows, it's really bad form to drink anything but Bud or maybe Miller Lite at a bowling alley (or, okay, maybe if you live in Pennsylvania and bowl you can drink the local favorites, Yuengling or Rolling Rock). But remember: this was San Francisco, where everything is precious or, if it's not yet, soon will be. So I liked the fact that even the relentless pressure of San Francisco preciousness couldn't bully gay bowlers into drinking imported beer.

There was one sour note in our otherwise convivial relationship with our gay bowling brethren: names. As you know, we were quite proud of our choice of the Pinheads, so imagine our surprise when members of the Gay Bowling League started showing up in their bowling shirts with their team names embroidered on the backs and we realized that, slam-dunk, we had been badly outnamed! I'll leave it to you to judge, but it seems impossible to argue that Oh, Spare Me!, Bowling for Husbands, and, my favorite of all time, the Meet Balls were not all superior to the Pinheads.

However, what really sealed the bar at Japan Town Bowl in my beer joint memory was the improbable night that we, the Pinheads, found ourselves in the league *championship* match against our arch-nemesis, a team with a name so boring that I have long forgotten it. Unforgettable, though, was their anchor bowler, a man who physically resembled Pavarotti but who bowled monstrously well; he bowled with grace and style and had an average around 200. He moved like a ballerina with a bowling ball in his hands.

A bowling match is three games, with a fourth game awarded for the team that racks up the most total pins in the three games. We won the first two games, and went into the final game leading by about 80 pins—a comfortable margin, we figured. We could lose the game but still win the match and the championship so long as they didn't beat us by more than 80 pins. Alas, in the final game, after two opening spares, Pavarotti got hot and started bowling strike after strike after strike. Around the seventh frame it was clear he was on fire and I recall one of my *Wall Street Journal* colleagues crying out: "Oh, no. He's gonna bowl his weight!"

Well, he didn't quite make it. He only bowled a 279, but that was enough to erase our 80-pin advantage and crush us. We accepted the exquisitely faux-gilded, three-foot-high second-place trophy, being denied the even more exquisitely faux-gilded, six-foot-high first-place trophy.

Though battered and demoralized, we retreated to the bar and were saved from what well might have been our fate—going home and getting a good night's sleep. Instead, we sat at the bar, nursing Budweisers and our wounds and playing "Crazy" over and over again until, feeling better, we switched to "New York, New York" over and over again until people started screaming at us never to play either of those songs again. Sometime later a man with a broom—the same man who had finally unplugged the jukebox—came and kicked us out, whereupon we discovered that all mass transit had stopped running.

Well after I left San Francisco, they tore down Japan Town Bowl and the bar with it and are planning, no doubt, to put up something precious in its place. But the bar lingers forever in my beer joint memory.

It was a benchmark to keep in mind as I headed down the Mississippi.

* * *

My idea to not overly plan my trip didn't seem quite as clever when, sitting in my hotel in Minneapolis, I realized I would have to first head *up* the Mississippi River if I truly wanted to begin at its headwaters at Itasca State Park. In fact, MapQuest told me I faced at least a four-hour drive north by northwest. Beyond that, I knew that the river is but a mere stream at its headwaters, and little resembles the Mighty Mississip' till it clears the Twin Cities. So I decided I would cop out and start on or near the real river.

As for beer joints, the Minneapolis–St. Paul Yellow Pages weren't yielding much more than clutter and confusion when fate seemed to intervene. Rummaging through my downloaded Orbitz travel documents, I stumbled upon a "Things to Do" printout and there was a prospect: Schone's Gasthaus Bavarian Hunter. "Expect big sausages, large steins of beer, and rowdy polkas at this authentic German beer garden in the charming river town of Stillwater," the promo said. "If you're lucky, you'll stop on polka night."

Given the dominance of German-styled lager and the role of German beer barons such as the Busches, Pabsts, Schlitzes, and Millers in shaping—actually, conquering—the American beer market (a matter I deal with in depth later), this seemed an appropriate place to start a quest for the Perfect Beer Joint. When I phoned to get directions, I learned the bar was about a forty-five minute drive east of the Twin Cities. And, alas, this being Saturday, I had missed polka night by one night.

Stillwater was as charming as advertised. It sits on the St. Croix River, a tributary to the Mississippi so handsome that it forms part of America's Wild and Scenic Rivers system. I arrived with the sun sinking behind me in the soft light of dusk and found a low-rise, turn-of-the-century downtown with quaint limestone and brick-front buildings. I later learned that in its nineteenth-century heyday, Stillwater, population 16,000, had been a thriving lumber town with obscenely rich lumber barons living in mansions on the bluffs above the river. These days it is mainly a tourist day-trip destination, with people driving in to take river cruises on period paddle wheelers or to poke around in the town's sweet shops, rare books and antique stores, and plentiful bars and eateries. The only people who probably aren't so keen on Stillwater, in fact, are those spending time in its regional state prison.

The Gasthaus Bavarian, however, wasn't in Stillwater proper; it lay in splendid isolation, surrounded by cornfields, a goodly ways outside of town. I did notice, as I pulled into its spacious parking lot that seemed about two-thirds full, a sign that warned not to park horses beyond a certain point. I looked around but nary a horse was in sight.

From the outside, the Gasthaus Bavarian looked like it could be any other Midwestern supper club. Up a set of broad wooden steps sat a wide veranda with outdoor seating, where a few people sat clustered around tables drinking mugs of beer. Inside, though, the place was bustling, and it was like being abruptly tossed into a beer garden in, say, Heidelberg, the place where as a traveler right out of college I was first introduced to robust German lagers. As part of the Gasthaus's bid for authenticity, the waitstaff all wore traditional Germanic garb—dirndls for the women, lederhosen for the men. The costumes didn't slow anybody down, though; they were either pouring big mugs of beer from ornate German taps or lugging unbelievably big platters of food to tables that were already crowded with beer and food. And whoever wrote the Orbitz promo wasn't kidding about the size of the sausages: I saw a platter go by with sausages lolling atop the red cabbage like pythons on a riverbank. Clearly, a lot of beer would be required to soak those things up. The place altogether seemed noisily happy.

I settled at the end of the bar and was greeted cheerfully by a bartender whose name tag read Mike. The Gasthaus had an impressive array of authentic German beers—and not a single concession to the latter-day American version of German lagers. In fact, Mike later told me that not only were Bud and its American competitors verboten but the clientele had risen up in protest when the bar put in a tap for Beck's. "Everybody bitched and bitched," said Mike. "They said, 'Beck's? That's an *American* beer!' We had to get rid of it." (Well, actually, Beck's is a German lager brewed in Bremen since 1533 under the *Reinheitsgebot*, the German Purity Law of 1516 that prescribes how German beer must be made. Its status as the most popular German import in the U.S. perhaps explains why the picky Gasthaus crowd shunned it.)

When I seemed befuddled by the beer choices, Mike suggested a Hacker-Pschorr, made by a Munich brewery in business since 1417. He poured it expertly and set it before me. I took a sip and it was smooth as a moonstruck night. One thing you can say about lagers: the good ones don't make you work very hard to like them.

Mike got busy so I struck up a conversation with my nearest bar mate, an affable workingman named Andy Holdorph who lived just a couple of miles away. Andy described himself as a regular who came in for the authentic German beer and the conversation. He said the Gasthaus was really just a neighborhood joint, even if the neighborhood was mostly cornfields and cow pastures, and that it had a very clear idea of its clientele. "I know a lot of people think Minnesota is full of Swedes but it's actually full of us Germans," Andy told me.

He then wanted to know if I was planning to come to the Gasthaus Oktoberfest next week. Since it was September 7, I was a bit surprised that Oktoberfest was falling so early. Andy rolled his eyes; it became obvious to him that he was dealing with an Oktoberfest ignoramus.

Yes, he told me, the German beer festival got its start in October 1810 as a public wedding reception for Bavarian Crown Prince Ludwig and his bride Princess Therese. "But the weather was lousy in Bavaria in October so they moved it to September. The Germans are practical people, you know," Andy said. American Oktoberfests generally follow this later calendar. I eventually learned that Oktoberfest in the fatherland had mutated into an annual beer blowout in Munich at which literally five million liters of beer—about 85,200 standard U.S. kegs—are drunk over a sixteen-day period.

Andy said the Gasthaus did pretty well for a place out in the sticks. "There'll be 2,000 people here next weekend," he said. "There's deer stew on the menu."

Deer stew and beer didn't sound half bad, but I had a big river, and many other beer joints, to explore.

I told Andy about my Perfect Beer Joint quest. He thought about it a minute and concluded that the Gasthaus should certainly be in the running.

Mike the bartender, overhearing us, had a few of his own notions.

"It's got to be a workingman's bar," he said, "a place where you're welcomed, no matter what you do. But no BS. You don't want to have to be looking over your shoulder. Oh, and no peanut shells on the floor. And a guy can light up a cigar if he wants to."

He paused and then went on: "And it can't be politically correct. You should be able to tell a Michael Jackson joke and get away with it." (He meant the pop star, not the beer writer.) He had one last thought: "And, oh, yeah, there should be no Big Blues."

This term stopped me and I asked Mike what he meant. At the *Wall Street Journal* where I work, Big Blue is the corporate nickname for IBM, the computer giant.

He explained that this was a kind of German-American beer hall insider slang. Big Blues are bartenders or cocktail waitresses who wear blue lederhosen or dirndls; they have the uniform "and know how to sling gin and pour beer but they're either pompous or have no personality," Mike said.

I told Mike I'd never met a Big Blue but if I ever did, I'd ask for another bartender.

Andy drained his beer and bid us good-bye, lugging home a carton of Gasthaus homemade ice cream for his daughter, and Mike handed me a food menu. I'd studied German for three semesters in college and, as I said earlier, traveled in and around Heidelberg for about a week once, but I had no memory of any of these dishes outside of Wiener schnitzel. Some of the choices, like the fried bread dumplings and the five separate herring appetizers with various cream sauces, seemed a little rich. And I didn't know what to make of *jagerschnitzel*, described as "two breaded pork cutlets in mushroom sauce with potato dumplings and cabbage." *Jagerschnitzel* portended a massive meal. So the Wiener schnitzel it was. It, too, came as a gargantuan heap of food—it could have fed a six-pack of small people, easily. It was tasty but I could only get through about a third of it.

Around 9:00 P.M., as the bar started to thin out, I walked out onto the veranda. It was a gorgeous, mild night, summer stars painting a dark, rustic sky. I got invited to sit with the Baumann brothers, Ian and Joel, friendly young locals who hung drywall by day and hunted for good beer at night. Anyone who's ever hung drywall understands that it's a tedious, hot, dusty job and thus excellent preparation for beer drinking. We were later joined by Mike, the bartender (whose last name I learned was Seggelke), and Jade Harris, Ian's girlfriend and a waitress at the Gasthaus. Jade told me that the bar was such a pleasant place to work that her four years there made her the junior person on the staff. One waitress named Billy Jean was a twenty-year veteran.

I was interested in the Baumanns' opinion of the place because the Gasthaus crowd I'd seen so far was pretty middle-aged. Ian turned out to be thirty and Joel twenty-seven. Ian said that when he was in the mood just to drink beer and talk, this was his favorite place.

"It's very easygoing out here," he said. "It's a very civilized notion of beer. It's not a bunch of young kids just turning twenty-one and seeing how many beers they can pound down."

The Baumanns were of the demographic profile that the big beer companies love—males between the ages of twenty-one and thirty-four who statistically account for about 60 percent of all beer consumed in beer joints, and who drink 59 percent of all light beer. But they were decidedly *not* in the light beer camp and decidedly *not* America's typical Bud/Miller/Coors drinkers.

"Bud uses rice in its beer," Ian told me. "That's a crime. How can you make beer from rice?" (Well, the Bud people say that because the American malt they use is a bit stronger than European malt, using rice helps mellow the beer's flavor. Of course, some beer purists scoff at this.) On the other hand, the Baumanns conceded that their uncle by marriage, a Bud drinker, was always telling them that they were being far too picky. "My uncle has a saying that any beer is better than no beer," Ian said. He laughed and then added, "Well, he's only been my uncle for a year."

The Baumanns said that when they didn't drink here, they sought out places in and around Stillwater that served a burgeoning number of craft beers that had been popping up in the Midwest. They particularly liked Summit, brewed by a small Twin Cities brewer, and were shocked that I hadn't tried one yet. They let me off the hook when I said I'd just blown into town but made me pledge we'd go find one before the night was over. (Beer people everywhere, I came to learn, were zealously missionary about their local favorites.)

"Oh, man, that place rules," said Ian. "I love their beer. When I die, just put me in a keg of Summit."

"Kinda like our friend Kevin," said Joel.

Kevin, I learned, was an old friend of theirs whose family history has been marked by early death; he is the last one standing. Kevin is convinced that, though only fifty, he will die early, too. "That's why he drinks hard," said Ian. "And whenever he gets on the subject, he says, 'I'm gonna miss you, man. But when I die, just come bring a beer to my grave and have a beer with me.'"

Ian stopped to sip his beer, then smiled. "I dunno—I think that's pretty cool."

Jade laughed. She said, "What are we supposed to do? Pour it on his grave?"

While beer and death is an intriguing subject, we moved on, mostly to beer talk and then to small talk. Beer joints are great places to pick up on local peculiarities. The Baumanns spent some time describing the difference between Minnesota and the neighboring Wisconsin when it comes to drunk driving laws. For example, they told me people have been arrested in Wisconsin for drunk driving while operating their riding lawnmowers (but not, to their knowledge, in Minnesota).

Awhile later we heard a whistle blow. Mike, the bartender, said it was a dinner train full of tourists that made a run from Stillwater and was probably returning to town. He suggested we all march up to the nearby tracks, line up, and moon the passengers.

This got about six seconds of gleeful consideration but the prospects of being arrested for public lewdness didn't seem a good way to begin my beer quest. And anyway, the Baumanns and Jade were anxious to take me on a Summit run. So I followed them into Stillwater, leaving the train and its tourists un-mooned. I sipped a very nice Summit Porter—roasty and smooth!—at a place called the Mad Capper. But music crunching from the bar's sound system was so loud that it soon pounded me out the door, and I bid the Baumanns and Jade good night and headed back to Minneapolis.

Back at my hotel, I took out my road map and stabbed a finger at Wisconsin. It landed close enough to La Crosse for me to figure that that was my next destination.

Author's note: Michael Jackson, inarguably the world's best-known beer writer, died in September 2007 of a heart attack in his London home.

3

A Diversion to Consider the Beer Cure

Beer, if drunk with moderation, softens the temper,
cheers the spirit, and promotes health.
—Thomas Jefferson

New York, N.Y.—A couple of months before I began my trip down the Mississippi, an odd invitation came in the mail from the National Beer Wholesalers Association (NBWA), the powerful trade group representing the nation's 2,300 beer wholesalers. "Intellectual Brew," the invite proclaimed, but the subtext was more scientific than intellectual. People were coming to speak at this event from places like Harvard, and the topic was "beer and health."

If this sounded like an oxymoron, I was assured it wasn't. In fact, based on a little pre-reporting, I found out that people were apparently coming to say: Beer is good for you!

"Eat right, exercise and drink a beer a day may be the way to keep the doctor away," an NBWA press release exclaimed.

Red wine, I knew about. But beer?

Yes, beer. The thesis was that beer was slowly bubbling to the top as a beverage that not only lifts spirits but coincidentally delivers statistically relevant protection against heart attack, stroke, hypertension, diabetes, and dementia. As someone facing long months of beer research, the dementia angle particularly interested me.

And if perchance anyone might worry that the event would be one of those droning recitations of statistically significant data, the NBWA, no slouch in the PR department, had organized a fun component as an inducement. We would all show up at Manhattan's elegant Tribeca Grand Hotel, where the hotel's executive chef, John DeLucie, and Daniel Bradford, a certified beer expert, were to run through pairings of ten elegant dishes, all cooked with beer, and the proper beers to sip while dining on these delicacies. Bradford is a founder and onetime director of the Great American Beer Festival held annually in Denver, and is currently president of the Brewers' Association of America (BAA), a group largely composed of the nation's craft and microbrewers. I'd never met Daniel but I'd spoken with him on the phone numerous times and knew him to be not just a fount of beer knowledge but temperamentally of a type I would increasingly run across on the River of Beer: a total Beer Guy, magnificently obsessed by beer and everything about it. Bradford, in fact, has a beer marriage; his wife, Julie, is editor of *All About Beer*, a beer drinkers' magazine with about 25,000 subscribers that she and Daniel bought about ten years ago.

The newsy health angle aside, such an event also seemed a good way to get a ringside seat to the craft beer phenomenon, or what seemed to me could be called the Uptown Beer Movement. The folks in Bradford's organization prefer other terms: the Real Beer Movement is one, the New Brewing Movement another. These designations, I came to learn, were essentially the result of the microbrew crowd—a quarter of a century into their effort to remake beer—seeking a better description of what they were about.

The technical definition of a microbrewery is one that brews 15,000 barrels of beer or less annually. (Bud, by comparison, brews more than 100 *million* barrels a year.) But size alone seemed an odd barometer of quality, and it didn't necessarily describe the kind of beer being brewed. Plus, it didn't fit onetime microbreweries, such as Sierra Nevada, that have grown too large to fit the definition, or well-thought-of regional breweries, such as Yuengling—a family-owned enterprise in Pottsville, Pennsylvania—that make some beer styles interesting enough to fit into the craft beer mold.

The pairing-beer-with-food wrinkle was new to me—it was clear that this was not about washing down pizza with beer. In fact, I'd learned that craft brewers like Garrett Oliver at New York's Brooklyn Brewery were these days seeking to align themselves with the Slow Food Movement, a kind of confederacy of high chefs, restaurateurs, and winemakers organized in Italy in 1986 that styles itself as the anti-McDonald's. Adherents advocate a return to a kind of old-world quality and craftsmanship in the preparation and consumption of food and drink, with an emphasis on using ingredients made by local or regional artisans—the mom-and-pop cheese and bread makers, the free-range chicken grower, the organic olive farmer, and the like.

Oliver, Brooklyn Brewery's brewmaster and one of the few high-ranking African-Americans on the U.S. beer scene, had dedicated much of a recent book he'd written, *The Brewmaster's Table*, to the notion that craft beer belonged in this company, arguing that well-made beer can be as rich, flavorful, and interesting as fine wine, and thus an able companion to food. Indeed, I'd heard him and other craft beer people make the argument that because beer has more ingredients than wine—malted barley, hops, yeast, and water compared with grapes, yeast, and water—it potentially offers more complexity of flavor.

Now, this view—indeed, the very notion of haute beer—may strike the Bud crowd or even more neutral observers as more than a bit overblown. But I'd chatted with Oliver one evening at a craft beer bar in Manhattan called the Blind Tiger, where he'd come to flog his book. His main point was, "Real beer is to mass-market beer like a loaf of fresh-baked bread is to store-bought Wonder Bread. My feeling is that both wine and beer reach their best expression with food, but that beer is by far the most versatile partner."

The seeds of all this got planted (where else) in California in the 1970s. First came Fritz Maytag's revitalized bottling in 1971 of Anchor Steam ales at the Anchor Brewing Co. in San Francisco; then an ex-navy man named Jack McAuliffe, longing for the English-styled ales he'd enjoyed during a tour of duty in Scotland but couldn't find in America, opened the nation's first microbrewery, called New Albion, in Sonoma in 1976. Maytag, scion of the washing machine fortune whose operation has always been too large to be considered a true microbrewery, is still doing great business producing what were, when they were first introduced, positively countercultural ales. McAuliffe's venture was short-lived. Nonetheless both men are credited with jump-starting the craft/microbrew phenomenon at a point when the number of breweries in America was heading for an all-time low. The U.S. entered World War II with about 750 breweries; by 1983, there were only 80 left, consolidated into about fifty owners. The Big Beer juggernaut, led by Bud and followed by Miller and Coors, had among them 92 percent of the market. Craft brewing has had its own ups and downs, but the movement has since put about 1,500 new breweries and brewpubs into operation, creating a renaissance that has made America "the best place in the world *ever* to drink beer," Jim Koch at Boston Beer told me. (Much more about this later.)

At any rate, I'd been to formal wine tastings before, but never to a formal beer tasting. I was curious to see what it would be like.

I arrived a bit early and got a chance to schmooze with David Rehr, the NBWA's congenially pugnacious president, whom I'd met earlier at his Alexandria, Virginia, offices on an early fact-finding and source-scouting mission. Rehr is a stocky man with a quick smile, who carries himself with the bearing of a prizefighter. He is nothing if not plainspoken—well, actually, outspoken—and the NBWA reflects his cheerfully combative attitude. It takes a certain kind of personality to stand toe-to-toe with, for example, Mothers Against Drunk Driving (MADD), the organization that has successfully pushed for stringent drunk driving laws in America, and to argue that lowering the drunk driving threshold from an alcohol blood level of .10 to .08, as MADD has pushed for, is wrongheaded because it diverts attention from the fact that it's the .10 and above offenders who are chief culprits in *fatal* accidents. But Rehr (pronounced Rare) does this kind of thing matter-of-factly, mostly because he is positively missionary in his belief that beer, consumed responsibly, is good for the body, soul, and spirit, not to mention good for the economy and thus good for the country. The main function of the NBWA, along with the Beer Institute—the lobby arm of the big beer makers—is to keep a keen and protective eye on Washington and the statehouses for Big Beer.

Outwardly, in fact, this event seemed an odd pairing, since Rehr and Bradford essentially represent the opposite ends of the industry: Rehr, Big Beer; Bradford, Little Beer. I was starting to learn that tensions between the camps are real and sometimes palpable. They try not to squabble publicly because that's considered bad for beer as a whole, though public squabbles happen. In a nutshell, Little Beer chafes at Big Beer's power over the channels of beer distribution (most beer wholesalers in America make their money off of Bud, Miller, and Coors), not to mention Big Beer's gorilla-sized marketing muscle. Big Beer gets tired of what it sees as Little Beer's constant self-adulation and its chronic insinuation that Big Beer makes mass-market swill that Americans drink only because they're suckers for glib advertising. (It's actually more complicated than this, but more about the NBWA and beer politics later.)

However, this was exactly the kind of event—good news about beer—that Beer People of all stripes like to rally around. Beyond that, beer makers themselves are constrained from directly touting any health benefits on labels or in advertising; thus it's up to trade groups like the NBWA to spread the word on their behalf.

About fifty people showed up for this, most of them fashion, spirits, or food journalists who had come for the beer and food. But we all had to take our medicine first (a shrewd move when dealing with the notorious eat-and-run press). We sat through about an hour of presentations by Dr. Eric Rimm, an associate professor of epidemiology at Harvard's School of Public Health, and Dr. Norman Kaplan, a professor of internal medicine at the University of Texas Southwestern Medical Center in Dallas.

If it seemed odd at first that two such learned men had come to talk about beer, it soon became clear that their beer research was an adjunct of much more serious matters. Dr. Rimm had spent much of his professional life studying associations between diet and lifestyle in relation to the risk of obesity, diabetes, heart disease, and stroke. Likewise, Dr. Kaplan had wandered into the beer-and-health frontier as part of forty years of research on the causes and prevention of hypertension, which, as a leading factor in strokes, is one of the nation's biggest killers. Given that as many as 120 million people in the U.S. drink some form of alcohol and collectively consume more than seven billion gallons of it annually, the effects of alcohol on health—bad and good—is a monumental public health issue.

And both researchers told me later that their findings on beer were really a refinement of the knowledge that began trickling to light more than twenty years ago when credible medical research began to hint at the health benefits of moderate alcohol consumption. The most famous report on that subject appeared in the mid-1990s, when news burst onto the scene that red wine was thought to have special properties that made it essentially *the* healthy alcoholic beverage. At the time, researchers reported the phenomenon as the "French paradox"—the fact that, though the French eat a diet even more fat-rich than that of Americans, they have lower coronary disease rates. Looking for an explanation, researchers settled on the red wine that is a staple in the French diet. Red wine contains goodly amounts of chemical compounds called flavonoids—antioxidants that appear to help lower cholesterol levels and hence help prevent the arterial clogging that is a major component of heart disease.

But a fresh look at that research, plus a raft of new findings, has led scientists to conclude that the original study oversold red wine's singular advantage. For one thing, the French are thought to underreport coronary deaths and heart disease. And most researchers—Dr. Rimm included—say the original French study didn't take lifestyle biases into account. "Wine drinkers tend to be people who eat better and exercise more" than the drinkers of beer or spirits, Dr. Rimm told me. "If you don't factor that in, it makes wine look better." Dr. Kaplan was a little more blunt. "The wine people have done a major snow job" in peddling the notion of red wine's position as the only healthful alcoholic beverage.

The upshot of their presentation was that there have now been so many validated studies on the health benefits of moderate drinking—"moderate" being the pivotal word—that Dr. Kaplan could proclaim the evidence in alcohol's favor "is now incontrovertible." Dr. Rimm added: "My opinion is that regardless of what you die from, it's better to die as a moderate drinker."

And beer, according to Dr. Rimm, absolutely belongs on the list of alcoholic beverages with sanguine effects, though he was reluctant to characterize it as more efficacious than, say, red wine or any other comestible spirit for that matter. Dr. Rimm thinks much of the health-and-alcohol research is pointing toward alcohol's key component, ethanol, as the chief palliative, though no one knows quite why. One theory is that it acts much like aspirin, helping to thin blood and reduce clotting and arterial plaque, thus helping to prevent heart attacks and strokes.

Dr. Kaplan, though, was willing to go out on something of a limb for beer. As for beer's specific virtues, he cited two recent large-scale studies: in one, a look at 70,000 female nurses showed that those who drank moderate amounts of beer had less hypertension than did nurses who drank either wine or spirits. He also pointed to a survey of 128,934 adults in the Kaiser Permanente managed care system. It showed that male beer drinkers among the group were at a statistically significant lower risk of coronary artery disease than were men who drank red wine, white wine, or spirits.

Dr. Kaplan said new evidence also suggests that beer, because of mechanisms that "are not all clearly understood," may help raise by 10 percent to 20 percent the so-called good cholesterol levels in some people, thereby helping to ward off heart disease and related afflictions such as dementia. Beer is also rich in B vitamins and folates (an enzyme also found in green leafy vegetables), both of which help keep homocysteine blood levels in check. (Homocysteine is a chemical that, in elevated amounts, has been linked to an increased risk of heart disease.) For those reasons, said Dr. Kaplan, "beer drinking has equal or perhaps more benefit" than its rivals, wine or spirits.

Of course, before the Joe Six-Packs of the world rush out to quaff a few in celebration, the researchers offered a major caveat. They generally define moderate drinking as one drink a day for women and two a day for men (a drink itself being a 12-ounce beer, a 5-ounce glass of wine, or 1.5 ounces of distilled spirits). Conversely, studies show that binge drinking—considered to be the consumption of six or more drinks in a day—not only obliterates the benefits of moderate drinking but puts drinkers at increased risk for obesity (the notorious beer gut being one manifestation) and certain types of cancers, liver failure, and stroke.

And there are statistics—generally published by anti-drinking groups—that tend to dim this bright news about beer. The Public Health Institute affiliated with the University of California–Berkeley, for example, published a report in 2000 that estimated that 10 percent of beer drinkers account for more than 40 percent of all beer consumption. Though the beer industry disputes this as wildly inflated, it acknowledges the existence of a pre-ponderantly young male group of consumers who don't exactly fit the profile of moderate drinkers.

* * *

As appetizer-sized servings of gravlax with beer and cilantro arrived, followed by the beer-braised chicken and salad with Corona Beer dressing, the question of whether drinking beer was good for you was easily replaced by the conclusion that it was certainly fun. The beer in the gravlax dish turned out to be Budweiser, and the beer Daniel Bradford asked us to take from the ice buckets at our table and open turned out to be Bud's fancy brother, Michelob.

This just showed you how catholic this event was. Of the ten beers we were to sample, eight of them qualified as craft brews. But Michelob and Corona are popular light lagers, and not of a style in favor among the Ale Heads who predominate in Bradford's organization. The Ale Heads represent a return to pre-lager America before the 1870s, when lager began to predominate, and they pay homage to Britain and Belgium, the only two countries in the world where ales still predominate. Ale Heads believe that ales, brewed from feisty yeast strains that ferment at higher temperatures than do lager yeast strains, have more character and range than do lagers and their derivations, such as pilsners, bocks, and Märzens. Most Ale Heads think lagers, even the good ones the Czechs, Dutch, and Germans make, are boring. (An eloquent counterargument on the merits of lager and the cool-loving, bottom-fermenting lager yeast appears later in a chapter exploring the beer yeast underworld.)

At any rate, we popped open the Michelob and everyone poured a couple of fingers into crystal wine goblets.

"Notice the great aromatics in this," Bradford intoned, nosing his glass. "It's light and very delicate...Do you get a kind of tingly taste in the back of your mouth? That's the hops."

I have to admit I'd not drunk Michelob in years and hadn't in the past nosed it, or spent much time noticing its hoppy aroma. But I dutifully sniffed my glass and concluded he was right. And the salmon appetizer marinated in Bud and cilantro was good, too, though it seemed to me there wasn't much beer taste in it. But maybe that was the point. Beer in food, Chef DeLucie would later explain, wasn't supposed to be the main show but to act pretty much as oils and spices do, helping to enhance flavor.

I was wondering what Bradford would say about Corona, these days a light lager most consumers know for the slice of lime you're supposed to force down the bottle neck. I'd drunk a lot of it on a few beach trips to Mexico, and I found it pleasant on a hot day, but it seemed something of an odd pick for a fancy beer tasting.

I also knew that Corona had gotten its U.S. start in the 1960s as a kind of cult beer, winning word-of-mouth endorsement from young American adventurers who had discovered it while surfing in Mexico. From there, it had grown into an import juggernaut, in 1997 racing by Heineken to claim the spot as America's number one imported beer (startling, given that Heineken had held that spot since 1930). In fact, as of this writing, Corona was, by sales, the sixth most popular beer among *all* beers sold in America.

This seems all the more astonishing given that in the late 1980s, the brand, owned by Mexico's Grupo Modelo (and now part-owned by Anheuser-Busch, which in 2000 bought a 50 percent nonmanagement stake), withstood one of the most bizarre smear attacks in corporate history. Salesmen for a Nevada Heineken distributor, jealous that Corona was taking business from its brand, began spreading the word that brewery workers urinated in the beer before it was bottled. The entire affair was the subject of a *Wall Street Journal* feature story in 1987 and ended when the distributor, sued for $3 million in damages by a Corona importer, retracted the slander and apologized. Talk about rebounds: by 2002, Corona was selling 90 *million* cases of beer in the U.S., and as of 2006 it was the fourth best-selling beer in the world.

Bradford seemed to agree with the growing hordes of Corona drinkers, calling the beer "refreshing and tasty with a hint of citrus" and, using a wine analogy, "easy to drink, just like a zinfandel."

I was wondering if Bradford was perhaps just being politic. So I later asked another certified Ale Head, Jim Koch at Boston Beer, what he thought of Corona. He was surprisingly complimentary, too. "It does have its own unique flavor—kind of a grape soda-pop fermentation ester. You wouldn't mistake Corona for Miller or Bud. It's somewhere between a Bud and a Heineken."

I perhaps understood this a bit better when Fritz Maytag at Anchor Brewing, the dean of craft brewers, told me, "Well, you know, once beer drinkers try Corona, usually there's no going back to Bud." Or put another way: the craft beer folk take a reasonably charitable view of most imports, considering them to be the portal through which Bud, Miller, and Coors drinkers, if they are ever going to cross over, are drawn to microbrews. This is kind of like the argument that pot leads to heroin—except the spin (if you're a craft brewer) is positive.

Bradford then moved on to more exotic beer: Goose Island Hex Nut Brown Ale (Chicago); Samuel Adams Boston Stock Ale (Boston); Anderson Valley Barney Flats Oatmeal Stout (Boonville, California); Deschutes Black Butte Porter (Bend, Oregon); New Glarus Belgian Red Ale (New Glarus, Wisconsin); and Ommegang Abbey Ale (Cooperstown, New York). It occurred to me how much like a wine tasting this was—though Bradford insisted that though the style might be borrowed from wine events, the beer writer Michael Jackson is "quite correctly credited with beginning the development of a real vocabulary for beer. We talk about the malt-hop balance, things that actually apply to beer."

But like at a wine tasting, Bradford used the pauses between samplings to impart knowledge, much as a wine steward might discourse on the origins of a certain vintage. He tackled a question about proper beer serving temperatures, for example, noting that lagers, because they are made at colder temperatures, are best served at colder temperatures, whereas ales and their darkish derivations, such as stouts, are best served in the range of cellar temperatures.

He ventured into beer color, entirely a function of malt. "Malt is barley," he said. "You let it sprout. Then you kill it. Then you roast it in a kiln." Typically, the darker you roast the malt, the darker the beer. This explains why Guinness is black.

As we moved deeper into the menu and got to the grilled steak with stout-beer sauce, I thought Bradford might fall over. "This is almost like veal stock," he said, savoring a bite. Then, sampling the paired beer, the Anderson Valley Barney Flats Oatmeal Stout, he described it as "deliciously smooth. This is black malt with oats added. The oats help smooth it out."

He stopped and offered a confession that showed his private beer tastes were not quite as catholic as his public ones. "I love stouts," he said. "It's all I have in my refrigerator."

By the time we got to dessert—beer floats made with vanilla ice cream, Pyramid Apricot Ale, and Fat Dog Stout, and paired with New Glarus Raspberry Tart—I had to admit that I'd gone from being somewhat dubious of the Uptown Beer notion to being charmed by much of what I'd heard and tasted. It was hard to tell much about the beers that were churned up in ice cream, but the New Glarus Raspberry Tart was surprisingly tasty for something I didn't think I would like. It was as if beer had somehow been married to sparkling wine.

I later looked up the Raspberry Tart on the New Glarus website, and this is how it was described: "The voluminous raspberry bouquet will greet you long before your lips touch your glass. Serve this Wisconsin framboise very cold in a champagne flute. Then hold your glass to a light and enjoy the jewel-like sparkle of a very special ale. Oregon proudly shares their harvest of mouth-watering berries, which we ferment spontaneously in large oak vats. Then we employ Wisconsin farmed wheat and year old Hallertau hops to round out this extravaganza of flavor. Why wait for dessert?"

Okay, that's a bit of precious New Brewing preening, perhaps. But then again I had to admit: it wasn't my father's Falstaff.

Author's note: In 2004, the Brewers Association of America merged with a rival trade group to form a single representative for the craft beer industry known as the Brewers Association.

On the Road Again

In the Shadow of the World's Largest Six-Pack via La Crosse, Wisconsin

Drinking beer . . . educates, creates friends, and enlarges humanity's grasp of its own commonalties.
—Los Testigos de Cerveza

I didn't really get out of Minneapolis until Monday morning.

Sunday can be a desultory day for beer anyway, so after sleeping off (and exercising away) my Gasthaus Wiener schnitzel, I'd pitched up early in the evening at Great Waters Brewing Co. and Brew Pub in Minneapolis's twin city of St. Paul. It was a *very* slow night, however, and after taking a gamble on the Cajun jambalaya (which turned out to be pasta), I ordered my one and only beer for the evening before succumbing to Gasthaus lag.

The beer was one of Great Waters' cask-conditioned ales, beers stored and served at cellar temperatures in a tradition owing much to the British. I'd drunk quite a few of those during my reporting days in London, when I would occasionally amble into Ye Olde Cheshire Cheese, a pub off of Fleet Street, where Samuel Johnson spent salubrious evenings after laboring the day over his famous dictionary. The Great Waters rendition was called Old Bastard IPA (IPA being an abbreviation for India Pale Ale). I liked the name and it was tasty—a big beer, nicely hopped, as Daniel Bradford might say. In fact, ever since my Bradford encounter at the beer-and-health seminar, I'd found myself sniffing beers for hops—and feeling a little silly about it. But that didn't stop me, for Bradford had clearly planted a seed of something.

I realized I actually might have a strong beer preference, other than for cold lager on a hot day: I was perhaps a Hophead, or on my way to becoming one.

"Hophead" was a term I'd heard from the Beer Geeks, which itself was another term I'd just learned. "Beer Geek" may sound like a pejorative, but it isn't; it's an honorific bestowed upon Beer People of unusual enthusiasm and knowledge. And it is considered kinder than Beer Snob (which is also subject to be derided as an oxymoron) and most certainly kinder than Beer Nazi, a term I'd heard to deride beer know-it-alls who sought to impose their beer tastes on others.

At any rate, thanks to Bradford's prodding, I'd done a little studying on IPAs and learned that India Pale Ale wasn't made in India (the same as Russian Imperial Stout wasn't made in Russia). It was made by British brewers for expatriates in India during that long colonial experiment known as the Raj, to wash down all those fiery curries they were eating. And its hoppiness was more than just a flavor play: hops serve as a preservative (as can high alcohol content). So IPAs were made strong (typically 7 to 8 percent alcohol by volume) and with lots of hops, to survive the long sea voyage to the subcontinent. It was dawning on me that if you were a Hophead, IPA might be your beer.

I had no way to judge, on a dead night, whether Great Waters was a candidate for the Perfect Beer Joint. But I left it very happy after sampling the Old Bastard IPA.

On Monday morning, I found myself at the doors of the

James Page Brewing Co., a microbrewery in Minneapolis that I knew about because I'd noticed its beer being offered aboard the Northwest Airlines flight I'd flown in on. I'd looked up the address online from my laptop and was pleased to learn that the brewery sponsored an annual Blubber Run, a five-kilometer race that featured a beer-keg stop at the halfway point. As a beer-drinking jogger, this was my kind of race.

I found a small brewery in an antique low-rise brick building tucked into an otherwise nondescript industrial area. I went in and was greeted by Christopher Dunn, an energetic, lanky, sandy-haired man wearing khaki shorts, a green polo shirt, and Top-Siders. If you were looking for a brewer to pose for the L.L. Bean catalogue, this would be your guy.

The first thing I did was to ask Dunn about the dense green vine I'd noticed that was growing up the front of his building.

"Hops," he said.

Hops!

Though I would see fields and fields of hops later in my journey, this was my first hops encounter. Dunn dragged me outside for a closer look.

The vine was climbing Jack-and-the-Beanstalk style up the building. "Hops grow like weeds," he said. Then, examining the vine more closely, he pointed to a mildly alien-looking pod. "See that little piney-cone thing? That's the hop flower. If you take one of those and break it open, you can smell the hop oils and resins that provide you with the aroma and bittering in beer. It's pretty pungent stuff."

Dunn plucked the pod, broke it open, rubbed the separated parts together, and held it to my nose. It was mildly bittersweet and herbal-like, but with a definite bite—exotically pleasant.

Dunn told me that some brewers (Bud is one) actually use the dried flower-cone (pressed into bales) in the hopping process. But most hops these days are processed into hops pellets that Dunn said "look like gerbil food. I'll show you some we have stored in the freezer. The aroma is something else."

Back inside the brewery, we settled at a table near a small bar area where Page serves sample beers to tourists, and Dunn did what any good microbewer would do: he told me something about the brewery while offering me a beer. It was morning yet, but work is work, so I accepted a half pint of his Iron Range Amber Lager after reading a sheet describing Page's five regular and four seasonal beers. One of the brews, called Boundary Waters Golden Lager, was made with Minnesota wild rice. (I wondered if that would make Ian Baumann think better of Bud's use of rice in its beer.) I chose the Iron Range because it had won a gold medal at the Great American Beer Fest in 1999, so why not the best?

I sipped it; now that I was beginning to accept my Hopheadism, I could say that the hops profile was a bit understated for my tastes. But it was malty, smooth, and highly drinkable. Maybe I'd discovered a great breakfast beer.

Dunn told me Page was started in 1987 by a Minneapolis homebrewing lawyer for whom the brewery was named and had an initial output of about 650 barrels a year. A team that included Dunn—a Milwaukee native who confessed to being a Pabst and Miller drinker in college—took it over in 1996; in 1999, the brewery undertook a limited offering to 100 shareholders as a way of raising capital. Output had climbed to about 10,000 barrels a year, and Dunn said he was optimistic the brewery could grow about 20 percent a year over the next several years. Its marketing plan was pretty typical of what I came to learn that microbreweries tried to do: squeeze into a niche built upon good, somewhat exotic beer; build a core of enthusiastic and loyal local drinkers; and use their good word of mouth to spread brand appeal to an ever-widening area. Already Page's brews were being distributed throughout Minnesota and in western Wisconsin, the Dakotas, Chicago, and as far away as California. The brewery here strictly made draft beer. Page had for a while farmed out its bottling operations to Minnesota

Brewing Co., a respected regional brewer that made a popular lager called Grain Belt Premium.

But Minnesota Brewing, like many regionals that had to scrabble in the lager market against the marketing and distribution muscle of the Big Three, had recently given up the fight, Dunn told me, throwing 200 people out of work. This forced Page to shift its bottling business to another regional brewer, August Schell Brewing in New Ulm, Minnesota, about two hours south of Minneapolis. All that remained operating at the 150-year-old Minnesota Brewing plant was a small, smelly, and locally unpopular ethanol-making operation—ethanol being fuel made from corn—that the brewery had taken on in a last-ditch effort to supplement its income and perhaps save its beer-making operations. "It's a nightmare from a PR standpoint," Dunn told me. "But you're seeing more of that across the country as these regional brewers try to hang on." In fact, as I moved down the river, dead regional lager breweries became a mainstay of the landscape—victims of a consolidation trend, the latest round of which I'd come to learn had begun after World War II and had continued unabated since.

We then headed off for a quick but enthusiastic tour of the place. Breweries regardless of size have an essential smell—a signature sweet-and-sour odor of warm malt and fermenting liquids that's perhaps best described as beer in the raw. This one was no different. Beer making is relatively simple, though brewers do tend to throw around a bit of jargon when they describe it.

"Here," Dunn said, as we stepped inside a warm, steamy room stuffed with a large stainless steel tank, "we mash barley in the mash tun." That simply describes brewing's first step, which is transferring malted barley from a storage silo into a large, primary brewing vessel (the mash tun), where it is mixed with water and gently heated in a process called mashing. The mash that's produced is essentially a porridge of fermentable sugars. The mash is rinsed in hot water. The result is a sweet, amber liquid called wort. The wort is drained off, usually by gravity through a false bottom in the mash tun, and the spent, soggy grains usually go to feed some lucky local cattle.

The wort, Dunn went on to explain, then goes into another big tank called a boil kettle and is brought to a boil for about ninety minutes. As the boil begins, hops are added for the first time— these hops are usually of a variety known as bittering hops. "Most of our hops come from the Pacific Northwest, though we still use some from Europe," he explained. "It's similar to wine. Thirty or forty years ago you didn't think of the U.S. as a great wine region, but it is. It's getting to be the same with hops." Toward the end of the boil, the beer is usually hopped again, this time with so-called finishing hops that boost its aroma and smooth out its flavor.

The boiled, hopped wort is then spun by whirlpool to rid it of spent hops and any remaining malt solids, cooled to room temperature through a heat exchanger, and moved to a fermentation tank. There, fresh cultured yeast is added—"pitched," in brewer jargon. The wort is now called beer and over a period of about five days undergoes fermentation as the yeast feeds on sugars and gives off alcohol and carbon dioxide. In some cases, the beer undergoes a secondary fermentation, which can boost carbonation and alcohol levels, or smooth out the taste. The beer is then transferred through a filter to a tank (known as a bright tank), where it is brought to optimum carbonation levels, often with the help of the injection of carbon dioxide.

Some ales can be ready to drink in as little as two to three weeks and lagers in as little as thirty days—Bud is. But many ale and lager styles take much longer, particularly stronger beers that require extended fermentation periods.

Page, like many microbrewery start-ups in the 1980s, began its operation by using refurbished and modified equipment scavenged from defunct dairy-farming operations. It operated a simple two-vessel brewing system, meaning a mash tun and a boiling kettle. "It's not one of the prettiest breweries you'll ever see," Dunn told me, "but we put our money into the end product."*

We then made a detour into the freezer room, where Dunn rustled up a box of pelletized hops to show me. They looked exactly like gerbil food but they smelled a lot better. As I was leaving, he told me that hops are actually a close relative to the cannabis family. "So we do have a hop bong out back if you want to try it," he joked.

I laughed and said I'd skip the hops smoking this time. But it did occur to me that this connection to marijuana must have been the derivation of the 1920s term "hopped-up," a euphemism for a drug high.

Before leaving, I did ask Dunn about the Blubber Run, and whether Page actually did station kegs at the halfway point. "Absolutely," he said. "In fact, this year we're doing things a little differently. We have a bus at the halfway point to haul people back to the starting line, since a lot of people never get farther than the kegs."

* * *

By 1:00 P.M., I'd barreled south down the interstate to the junction of storied, scenic Highway 61, but not before gassing up at a bustling Mobil station where a Shania Twain country music video blared from an amplified LCD screen on the gas pump. I didn't think I needed to be entertained while pumping self-service regular, but I guess the theory these days is to let no moment pass in America without a mass media fix. What'll they think of next—MTV screens in the bathroom stalls?

Bob Dylan, in his satirical 1965 breakout album, *Highway 61 Revisited,* may have introduced Highway 61 to the global music world, but the route it follows, hugging the Mississippi

---

* James Page has since closed its small Minneapolis brewery and contract-brews all of its beer through the August Schell Brewing Co.

for most of its length, is an ancient one, heavy with echoes of Native Americans, frontiersmen, fur traders, riverboaters, and settlers, and, more contemporarily, grifters, madmen, and religious visionaries, not to mention visionary musicians, poets, and writers. Also known as the Great River Road, the official highway was created in 1938 out of existing federal, state, and local routes. Its original purpose, as a major north–south thoroughfare, has been largely subsumed by the construction of quasi-parallel four-lane interstate highways that lop off hundreds of miles from Highway 61's more meandering path. One perhaps unintended virtue of this: traffic and attention have been diverted from long stretches of the Great River Road, which at least has kept the strip mall developers from lining every mile of it with the tacky, kudzulike sprawl that now blights the entrances to an astonishing number of American towns.

Indeed, as I nudged into Wabasha County, I passed through rustic river hamlets with names like Wabasha, Weaver, and Minneiska: I motored up and down bluffs, watching pleasure boats etch silver wakes upon the broad river below; I glided past endless stretches of tasseled cornfields and low-cropped soybean fields, all being nudged slowly toward harvest by a cheerful and unrelenting sun. It was only when I entered the semicluttered outskirts of Winona, Minnesota—an otherwise pretty town with a population of 27,000—that I was suddenly jolted back into beer world.

I swore I saw what seemed to be an improbable sign: for a bowling alley/brewpub.

As soon as I could, I made a U-turn on the four-lane highway and doubled back, and sure enough, I wasn't wrong. Tucked into a shopping center, I spied a sign that read: "The Westgate Bowl/Wellington Pub and Grill/Backwater Brewing Co."

That seemed a lot for a bowling alley to take on. It was about 3:30. I pulled into the parking lot and went in.

The place was almost empty (unsurprising, given the hour)

but seemed as advertised. A long wooden bar, with an impressive array of beer taps, fronted a glassed-off sixteen-lane bowling alley. A woman sat at one end of the bar nursing a beer and talking to a waitress. The occasional thud of bowling balls thumping the floor came from behind the long glass panel behind the bar. I peered through and saw a cluster of kids staking out a solitary lane in a sea of empty ones.

I settled in at the bar and was greeted warmly by the waitress, whose name was Jody Wilkins.

"Yes, we do brew our own beer," she said, in response to my question. "Of course, we serve Bud and the like, too."

I told her I'd never heard of a beer-brewing bowling alley. She said she hadn't either until she worked here and that if I hung around for a while, I might snag the owner-brewer, Christopher Gardner, and have a chat. "He's around here someplace," she said. "You want a beer?"

I actually didn't want a beer, but since I'd had a research beer for breakfast, I couldn't very well pass up a research beer at tea time. I looked the taps over and settled on a Backwater IPA. (Hops again!) Jody poured it and sat it before me, and I sipped it. It was a worthy, well-balanced IPA—and by far the best microbrew I'd ever had at a bowling alley (and, okay, the only one so far).

I nursed my beer for about a half hour and was about to give up on the proprietor when he sauntered out of a back room with a man dressed like a chef, heading outside.

"That's him!" Jody said, pointing.

They'd cleared the door by the time I could respond, but I chased them down in the parking lot.

Gardner at first seemed confused as to why a man with a notebook and pen was running after him and shouting, but said he had a few minutes to talk when I explained my mission. We walked back into the bar/alley and sat at a table where Gardner, a cheerful, middle-aged man who looked like he liked his beer, told me the bowling alley had been started by his father in 1961, with never a thought of adding a brewpub. But Gardner got the idea from his brother, a homebrewer, and started making beer on a shoestring, at first using an old retrofitted soup kettle in place of a mash tun and boil kettle. "It's just a little system," he said. "We brew two barrels a week, usually. When we're busy, we'll brew eighteen barrels a month." (A barrel is 31.5 gallons.)

Gardner said that when he started he had no idea how his bowlers would go for microbrew but he was pleasantly surprised. "I'd guess we sell 30 percent of our stuff and 70 percent of the other stuff."

I asked him if he thought he might be the only brewpub/bowling alley on earth. He said he'd never really considered the question; the town was just a good place to sell beer.

Winona, I learned, was built atop a large Mississippi River sandbar flanked by bluffs on each side. Mark Twain, in his pilot days, called this stretch of the river the "Thousand Islands" and didn't care for all those shifting obstacles the islands created. Winona was largely settled by working-class Poles who came in the 1850s to cut timber for the lumber barons who dominated the town well into the nineteenth century.

"Heck, at one point back then, Winona had more millionaires per capita than any place in America," Gardner told me. These days, Winona was solidly Middle America—a mix of blue-collar workers and a fairly large contingent of white-collar employees and college students, mostly owing to the presence of two colleges, Saint Mary's University, a 1,600-student Catholic-affiliated college, and Winona State University, an 8,000-student state school.

"So we get everybody in here—white-collar, blue-collar, college kids," Gardner told me. "Fall and winter are the busiest, when all the students come back."

Gardner then introduced his sidekick in the chef's uniform, Chad Peters. He turned out to be not only Wellington Grill's actual chef but also the alley's current brewmaster. He'd just come from his lunch shift, and his white chef's jacket looked like it'd had a losing argument with an obstreperous deep-fat fryer. "I started here in '99 as a cook," the thirty-something Peters said. "I became an accidental brewer. I used to brew a lot at home and one day they just said, 'Hey, you wanna brew?' I said, 'Okay.'"

Peters said his philosophy was to keep the beer fairly simple and fresh. "It's all kegs. We don't bottle anything. We make it in small batches and it rarely stays around long. We'll switch our beers from time to time—we'll choose a pale ale over an IPA in the wintertime."

I actually think of pale ale as a summer beer, but whatever, that meant Peters made quite a bit of pale ale. The town gets about four feet of snow annually and a goodly number of zero-degree days, and is frost-free only about five and half months a year. On the other hand, it's probably fair to say that the drinking season in bowling alleys is perpetual summer (though statistics I unearthed indicate that bowling alleys as surrogate beer joints may be somewhat overrated—they only account for 3 percent of all on-premises beer consumption).

At any rate, that's all I got out of Gardner and Peters—they had to run off to an appointment. I thanked them for their time, headed out the door, and steered the rental car back south into early rush hour traffic on Highway 61.

Thus, I drove out of Winona without learning perhaps the most interesting thing about the place: that the aforementioned Saint Mary's University, which Gardner had made a point of telling me was "just up the road" from the bowling alley, was haunted by the ghost of a murderous priest who, having shot one of his brethren of the cloth on campus, had been floating through one of its dormitories for the past forty years. This news came to me during a late-night beer joint conversation in La Crosse, and I later "confirmed" it on a website called Ghosts of the Prairie. But, alas, though the priest apparently liked guns, he was not a beer man so far as I could learn, so I didn't go back to check it out.

* * *

By 4:30 P.M., spying no more beer oddities along my route, I had quit Minnesota for Wisconsin. By 6:00 P.M., after a bit of a look around, I'd settled into a Marriott Courtyard on the river in La Crosse, partly because it had a river view and partly because it was close to Old La Crosse; thus, I could walk in search of the Perfect Beer Joint. Walking was certainly the preferable mode of transportation if I wanted to cover more than one or two beer joints in a night and sample beer at each.

I liked the looks of La Crosse, which an entrance sign told me was the pride of "Wisconsin's west coast" and a tourist brochure I'd picked up at a visitors center said was home to about 52,000 people. The town seemed to have its share of outskirts sprawl and its isolated pockets of neglect, but its downtown and old town were quaint and impressive. French fur traders were the first Europeans to arrive; in the late 1700s they named it La Crosse after watching some Winnebago Indians play a stick-and-ball game that reminded them of a game by that name that they'd played back in France. Today, the game, spelled "lacrosse," is played by an estimated 250,000 kids and college students in the U.S., though in somewhat more genteel form than the original Native American version. Original lacrosse could be a rowdy and even bloody and violent game that some tribes used to settle scores in lieu of war.

In its heyday, La Crosse had also been a timber town and a bustling port, handling as many as 300 steamboats a month. It sits not just on the Mississippi but also at the Mississippi's confluence with the Black and La Crosse rivers. A twenty-five-foot-high, twenty-five-ton statue of Longfellow's mythic Indian, Hiawatha—arms folded, peace pipe at repose—has marked this spot for more than forty years. I found it bizarrely charming, but I guess I'm fond of kitsch. Depending on your politics and sensibilities, it is either an impressive tribute to Native American culture or a caricature thereof (and thus presently a matter of some local controversy). But the spot is considered unique to Native Americans for another reason: tribal lore has it that any place that sits on three rivers will forever be immune from tornadoes. (And for as long as records have been kept, La Crosse hasn't had one.)

Mark Twain called La Crosse a "choice town," and during the late nineteenth and early twentieth centuries it was also a choice brewing town, supporting more breweries than any other Wisconsin town save Milwaukee, which was on its way to becoming the beer capital of America (a title that it some time ago surrendered). Today, many La Crosse residents refer to it as "God's Country," and not necessarily because it has sixty churches, one-third of them Lutheran. Around sunset, at the top of Grandad Bluff, reachable by a winding road 500 feet above the city, La Crosse preened for me, in colors I could scarcely describe, like a postcard in otherworldly light.

It was also edifying (strictly as a beer scribe) to learn that La Crosse has more bars and beer joints than churches—eighty by actual count. I'd have my work cut out for me.

After a nice long jog (a beer pilgrim has to stay in shape), I ended up after dark just a couple of long blocks from my hotel at a place called Buzzard Billy's—well, actually, the trying-very-hard-to-be-wry name on the neon sign out front was Buzzard Billy's Flying Carp Café. Above the neon sign was a wooden one, hung from a substantial iron pole, of a cartoon buzzard clutching a mug of beer. The name made me think Billy's was either part of a chain or a tourist joint. (It turned out to be one of a small chain; one Billy's is in Waco, Texas.)

Still, it sat in a lovely, stand-alone redbrick building, obviously restored with some care, that literature inside would tell me had been a historic 1860s hotel. I have a soft spot for people who preserve antique architecture in lieu of tearing stuff down and replacing it with the squat, East German–styled cinder block squares or neon-lit plastic-and-glass boxes that seem to be required in most contemporary strip malls. And anyway, I was hungry, food being a wise pre-beer-sampling ritual, so I went in.

It was about what I expected: tray ceilings, hardwood floors, exposed brick walls hung with antique Coca-Cola signs, faded beer signs, old thermometers, and various bric-a-brac and whatnots. It might one day look like the Flora-Bama down on the Gulf Coast if it were allowed over time to slide slowly into half ruin. (Live buzzards on the counter: now *that* would be something to see.) The bar had an impressive array of beer taps, flanked by two ole-timey Texaco gas pumps. I puzzled on the gas-and-beer juxtaposition as I settled in at a table and an enormously cheerful waiter brought a menu.

I scanned it and gulped—it was pretty much all Cajun food!

Okay, well, I figured this was some sort of weird fate, testing both my palate and my sense of humor, so I didn't hesitate: I flipped through the menu and ordered the red beans and rice with sausage. I could hardly wait to see what mutation of that most simple of Cajun staples would appear before me.

I was actually much more interested in the beer menu. Not only did the Buzzard have an impressive range of microbrews on tap (plus Bud Light and Miller Lite) and about thirty bottled beers, it also offered a number of relic beers in cans: Schlitz, Falstaff, Old Milwaukee, Old Style, and Stroh's, among them. These were all once proud national or large regional lager makers, with thousands of well-paid, unionized employees (Schlitz, in the late 1940s, was the best-selling beer in the *world*), that had been killed off in recent decades in what might be termed the Lager Wars—a struggle for market shares dating back to the 1870s, characterized by extreme competitive pressures, consolidations, technological upheavals, management misfires, fractious and costly union bust-ups, or some combination thereof.

The beers mentioned above—the labels, not the breweries—

had all been resurrected in the past few years by Pabst Brewing Co. Pabst, in its turn-of-the-century heyday, had been the number one brewery in America and, through the 1970s, a worthy competitor to Anheuser-Busch. But since the 1970s it has been in a slow decline, owing to some extent to its own management gyrations. After swallowing up the Olympia Brewing Co. in 1983, it was itself the object of a hostile takeover in 1985 by secretive California billionaire Paul Kalmanovitz. After buying the company, Kalmanovitz proceeded to plow much of its profits into real estate—as Pabst all the while continued to bleed market share. Kalmanovitz died in 1987, and Pabst's ownership passed to a kind of self-dissolving charitable foundation obligated to sell itself off by 2005 (indeed, as of this writing, Pabst was for sale). Meanwhile, in 1999 the company bought the much depleted Stroh's Brewing Co. operations—a transaction that gave it the Stroh's label and the majority of the other twenty-nine beer labels it now sells.

But Pabst no longer brews beer; it closed its last actual brewery in 2001 and has contracted out all of its brewing operations to SABMiller. Headquartered in San Antonio, Texas, and run by Brian Kovalchuk, formerly an executive with Italian fashion maker Benetton, Pabst's strategy is to spend almost no money on advertising but instead depend on consumer recognition and nostalgia for these relic labels to sell enough of the beer to turn a profit.

The ultimate success of this is still to be measured, though Kovalchuk, in a later interview, told me he was optimistic. Pabst, though still the nation's fourth largest beer company, has been relegated to a minor player in the lager world: its sales have slipped sharply from more than $1 billion in 1999 to about $575 million these days, making it about one-sixth the size of third-ranked Coors. But one curious outcome is that its flagship Pabst label has enjoyed surprising growth in an unanticipated niche—among young, urban countercultural types, represented by the bike messenger and anti-globalization crowd, who have swarmed to it as an antidote to mass-market lager. (Never mind that it is mass-contract-brewed by mass-market lager maker SABMiller.) The beer has slipped into *The Hispter Handbook* (think *The Official Preppy Handbook*, but for the young urban crowd). And in Portland, Oregon, the epicenter of the American craft brew market, Pabst Blue Ribbon outsells Miller Lite in supermarkets and is the beer of choice at the city's one anarchist bar.

I decided not to order a Pabst, having had one fairly recently, but I did briefly consider ordering a Falstaff in homage to my father (and wondering if I would recognize the taste). But, being in Wisconsin, I wanted to try a Wisconsin beer. And there on the menu was a name I recognized: New Glarus, the Wisconsin brewer that had made the fruit brew I'd had at Daniel Bradford's health-and-beer tasting. The beer was called Spotted Cow and it was a cask-conditioned ale.

I wondered if Bradford would recommend pairing it with red beans and rice? Probably not, but I went for it anyway. It was a bit on the fruity side, I thought, but I liked it nonetheless.

My red beans and rice came, too, and here was the shocker: they were terrific—pretty close to what my friends in Louisiana would call N'awlins cookin'. I asked the waiter if the chef had a Louisiana connection. He said he'd ask and came back to report that the answer was no.

The Buzzard was a little too cute and put together to qualify as the Perfect Beer Joint, but I left a nice tip and struck out for beer joints unknown. Ninety minutes later, I'd covered most of the ones within walking distance, including a decent brewpub called Doc Powell's. It served an ale in the British brown ale tradition called Downtown Brown that was quite good—smooth, malty and fruity. However, the place had a sparse Monday night crowd, and beyond that, I was beginning to realize that what I admired about brewpubs was the creative beer, not necessarily the ambience. Most brewpubs always struck me as being essentially Applebee's or Bennigan's or T.G.I. Friday's with indigenous, exotic beer. Now, to be fair, I would meet many people on the River of Beer, including certified Beer Geeks, who loved certain brewpubs and had adopted them as their local beer joint the same way some people adopt the slightly dilapidated beer joints down at the corner of their streets. But I guess I like my beer joints with at least just a hint of grit and, well, maybe even a touch of sleaze.

I was about to give up on downtown, thinking I might have to flag a cab to another part of the city, when rounding a corner of a darkened street I spied a neon sign in the distance. It said, unless my eyes were deceiving me, "Lousy Service." After the relentless cheerfulness of the previous places, maybe I was ready for a little abuse. I headed that way.

The joint was called the Casino, and from the outside it had dive bar written all over it. Inside, it was a time warp—an art deco cocktail lounge that looked like it could have been uprooted from Vegas in, say, 1957, and moved here by large flatbed truck, lock, stock, green rotary telephone, jukebox, beer taps, and all. It was deliciously dark, and as soon as my eyes adjusted I saw an arched entryway; snug, leatherette booths curving against a wall; and a longish bar lined with stools. There wasn't much of a crowd—maybe a dozen people scattered about. I made for the bar and wondered about the icicle lights hanging from the ceiling. Maybe it was always Christmas in here.

I was greeted by a blond, stout, amiable young woman named Tracy, who presented me with an astonishing beer menu—more than 300 beers in bottles alone, never mind the stuff on tap. I looked around, wondering where they kept it all, and anticipating my question, Tracy told me the bar had a beer cellar where it locked away a lot of the good stuff. I noticed a Belgian ale on the menu priced at $25 a bottle—my first encounter with twenty-five-buck beer. What the hell: I ordered it. And, well, just my luck—Tracy rummaged through several coolers and even disappeared into the cellar, but the prize was not to be found.

While I pondered other choices, I told Tracy of my mission.

She laughed and said she could easily describe the Perfect Beer Joint. "It would be a place where I could go in and get a beer for free. And I wouldn't really care what kind of beer it would be. In fact, it would be a bar that would give you *everything* for free—free pizza, too!"

Tracy then proceeded to reveal herself as a fountain of beer knowledge—a Beer Geek (though catholic in her tastes), not to mention a certified mixologist who had attended formal bartending school. This was a refreshing turn of events on the River of Beer, which, for better or worse, I was finding to be a very male-dominated place. All the Beer Geeks I'd met so far had been men. But, then again, about 86 percent of all beer drinkers are male, and there are only a handful of female brewmasters or brewery owners in the business.

Tracy was a twenty-something Milwaukee native who'd moved here a few years back because "it was a pretty town." She worked at the Casino for the past year to earn money—and drink quality beer—while attending the University of Wisconsin–La Crosse. She used to play saxophone in the college marching band, but a bad back had put an end to that. "Now I'm into playing the jukebox," she said.

She went on: "I'm a beer drinker, and this is a good drinking town. With three colleges here, the bar ratio is insane. I pretty much drink everything, and when I'm broke I'll drink what's cheap—Bud Light or Busch Light. But working here, my hardest problem is deciding what beer to try next."

She then wanted to know if I'd yet seen the World's Largest Six-Pack.

I said I hadn't—in fact, I hadn't even heard of it.

"When I was moving here, my dad told me it was the first thing I should see," Tracy said.

She explained: the G. Heileman Brewing Co. had operated a large brewery in La Crosse for almost a hundred years, making a popular regional lager called Old Style. Heileman's giant beer storage tanks sat on the outside of the brewery next to the street—six of them lined up just like a six-pack of beer. Until Heileman went under a few years back (yet another victim of consolidation), the tanks had been painted like cans of Old Style—hence the moniker, "the World's Largest Six-Pack."

Tracy said the brewery was now called City Brewery and was trying to come back to life, in part by brewing its own beer, in part by contract-brewing so-called malternatives or alcopops—beverages such as Smirnoff Ice, malt-based alcoholic concoctions whose taste profile is closer to soda pop than to beer. About all I knew about them was that they seemed to be largely pitched at women drinkers as a beer alternative, and that they were roundly despised by the Beer Geeks.

In the meantime, Tracy told me, the Old Style tanks had been painted white and now looked like a six-pack of some generic beer you might find at a discount warehouse outlet.

I told Tracy I would check the tanks out on my way out of town.

As for the Casino, it had been operating since 1934, for the past twenty-five years under the ownership of Don. He was a seventy-eight-year-old World War II marine, who lived in an apartment above the place and conducted most of the bar's business by phone, usually appearing just once a day. Tracy said Don's joy had been to "go beer drinking all over the world—Europe and Russia—and all over the U.S.—Iowa, out West, or wherever, visiting pubs and breweries." In the glory days of Heileman, he had actually been a Heileman beer taster; the bar was his effort to bring world-class beer to La Crosse.

Tracy stopped and said, "Somewhere around here I have a little tidbit I could show you about Don's philosophy."

She went rummaging around on a shelf behind the bar and came up with a sheet of paper. It was Don's beer manifesto:

"At the Casino La Crosse, we will not become prostitutes to profit. We will serve only brews we will not be ashamed of from the best available around the world. Life is too short to drink cheap brews.... We serve no headache beers from national brewers. Nor will you find Canadian beers here—they are not import quality. Enjoy the best in world-class ales and beers in moderation at the Casino."

Don added a parting shot: "Please don't ask for Bud.... Remember, what Don drinks today is brewed downriver in St. Louis next week."

I told Tracy I'd like to meet Don. She phoned upstairs but after a brief conversation reported that Don wasn't coming down tonight.

Just then, I saw a man get up from a booth against a wall and dart for the door.

Tracy called out, "Hey, how ya doin', Tom?" but Tom disappeared without saying a word.

I found this odd, and before I could inquire about Tom, Tracy went over to wait on a new customer. But a guy sitting two bar stools away from me, noticing my puzzlement, explained Tom's abrupt departure. "I guess you could call Tom a regular. He's a homeless guy who likes to sleep in here sometimes. Nobody minds."

The speaker was a twenty-something, lanky, dark-haired guy, who introduced himself as Clay Holman. He said, "I overheard you telling Tracy about your book on beer culture. That's my area."

"Oh, how so?" I said.

Clay smiled. He said, "I've invested more years than I probably should have exploring beer culture. And I mean that with wisdom. I was just thinking about how much money I've pissed away on beer."

Clay then explained that he was a regular here, too, and, well, a regular in lots of other La Crosse beer joints. And my stumbling in here was propitious, he told me, because, "I'm a serious beer drinker and, for this town, this is absolutely the place."

I got up off my stool and filled in the one next to Clay so I could hear him over the jukebox, which in my short stay thus far had played pieces by Dean Martin, the Band, Frank Sinatra, contemporary jazz diva Diana Krall, Louis Armstrong, Benny

Goodman, and the godfather of smooth soul himself, the Reverend Al Green. The music was clearly as eclectic as the beer. I could feel my Perfect Beer Joint detector start ticking like a Geiger counter.

Clay then proceeded to fill me in on the La Crosse drinking scene. On the plus side, "the drink prices here have to be the best you can get in the States." On the downside, "Oktoberfest here is your quintessential drunken powwow...Actually, when I think about it, the per capita number of bars here is deeply troubling."

Of course, the silver lining to this, Clay said, is that La Crosse seemed to offer something for everyone. There was a hippie bar "with all kinds of trippy stuff in the back" and a bar serving 25-cent shots during something called "power hour," where "all the hard-core alcoholics go." There was the requisite cowboy bar and a "heavy metal bar, but I don't go in there because the music's too loud." And, of course, a brewpub or two and a few other "classier kinds of joints." But of all those choices, Clay told me, "I come here because it's a place for brainy people. It's where you have your little extended family when you go out drinking. I like filtering out run-of-the-mill people, and this place doesn't get many."

I realized, of course, that Clay was basically describing Cheers with an edge. Well, actually, I couldn't imagine Woody or Sam or the Coach—and certainly not Carla—letting Tom, the homeless man, sleep in a booth at night.

As if to prove his point about no run-of-the-mill people, Clay said: "On Saturday night, there was an Amish guy in here. You gotta know that when an Amish guy comes into a bar, he's gonna be a bit bent."

"Get out!" I said.

"I'm serious," Clay replied. "One of the regulars was talking to him."

I had two questions: Did he have a horse and buggy outside, and what was he drinking?

Clay shrugged off the horse question. "And I didn't really notice what he was drinking. I was having a bad night. I really didn't care."

We slipped into a brief silence, and I thought we were done with the Amish, but Clay said that same night he'd heard a story that he thought perhaps could explain why an Amish man would come to a bar in the first place. "Somebody told me that somebody had introduced crack into the Amish community around here. The guy who told me said he'd heard it from a TV reporter."

I burst out laughing at this and even Clay smiled. (I made a note to delve into this later, and a search of the *Wall Street Journal*'s extensive electronic database covering hundreds of newspapers and other publications turned up nary an Amish crack connection in and around La Crosse.)

Clay then stopped to drain his beer, a stout of some kind, and then called Tracy over and ordered a porter. I didn't have a beer yet, and he asked what I wanted to drink.

I'd already figured Clay for a Malt Man (recall Daniel Bradford's explanation that stouts tend to be malt-accented styles). I confessed I was a Hophead, but that I would defer a choice to him as the knowledgeable regular. He puzzled over this for a second and then said, "Well, you need a stout on the bitter side." He told Tracy to bring me a Mackeson's, a British ale. Tracy delivered the drinks, and I told Clay it was his lucky night—as a beer scribe on expenses, I'd pay.

Clay thanked me and then told me something about himself— well, actually, a lot in just the first two sentences.

"Basically," he said, "I'm a slacker and I'm struggling and I'm stuck in this town. I'm a cartoonist, but this town isn't my market."

I'm hardly a student of cartooning, but I asked about his genre. He reached into a sheaf of papers he'd laid on the bar and came up with a thin, glossy book that looked, from the cover, to be a downsized comic book. The title said *Grumpy Dog: The True Story of a Living Legend*. A smug, impudent-looking mutt adorned the cover; he was wearing a blue suit and tie over a white shirt, and smoking a filtered cigarette.

Clay handed it to me and I studied it for a few minutes. The guy clearly could draw, though I didn't quite know what to make of the story line, about a dog named Rufus who had been a TV personality brought low by fame and feral dereliction. I could at least appreciate the back of the book, where he'd included a "Phony Letters Page" of readers who had sent in their reactions to *Grumpy Dog*.

One, from a bag-of-wind art snob, praised its "readable style of storytelling," not to mention that Holman's "sense of line weight and chiaroscuro are appealing." But a counterletter stated:

> *Clay, what kind of garbage is this?! "Grumpy Dog" is an unfunny, poorly drawn, predictable waste of paper. I want my money back!*
> *Love,*
> *Dad*

Holman later told me he had self-published the book with his parents' help after getting turned down by a number of publishers. He was selling copies in bars, and to his friends, for $2, which I couldn't imagine came close to covering the printing cost. So it was hard for me to know whether this phony parental letter was self-deprecating humor or something deeper. Thinking about it, Holman's work reminded me of stuff you'd see in the *Village Voice* or some big city alternative newspaper back in the 1960s.

Of course, this wasn't the 1960s and La Crosse wasn't a big city.

"That's the problem," he said. "I just don't like the odds. I don't want to go to some mom-and-pop publisher with this. I'd like to do something that would get me into Barnes & Noble."

I could tell we were skating toward one of those moments when you order another beer and curse the trenchant unfairness of life and punch up "Crazy" on the jukebox. To avoid that, I was thinking about diverting the conversation back to the purported Amish crack epidemic when the Marine Corps anthem and Abigail and Leah saved the day.

For just about the time that the "Halls of Montezuma" came blaring out of the jukebox (an antidefeatist number if ever there was one), Abigail and Leah, young, bubbly friends of Tracy's who had come in moments before, started kissing.

"Hey, no making out at the bar, lesbians!" Tracy shouted with obvious glee.

Even the author of *Grumpy Dog* was snapped from his torpor over this turn of events.

The cute couple broke off, and Abigail came over to us. She apparently knew Clay.

"Oh, is that the new comic book?" she asked Clay, noticing the copy of *Grumpy Dog*.

Clay nodded.

Then she said, "Did you hear we got married recently?"

Clay didn't know what to say to that.

I didn't, either, though I did wonder if I should offer a toast. Instead, I snapped into journalist mode and angled for safe territory.

I said, "So, what is it you do, Abigail?"

She threw her head back and laughed. She said, "*This! This* is what I do!"

She then went back to Leah. The Marine Corps anthem ended, and I heard Abigail and Leah ordering drinks called Jolly Ranchers. Tracy made them up and set them on the bar. Then a Diana Krall song came on, and Abigail and Leah went off to slow-dance.

"Hhm," said Clay, "I don't know about that marriage stuff. Is it an exaggeration? I've known Leah for a long time and it's news to me."

We then sat silently for a while, watching the lasses dance and frolic, and contemplating their happy "marriage," and I just knew after this there was no way we were going back to the depressing stuff. So Clay filled me in on more La Crosse lore, notably the mysterious question of whether all of downtown was connected by a series of secret tunnels that had been built during Prohibition, allowing people to move easily among the speakeasies and brothels that proliferated back then.

This question seemed to go round and round, the way questions do when it gets late in a bar and the beers keep piling up. A semidefinitive answer arrived around 1:45 A.M. from a guy who claimed to have intricate knowledge of La Crosse history. He said that though the tunnels once existed, they had been closed up during a construction project some time ago designed to make the streets tourist friendly. Until then, "this place had been prostitute heaven," he said. (This same guy then told me the story of the murderous priest up the road in Winona.)

On that note of resolution, and clutching the copy of *Grumpy Dog* I'd bought from Clay, I bid the happy Casino crowd good night and headed back to my hotel, only sorry that those mysterious tunnels no longer existed and that I hadn't met the mysterious Don. This was my kind of joint, and beer joints down the river would have their work cut out for them.

I headed out of La Crosse the next morning (not particularly early) and made a beeline for the City Brewery and the World's Largest Six-Pack. I thought I might even try to get a tour of the Smirnoff Ice brewing operation but found the brewery closed up like a church on Tuesday, though a placard did tell me that it was once the seventh largest brewery in America by volume.

But there loomed the six-pack, mighty even in its bland coat of white paint. I parked the car, got out, and walked up to see the behemoth. A sign in front of the middle tank told me all I needed to know. The six-pack was capable of holding 22,000 barrels of beer, or 688,200 gallons. That's enough beer to fill 7,340,796 cans, which, if placed end to end, would run for 565 miles and would keep a person in a six-pack a day for 3,351 years.

5

The Plymouth Rock Beer Detour (Or, a Pause to Consider the History of the River of Beer)

Fermentation may have been a greater discovery than fire.
—David Rains Wallace

If you doubt that the River of Beer runs deep into America's past, consider the following:

It's November 9, 1620, and there are the Pilgrims aboard the *Mayflower*, 101 in all, bobbing around off the gray, wintry Massachusetts coast, many of them seasick. They have finally spotted land after more than 2,500 miles and sixty-four miserable days at sea. But, alas, this isn't Virginia, their intended destination. It's Cape Cod, which will be a swell place to visit—in about 300 years. It holds no suitable landing spot, and the *Mayflower*'s crew must push on down the coast.

Two days later, though, the crew has had it and so have the passengers, who, though they've fled the Old World seeking freedom to practice their austere, separatist religion, are beer-drinking

Christians. They've arrived at Plymouth Bay, which does afford a safe place to come ashore, and decide to call it home. That's because, as the group's leader William Bradford writes in his diary, "We could not now take much time for further search...our victuals being much spent—especially our beere."

It isn't recorded whether any of the ship's beer got left on the shores for the Pilgrims, who, with the help of friendly Native Americans, went on to organize that famous party known as the First Thanksgiving. But it is recorded that the beer-short crew sailed back to England in a speedy thirty days—perhaps pushed on by the fear of no beer at all.

I digress from my narrative long enough to explain how the River of Beer came to be and what forces and events have shaped and transformed it as it flows through America today. Though you probably didn't learn of the *Mayflower* beer connection in seventh-grade history, it's clear that beer was present at the very beginning of the American experience. One lament of the poor Pilgrims in their first years in their new world was that they had no barley seed, thus could not make malt to brew proper beer. No matter: ingenious Native Americans graciously supplied tips on how to make beer from corn, pumpkin, and walnut chips. This was hardly surprising: Christopher Columbus, on his fourth voyage to the New World more than a century earlier, reported that the indigenous people of Central America brewed a corn elixir that reminded him of British ale. And such innovation, together with beer's chronic reinvention, either in substance or by marketing, along with waves of expansion and consolidation among commercial brewers, has been a remarkably resilient feature of the American beer scene.

But first a bit of background on the very beginnings of beer history. In 1952, a debate, prompted by a scholarly response to a scholarly article by anthropologist Robert Braidwood in *Scientific American* magazine, began that continues unabated today. It is over a rather startling question: Which came first—bread or beer?

Anthropologists speculate that both were discovered by happenstance. Somebody ground up or chewed up a primitive grain; it somehow got wet, by design or accident, and turned into a pasty glob, then was abandoned on a rock in the hot sun. It baked, in an early demonstration of solar power, into bread.

Or: Wild barley harvested by ancient hunter-gatherers got damp and sprouted, then got rained on and sat forgotten for a while in water. Wild, airborne yeast strains, which exist in every climate on earth, invaded the broth and induced the then unseen alchemy of fermentation. There you have it: beer.

Braidwood argued for bread.

I personally and with obvious self-interest vote for beer as the forerunner, buying the arguments of Jonathan D. Sauer, a University of Wisconsin botanist, who took the beer side of the *Scientific American* debate. For one thing, barley was among the first domesticated grains and eventually came to be used by bakers and brewers alike. (One widely known modern-day food use of barley is Grape-Nuts cereal.) But the work required to gather wild barley, and later domesticate it for food purposes, Sauer pointed out, would've been daunting for the ancients, who had only the most primitive tools and knowledge. Thus, the initial food payoff—a few lumps of hard, dry, unappealing bread—would have been scant inducement to abandon hunting for barley growing.

Accidental beer, on the flavor front, might not have seemed much better. It no doubt looked and tasted pretty foul—cloudy, sour, skunky to the smell, unrecognizable to any modern beer drinker. But, ah, the buzz it imparted, to use a modern term. This certainly would've gotten the attention of the experimentally inclined tribesperson brave enough to take a few sips. So taste be damned: the seemingly magical mind-altering attributes of accidental beer could well have provided a huge incentive for the first beer sippers to try to re-create the accident. They could've even hastened it by pouring a splash of the accidental beer into the hoped-for new batch, a lucky guess that would've introduced surviving live yeast to start fermentation all over again (a practice, in fact, that later brewers intuitively used, even before they had connected those invisible yeast organisms to fermentation). Historians and archaeologists believe that barley has probably been cultivated for at least 10,000 years, making brewing at least that old but probably much older.

History tells us (and so does the Beer Institute's informative Web site) that the first written record of beer anyplace is a 4,000-year-old Sumerian recipe carved into a clay tablet dug up from ancient Mesopotamia, the area between the Tigris and Euphrates rivers long considered the "cradle of civilization" and a known site of early mass barley cultivation. (Mesopotamia today is known by a different name and for a different reason: it's called Iraq. And the beer, including Miller Genuine Draft, found during the invasion phase of the Iraq War in the fridge in Odai Hussein's abandoned sybaritic pleasure pad, bore no resemblance to ancient Sumerian brew.)

The 4,000-year-old recipe wasn't just the musings of some scribe noodling in cuneiform, the pictograph form of writing the Sumerians invented. It was, according to the translation, given to the Sumerians by their chief god, Enki, in the form of an epic poem called the Hymn to Ninkasi (who, until some more ancient tablet is unearthed, can lay claim to being the original Beer Goddess). And there is good evidence that this beer, made from unleavened bread called bappir, was leaps ahead of the accidental swill of prehistoric times because, well, two Americans re-created it in 1989. Fritz Maytag of Anchor Brewing Co. and Solomon Katz, a respected bioanthropologist and beer historian at the University of Pennsylvania, working with a University of Chicago translator, decoded the Hymn to Ninkasi and figured out that it was essentially a primer on Sumerian beer making. Using Sumerian techniques and what they believed was a reasonably accurate rendition of the recipe (a mixture of dried barley-dough bread to form the mash, plus dates, honey, and a mystery fermenter known as gestin), they brewed up a ceremonial batch, substituting brewer's yeast for gestin. The taste, Maytag now recalls, was "better than you might have expected—not much like beer but pleasant, and similar to homemade apple cider."

In fact, archaeologists would be hard-pressed to name many ancient civilizations, including wine-loving Greece and Rome, in which they haven't found, in the ruins and rubble of tumbled-down cities, images of people making, delivering, or drinking beer. Plato even said, "He was a wise man who invented beer," though Herodotus didn't think much of it, preferring wine while conceding that beer was extremely popular in the "barbarian states," such as the Roman colonies of the British Isles.

Hammurabi, whose Amorites conquered Mesopotamia around 1800 B.C. and set up the kingdom of Babylon, was known as a great reformer and early codifier of laws known as Hammurabi's Code. But here's something else you probably didn't learn in seventh-grade history: beer was so important in Babylonian culture that a portion of the code was given over to the intricate regulation of beer parlors. It certainly put drama into beer drinking: tavern keepers who overcharged customers were put to death by drowning, while any high priestesses caught frequenting beer parlors were condemned to death by fire.

The ancient Egyptians likewise brewed beer, and the barley-and-wheat-based beverage was so treasured that the Egyptians believed it had been delivered unto the people by the god Osiris himself. Hek, as it was originally called, was the Egyptian national drink, and the pharaohs strictly enforced beer quality with official beer inspectors. British archaeologists found an entire kitchen/brewery while sifting through the tomb of boy king Tutankhamen; beer scholars in 1996, with the help of U.K. brewer Scottish & Newcastle, deduced the recipe from writings and wall paintings and produced 1,000 bottles of Tutankhamen Ale. The first bottle sold for $7,200 at auction at Harrod's of London—a record price for any bottle of beer.

University of Pennsylvania Museum archaeologists, on a dig in central Turkey in 1957, unearthed a gold-laden royal tomb that scholars believe belonged to a ruler who was likely the inspiration for the legendary King Midas. (In legend, at least, the king nearly starved when everything he touched, including his food, turned to gold.) Among the relics found in the 2,700-year-old tomb was the largest set of Iron Age drinking vessels ever discovered. Some forty years later, Patrick McGovern, a University of Pennsylvania Museum archaeological chemist, ran biochemical analyses on the vessels' residue and determined that it was the dry dregs of an ancient elixir whose components included barley beer, grape wine, and honey mead. (This beer, too, is being made commercially, but more about that later in a chapter on Extreme Beer. Suffice it to say that replicating ancient beers has become a niche in commercial brewing and is also big among U.S. homebrewers.)

Beer was a central fact of life in much of Europe by the eighth century A.D., treasured not only as food and a mild intoxicant but because it didn't kill you like the water of the time did. The Vikings were great beer swillers, brewing on ships as they sailed up and down rivers and oceans looking for places to plunder. Beer-induced hallucinogenic stupors were part of a quasi-spiritual exercise that worked the Vikings into a trance on the nights before they sent out raiding parties.

An epic poem of Finland, known as the Kalevala, devotes an entire rune to brewing, not to mention a passage in which a heroic protagonist, served a tankard of beer brimming with toxic serpents, first dispatches the snakes by catching them with fish hooks, then drinks the beer (yuck!) and kills his inhospitable host in a sword fight.

By the eleventh century, the Germans, Dutch, and brewers in the Czech lands, known then as Bohemia, had introduced hops into beer—until that time beer had been flavored with herbs such as rosemary, bog myrtle, thyme, and yarrow. These early brewers first noted the preservative qualities of hops, important because before this discovery, beer spoiled quickly. Brewing, until the Middle Ages, was largely an enterprise carried out at home, mostly by women.

By the thirteenth century, that began to change as beer making became a thriving commercial trade in Germany, Austria, Bohemia, and the British Isles. About that time monasteries, where literate monks started writing down recipes and techniques and turning their energies toward scientific brewing, began playing a significant role in beer production, as they still do in modern-day Belgium and a handful of other countries. Meanwhile, a beer-friendly thirteenth-century German duke and brewer named Jan Primus was apparently so beloved by the beer-drinking hordes that after death he was made the patron saint of beer and idealized with a new name, King Gambrinus. (At least, that's one of the theories of the origin.) Flash forward to the 2003 Oregon Brewers Festival in Portland, where a brewer dressed up like King Gambrinus wended his way through admiring crowds. Indeed, breweries and beer festivals all over the world honor this king who was never a king at all.

By the mid-1500s, Bavarian monks, looking for a way to defeat the summer heat that spoiled beer all too quickly, began storing beer in cool cellars and even caves in a process they would call lagering. The connection of yeast to fermentation, not to mention the development of a pure strain of lager yeast, was still at least 300 years away, but never mind. This was the beginning of the beer style that would one day change the beer world.

In Britain by the middle 1500s, beer was such a staple of life that Queen Elizabeth was said to enjoy a pint of strong ale a day—for breakfast. By this time, the British alehouse, a forerunner to the modern British pub and our beer joint, was already 600 years old. British literature, from Chaucer to Shakespeare, is rife with references to beer, the inns and taverns that served it, and ale-induced mischief. By Shakespeare's peak, in the late 1500s, beer still meant strictly warm, dark, and usually cloudy ale, but it was commonly categorized by strength—strong beer, table beer, ship's beer, and small beer in descending order. Small beer referred to a weak ale made by taking once-brewed mash, rinsing it with hot water to extract a diluted wort, and brewing a second batch of beer from it; many people drank it at every meal. (As an aside, Maytag's Anchor Brewing Co. makes a contemporary small beer.) The Bard was perhaps venting his personal beer tastes when, in *King Henry VI, Part II*, he has a character declare "I will make it a felony to drink small beer." Over time, the term became synonymous for a trifling thing (or person).

Shakespeare at least lived in the proper age to experience one revolution in British tastes—the introduction of hops to British brewing. One theory has it that the Brits, soldiering in the Low Countries, developed a taste for hopped Dutch beer and began importing hop vines by the early 1400s, more than 300 years after they had been widely used in the rest of Europe. Xenophobic Britons at first rebelled, calling the hops an "adulteration" and "wicked weed" and outlawing them for a while. The Brits came to their senses, and by 1700 British beer was thoroughly hopped. In fact, by the 1820s the now mad-for-hops English were shipping thousands of barrels of the strong, hoppy beers known as India Pale Ale to the subcontinent.

In the early 1840s, the world beer road would suddenly diverge when brewers in Pilsen, Bohemia (now the Czech Republic), introduced lager that was for the first time as clear and golden as much beer is today, a style that would come to be called pilsner. The development of pale malt was a major factor, together with the fact that lager yeast, unlike top-fermenting ale yeast, ferments and settles out at the bottom of brewing vessels and can thus more easily be removed. Coupled with the startling invention of clear glass for drinking ware (until that time, beer had been drunk in stone, ceramic, or metal vessels), beer was no longer simply nourishment and a mood elevator: it was beautiful.

American beer would be some derivation of British ale until lager reached these shores with the German brewing invasion starting in the 1840s. Since early colonists could hardly rely on

British imports for all their beer needs, they began immediately to brew their own. Virginia colonists were making beer with corn as early as 1587; in 1609, America's first "Help Wanted" ads appeared in London newspapers seeking brewers to come to Virginia. In 1613, Adrian Block, a Dutch explorer, set up a brewhouse in a log cabin at the southern tip of Manhattan Island, gaining credit for establishing the first brewery in the New World.

American colonists plotted revolution in their New World taverns. The famous Boston Tea Party of December 1773 inspired colonial rebels to converge over pints in Fraunces Tavern in New York City to plan a similar raid on British ships in the Hudson River. (You can still order a pint of British ale there today, or you can have a Budweiser.) Beer, in fact, had become as contentious as tea. As early as 1750, colonists had organized boycotts of British beer, accusing the Brits of dumping cheap ale on the colonies to suppress the nascent American brewing industry. George Washington was said to be fond of a new British style of beer called porter (a rich, dark ancestor to stout) but publicly agitated for his fellow citizens, in one of the first "buy-American" campaigns, to drink American-made porters. (One irony: porters have virtually disappeared from Britain but are being kept alive by numerous U.S. brewers, including Yuengling in Pennsylvania. In fact, America, thanks largely to the craft brew revolution, has become a kind of ark for numerous international beer styles that are no longer being made in their native countries.) During the War of Independence, Washington and his troops drank a concoction called spruce beer that was indeed beer flavored with an extract made from boiling spruce twigs (in lieu of hops). However it tasted, it offers one explanation for the term "spruced up"—for surely the world to Washington's soldiers looked brighter and snappier after they had drunk their daily quart allowance.

Beer took off after the Revolution, and by 1810 there were 132 commercial breweries pumping out 185,000 barrels of beer a year for a population of about seven million. That same year, President James Madison entertained a petition to set up a national brewery in Washington, D.C., the petitioners explaining that not only was beer good for American commerce but it was a foil against a rising demon stalking the land—whisky and other forms of hard liquor that were growing in popularity. But Madison demurred after his advisor on the matter, Thomas Jefferson, pointed out that private enterprise seemed to be handling America's beer needs just fine.

Beer was an early example of the industrialization of a popular commodity; the first American steam engine was installed in a brewery in Philadelphia in 1819, and brewing was largely a mechanized industry by the time of the Civil War, when the number of breweries had grown to more than 1,250. Beer was also an extremely lucrative business; Matthew Vassar, a self-educated man who became both a brewer and a barley malter, had done so well by 1861 that he donated 200 acres of land plus half of his ale fortune—$408,000, a huge sum for the times—toward the founding of the nation's first high-quality women's college. Though now coed, it is still called Vassar College, and its students still occasionally break out in grateful song, to wit:

And so you see, to old V. C. / Our love shall never fail.
Full well we know that we all owe / To Matthew Vassar's ale.

American beer's first truly golden commercial age still awaited it, however, and its foundations were laid by the arrival of an estimated one million or more German immigrants fleeing the royal revolts and counterrevolts, high taxes, and scarce land of the fatherland—and bringing their newfangled beer style with them. The beer, of course, was lager in the pilsner style, and the first American lager brewery is said to have opened in 1840 in Philadelphia. In less than three decades, immigrant Germans whose names would live long in American brewing would join the lager fray. In 1842, the Schaefer brothers opened a commercial lager brewery in New York City; in 1844, Jacob Best founded a lager brewery in Milwaukee and later bequeathed the operation to his partner and son-in-law Frederick Pabst. Jacob's son, Charles Best, also operated a Milwaukee lager brewery known as the Plank Road Brewery but sold it in 1855 to a newly arrived young brewer named Frederick Miller. Joseph Schlitz, who had worked as a bookkeeper for Milwaukee brewer August Krug, took over management of the brewery when Krug died in 1856 and two years later married Krug's widow. He renamed the operation the Joseph Schlitz Brewing Co. (and, alas, drowned in a shipwreck a year later). In St. Louis, a well-to-do soap manufacturer named Eberhard Anheuser bought out his partners in the small Bavarian Brewery in 1860 and a few years later put his son-in-law Adolphus Busch to work there. Adolphus later took over the brewery and changed the name to the Anheuser-Busch Brewing Association.

By 1872, the year Adolphus Busch first began bottling beer for shipping in a nascent and novel quest to build a national brand, lager was beginning to chase ale from the American beer scene. A surge in population and the popularity of this new, pale, easy-to-drink beer had pushed the number of breweries in America to 4,131—a record never since surpassed. That number is understandable given that beer didn't yet travel well; it was still mostly unpasteurized and stored in and poured from wooden kegs in taverns, bottled brew being yet a novelty. By necessity, then, beer was a localized enterprise, with breweries springing up on the fringes of working-class neighborhoods in easy access to the numerous and thriving saloons that served those workers. New York City alone once supported seventy-five breweries; Philadelphia and Chicago had more than fifty each (though Chicago had many fewer after a certain incident involving Mrs. O'Leary's cow). Meanwhile, Milwaukee, the self-proclaimed "Beer Capital of the World," staked that claim not on brewery numbers but on the basis of being home to many of the nation's largest breweries, including Blatz, Miller, Pabst, and Schlitz.

The neighborhood brewery model was soon rendered obsolete with the coming of ubiquitous railroad transportation, which made shipping easier and faster, and the development of mechanical ice-making machines and refrigeration, which was critical to the storing, shipping, and serving of lager, which needs to be kept and drunk cold. And not least, also, was the process of pasteurization developed by the brilliant French biologist and chemist Louis Pasteur. Having already shown that unseen microbes spoiled beer (and milk and wine) and could be eradicated by applying heat and pressure, Pasteur in 1876 rocked the beer world by publishing his treatise, *Studies on Beer*, proving definitively for the first time that distinctive strains of yeast were responsible for fermentation. (Pasteur had hoped this knowledge would get his fellow Frenchmen interested in beer, but it was the Germans, of whom Pasteur was not fond, who took advantage of it.)

In this new beer universe, where pasteurized, refrigerated beer could travel great distances, Adolphus Busch's notions of a national brand didn't seem so far-fetched. A single large brewery could operate on economies of scale heretofore unknown and replace a dozen neighborhood ones. Wave after wave of closings and consolidations followed, and the first rounds of the Lager Wars saw the number of breweries fall to about 2,800 by 1880 and to about 1,500 in the decade before Prohibition in 1920. (Among consolidation's victims was Matthew Vassar's ale brewery, which simply declined to make lager and went out of business in 1896.) By 1933—the end of Prohibition, that grand, failed experiment in temperance—there were only about 750 breweries left in the U.S. America would come out of World War II with fewer than 500—whereupon another round of consolidation would begin.

Prohibition, however, did give America a new approach to distributing beer: the Twenty-first Amendment, which rolled back the Eighteenth Amendment and ended Prohibition, also effectively ended the "tied house" system, through which brewers previously controlled bars and other outlets. The amendment cleared the way for Congress and the states to create what is known as the Three-Tier System, a highly regulated class of independent beer distributors to act as middlemen between the brewers and the retailers. One consequence of this has been the making of a resilient and potent grassroots political base for beer. (More about beer politics later.)

From the time of the German lager invasion through Prohibition, the Great Depression, and the end of World War II, American beer underwent not only further changes in style but also changes in perception. Many of America's early German lager brewers had brought with them a solemn adherence to the *Reinheitsgebot*, the German Purity Law of 1516, which mandates that all beer be made solely with malted barley and hops (and later amended to include yeast, once yeast was discovered). But early on, so-called adjuncts began to find their way into beer production, with brewers adding starchy grains—corn was popular, while Anheuser-Busch used rice—to their malt. Brewers saw two advantages of this: first, it produced a beer even paler, drier, and lighter tasting than the original pilsner model most brewed. Second: adjuncts also significantly shaved brewing costs by adding an inexpensive starch to the fermenting process—i.e., they were a cheap way to achieve alcohol levels. The move to adjuncts gained momentum during the Great Depression and later during World War II, when beer makers were forced to find cheap alternatives either to survive or because of shortages. Even when the shortages eased, many brewers, fond of the cost savings of adjuncts, never went back to pure malt beer. By the 1950s, this light, adjunct-adulterated style had a name: American Standard.

But it wasn't simply that lager had become paler and lighter and even easier to drink or that beer had become big business. Where once beer had been the beverage of kings, pharaohs, gods, and goddesses; where once the Founding Fathers of the new nation had expressed their fondness for beer as publicly as the tinker and the soldier, beer by the 1880s in America began to develop a distinctly working-class aura. The nineteenth-century beer hall became the favored meeting place of the rising trade-union movement, a movement that, though it unquestionably improved the lives of millions of American workers, also had at its fringes a violent and hooligan side.

In 1882, beer saw its first high-profile alliance with sports when the relatively new game of baseball underwent a schism and a group calling itself the American Association broke off from the National League. The issue: the National League had just doubled ticket prices, banned Sunday play (the working stiff's day of leisure), and, worse, prohibited the sale of beer at games, all in the hopes of attracting a better sort of fan. Franchise owners in major beer hubs like St. Louis and Philadelphia revolted and started their new league with rolled-back ticket prices, Sunday play, and plenty of cold, cheap lager for sale. The league, ridiculed as the Whiskey and Beer League by the opposition, didn't last long, but the equation—sports + beer = fun and working-class camaraderie—endures even now.

Of course, the working-class affection for beer had a dark side—the intractable problems of alcoholism and public drunkenness, both considered moral failings in the nineteenth century—and starting in the 1870s, there were many organizations happy to point that out. One was the Woman's Christian Temperance Union, whose most famous member would be the six-foot-tall, saloon-smashing Carrie Nation, who once said: "Men are nicotine-soaked, beer-besmirched, whiskey-greased, red-eyed devils." The Anti-Saloon League, formed in 1883, would join forces with the WCTU and others in the long and inexorable run-up to Prohibition.

Big Beer helped arm them. Given what a cutthroat business beer had become, numerous big beer companies engaged in rather appalling practices to lock up large numbers of saloons to sell their brands exclusively and offered devious incentives, like free lunches based on beer purchases, designed to relieve the workingman of his hard-earned money and send him home drunk and intemperate. The Anti-Saloon League—made up mostly of Eastern and Midwestern elites, many from the clergy class—conducted a particularly vigorous public relations campaign that painted beer joints as dens of crime and prostitution, and as the debauchers of the morals of American youth. In one measure of how far beer was heading down the class-ladder rung, consider the remarks by Richard P. Hobson, an Alabama congressman, in his vote in favor of an early form of the legislation that would eventually banish beer and booze from America for thirteen years. Its essence: that beer and moderate drinking were in fact *more dangerous* to the public health than drunkenness and whisky.

> Some are trying to defend alcohol by saying that its abuse only is bad and that its temperate use is all right. Science absolutely denies it, and proclaims that drunkenness does not produce one-tenth part of the harm to society that the widespread, temperate, moderate drinking does. Some are trying to say that it is only distilled liquors that do harm. Science comes in now and says that...malt and fermented liquors produce vastly more harm than distilled liquors, and that it is the general public use of such drinks that has entailed the gradual decline and degeneracy of the nations of the past.

The big brewers like Anheuser-Busch, Pabst, and Schlitz managed to survive Prohibition by switching to products like nonalcoholic near beer, candy, soft drinks, baker's yeast, and ice cream while gangsters such as Al Capone made tens of millions of dollars in illicit profits commandeering breweries through fraud or strong-arm tactics and brewing the real thing for the black market. (We catch up with Capone's brewing strategies in the next chapter in a visit to a bar he once owned.)

Prohibition had scarcely ended when the nation was plunged into World War II, and the big beer companies honored the

nation's call for sacrifice and dedicated 15 percent of their production to the beer needs of the U.S. servicemen—an act of
shrewd patriotism if there ever was one. Propitiously, the beer
can had been introduced in 1935 and perfected by wartime,
making mass quantities of beer ever easier to stack, ship, and
store. Hordes of young men (and women) came back from the
war with an appreciation for mass market beers like Budweiser,
Pabst, and Schlitz that they simply didn't have before.

Wherever craft brewers are gathered these days, you can
foment a lively debate about the ascendancy of American Standard lager merely by pointing out that much of the rest of the
world drinks lager, too. But many craft beer people and their
disciples are convinced that Americans drink mostly Bud,
Miller, and Coors because (a) in the thirteen years of Prohibition, with only near beer or bad bootleg beer on the market,
Americans actually forgot how full-bodied ales and lagers
tasted; (b) returning veterans, remembering that cold Pabst on
that sweltering day on the beach at Guam, came home with sentimental fondness for the stuff; or (c) wartime beer was actually
watered down to appeal to the masses of working women who
had thronged into the nation's factories in the absence of men.
(This debate *does not* take place in the halls of Bud, Miller, or
Coors, who see the ascendancy of American Standard as proof
that they make great beer.)

The postwar rise of television and the growing ability of
beer companies to reach a national audience would set off yet
another round of the Lager Wars and roil the beer markets as
much as the arrival of lager did 100 years before. An irony is
that small regional brewers were the first to use the newfangled
medium of television to advertise their products, but these early
attempts were local, somewhat primitive, and inexpensive. Nar-
ragansett Beer sponsored the first-ever broadcasts of a major
league baseball game in 1945, bringing the Boston Red Sox to
a sparse audience huddled before black-and-white TVs. But by
1975, when Miller Brewing launched its Miller Lite campaign

to a huge and relatively sophisticated national audience, TV beer advertising was well on its way to becoming a $1 billion a year game that only the big boys could afford to play well and with stamina.

Does it work? Well, Miller's sales rocketed from about seven million barrels in 1975 to over 31 million barrels in 1978—the most intense boom in sales in recorded beer history. Moreover, even the Beer Geeks stand in awe of the ability of Big Beer to use its huge financial reserves to bring to life creative ad campaigns that not only sell beer but roll like tsunamis through popular culture. One example is Anheuser-Busch's hilarious and stunningly popular "Whassup?" commercials that first aired during the 2000 Super Bowl. The skit, starring real-life moviemaker Charles Stone III, simply had Stone, who is African-American, and a few of his black friends holding cans of Bud and talking on the phone, greeting each other with the verbal high-five, "Whassup?"

The commercial, Stone told me, was actually built around a kind of video résumé he'd made for himself a year before. And it wasn't exactly a safe play for Anheuser-Busch, even from a marketing standpoint. Whites consume 77 percent of all beer in America; blacks only 10 percent. Yet the commercial was the highest rated of any at the Super Bowl, and it and its derivations still enjoy a spectacular afterlife on the Internet, where they are replayed again and again (for free) in the U.S. and scores of other countries.

It was during the mid-1970s that Miller, Anheuser-Busch, and that once middle-of-the-pack regional brewer Coors began to make the gains that now give them 80 percent of the American beer market—Bud, now 50 percent; Miller, about 20 percent; Coors, about 10 percent—virtually all of it at the expense of regional players who just couldn't spend to compete. To put this in perspective: in 1947, Anheuser-Busch was only the fourth-largest brewer in the U.S.; Schlitz, Pabst, and Ballantine & Sons held the top three spots respectively. Familiar names like

Schaefer, Rheingold, Falstaff, Blatz, and Hamm's helped fill out the top ten. The spread among the top ten then was such that *any of them* could have theoretically emerged as a contending brand for the top spot. Yet not a single one of those companies survives today, save Pabst, which, as noted earlier, soldiers on as a contract brewer of relic beers and a shadow of its old self.

Of course, it would be simplistic to lay this *all* at the feet of mass marketing. Anheuser-Busch, as you'll see in a coming chapter, is a ferociously shrewd and competitive company. Miller, though struggling for the past decade, built its empire on clever branding and chutzpah: its risky Lite Beer gambit paid off handsomely and put a huge fright into the Anheuser-Busch Goliath. Coors craftily took advantage of its status as a kind of regional cult beer in the 1960s to ramp itself up into a national player.

Moreover, competitors were sunk by more than clever and expensive advertising. Nervous antitrust regulators through the 1980s blocked or delayed some proposed beer mergers that might have saved big second-tier players like G. Heileman & Co. and Stroh Brewing Co., and perhaps might even have allowed Pabst to remain a real competitor. Blunders were made, the most colossal by Schlitz, which was in a neck-and-neck race with Anheuser-Busch to lead the American beer market in the 1970s. Whether out of greed or panic, it chemically shortened its brewing cycle and went to a recipe ever heavier with adjuncts, all with the hope of speeding up production and shaving a buck a barrel off its costs. The result was a beer, from all accounts, that tasted like tin, and coagulated, if stored improperly, into a kind of gelatinous snot. By 1980, Schlitz was on the auction block.

But while the Bud Blitzkrieg was winning the Lager Wars, a funny thing happened—some upstarts, tired of the same old beers, opened a kind of guerrilla front, producing ales (and some odd and well-hopped lagers) in a return to a tradition that was both subversive and would've warmed Matthew Vassar's generous ale-making heart. As stated earlier, Fritz Maytag fired the opening shot in 1969 by acquiring full ownership of the Anchor Brewing Co., and by 1971 he was brewing a head-turning beer called Anchor Steam; Jack McAuliffe's New Albion followed suit in 1976. New Albion could have just as easily been called a minibrewery as a microbrewery, but as Maytag pointed out during an interview at his San Francisco brewery, "micro" was a word suddenly being bandied around by dazzling new tech upstarts like Intel and Apple Computer, which were springing up in a place soon to be called Silicon Valley. McAuliffe intended his beer to be to old-line lager what the microchip was to the vacuum tube.

In 1982, Bert Grant, an expatriated Scotsman, opened the nation's first modern brewpub in Yakima, Washington, bringing back and even reinventing super-hoppy beers in the IPA tradition. By 1984, Jim Koch had founded his Boston Beer Co. and the Samuel Adams label. Given the lager taste spectrum at the time, Koch could without exaggeration apply the label "Extreme Beer" to his first products.

By 1995, regional lager companies were still failing, but the number of U.S. breweries, counting microbreweries and brewpubs, had radically reversed itself and spurted upward to 500. As of this writing, they number more than 1,400, and craft brew sales in 2006 reached a record retail volume of about $4.2 billion. That's still peanuts to Bud and even to SABMiller. But in a rousing speech to an Association of Brewers (AOB) conference in 2003, Kim Jordan, head of Colorado craft beer maker New Belgium Brewing, told the minions of Little Beer that there was no reason they couldn't capture 10 percent of the U.S. beer market—about triple their current market share—if they continued to mix innovation with rigid quality standards and aggressive marketing.

While even some craft brewers think this figure is ambitious, the larger point is that the Ale Genie has gotten out of the bottle and the Lager Wars simply aren't that interesting anymore because, in reality, Anheuser-Busch has won. The Big

Three, as they have in the past, will continue to duke it out—by ad spending or hardball distribution tactics—over market share. They will put out a new beer here and there; they will buy a craft brewer here and there; they will make alliances with foreign brewers here and there. (Indeed, as the first edition of this book was being put to bed, Coors merged with Canadian brewing giant Molson to form the Molson Coors Brewing Co.) But beer's creative and passionate center seems clearly to have shifted to the little guys, for when the beer guru Michael Jackson extols America as "the most interesting beer scene in the world," he isn't talking about the 206 million barrels of American Standard lager that the Big Three produced in 2005.

Or as Randy Mosher, a Chicago beer writer, historian, and homebrewer told me, "Bud does what it does very well and it will continue to do that very well. But when it comes to what's truly *interesting* about beer today, it's completely out of their hands."

I expected I might get an argument or two about this as I headed back down the River of Beer.

The Quest Continues
Motoring Toward Dubuque, in Search of the Brewer Al Capone

The road of excess leads to the palace of wisdom.
—William Blake

I left La Crosse in overcast skies and a cool drizzle and headed down State Highway 35 without a clear destination in mind. The gloom of the day couldn't hide the verdant, expansive beauty of the countryside as the highway hugged the river for the most part. Steering down a winding bluff, I watched a two-mile-long freight train chug up a bluff on the distant shore. At Genoa, Wisconsin, I stopped briefly to admire one of the biggest locks on the Mississippi (one of twenty-nine locks and dams on the river), and at 1:00 P.M. I pulled into the parking lot of Coaches Family Restaurant in Prairie du Chien.

I ordered the fried catfish lunch, though a kindly waitress informed me that the Flavor Crisp Fried Chicken was the pick of the menu. It was a perfectly fine fried catfish meal, though the highlight of my time at Coaches was listening to the local radio station over the restaurant's sound system. When an advertisement for a Prairie du Chien funeral home pitched its services as "celebrating the end of your loved one's life," I knew I had arrived at a place of wry humor if not savvy marketing. ("Uncle Joe's finally dead?—Call us to plan the party!")

Prairie du Chien, population 6,000, turned out to be a very old and historically significant town, though, driving in, much of it looked as if it had arrived yesterday. I passed strip malls and semimodern factories and a huge modular home sales lot, and large clusters of occupied modular homes. A cavernous superstore and warehouse for Cabela's, the national hunting and fishing catalogue retailer, anchored the outskirts.

Modern appearances aside, I learned that the French explorers Marquette and Jolliet first ran into the Mississippi River here in 1673 after adventuring down the Wisconsin River with the help of Native American guides. But the town's real claim to fame was mixed up with an episode that had at least an oblique beer connection. In the summer of 1900, the Ringling Brothers Circus, Buffalo Bill's Wild West Show, and a clutch of tourist trains called the Great Railroad Excursion all converged on Prairie du Chien. This surge of mass entertainment brought 30,000 visitors, many of them deeply committed beer drinkers, to the sleepy little town, apparently taxing the patience and tempers of the locals. By the time William Cody and his bunch arrived in August, some of the townspeople had had it; a small riot broke out between locals and some of Bill's fellows, with shots being fired and property being damaged. Buffalo Bill himself had to come galloping down the street on his impressive stallion and in full Wild West regalia to restore order.

My catfish lunch over and contemporary beer pickings looking slim, I moved on, crossing the river to Marquette, Iowa, and heading south on scenic Highway 340. Soon the river divided itself into two channels and I found myself in Dorothy Country, with endless, rolling cornfields on one side of the road and endless, rolling soybean fields on the other. Rain splattered my windshield and dark, menacing clouds boiled up on the distant horizon in a huge and glowering sky. It looked like one of those places that could easily hatch tornadoes (or the Wicked Witch of the West). It was extremely scenic, in an unsettling kind of way.

Two hours later the pastoral countryside melted into the sprawling fringes of Dubuque, population 62,000, where a welcoming sign said "Help Keep a Good Thing Growing." As I drove deeper into the city, the sprawl surrendered to what looked like a solidly working-class burg, faded and tattered in places, but with sections that suggested stability if not exactly prosperity: rows of tidy houses with American flags flapping from the eaves of front porches; white, clapboard churches; redbrick buildings housing barber shops and hardware stores. I also saw eighteen-wheelers parked up in yards; I passed Hawkeye's, a motorcycle salvage shop; a used CD- and record-trading place; and a half-dozen old-fashioned beer joints that looked like the painters hadn't been by in a couple of decades. A homeless man staggered down the street in front of one of them.

Dubuque looked like a town that had seen better days.

But then I knew, having helped cover the fringes of the American farm crisis in the 1980s for the *Journal*, that Dubuque was among the Midwestern towns that had taken the brunt of a sharp rise in interest rates and collateral collapse in commodities prices that had driven thousands of debt-laden family farms out of business. The town and county had been trying to claw its way back ever since.

I soon found myself downtown in Old Dubuque, a few square blocks of handsome redevelopment that provided a glimpse of the city's earlier glory. It had been founded in the 1780s by Julien Dubuque, a French Canadian fur trader who had also launched the region's once prosperous lead mining industry. Farming and farming-related manufacturing arrived after fur and lead ran their course. After driving around a bit, I parked at the river, where the impressive and new National Mississippi

River Museum loomed up, a picture of Mark Twain auspiciously adorning the entrance. Next door, as though attached, was the glittery Diamond Jo Casino and Riverboat. If this seemed an odd juxtaposition, it wasn't—Dubuque, since the farm bust, had decided to hitch its economic wagon to tourism and casino gambling, or so I learned later at a downtown visitors center. The town's new motto was: "Masterpiece of the Mississippi."

I'm not a fan of casinos but I do like museums, so I paid the $8.75 admission fee (which seemed steep) and went in for a gander, thinking perhaps I would stumble upon Dubuque beer lore. It was money well spent, for not only did I immerse myself in gee-whiz river facts (the Mississippi sends 2.3 million cubic feet of water *per second* into the Gulf of Mexico and transports 472 million tons of cargo annually), but I also got a great beer scoop. During a twenty-minute movie on river history, I learned that in the late 1800s the steamboat *Ophelia* of Dubuque "took a large party to Guttenburg" about thirty miles upstream, toting "50 half-barrels of lager and 1,200 pounds of ice" to keep the beer cold. Not an ounce of beer remained as the *Ophelia* returned to Dubuque, and as the wobbly passengers disembarked, "two men fell overboard." And later, a fellow museum browser with whom I chatted briefly about my beer quest asked if I knew who Dubuque's most famous—well, infamous—bar owner, brewer, and sometime resident happened to be?

I said I had no idea.

He said, "Al Capone. He owned the Julien Hotel in town and used to hide out there when things got too hot for him in Chicago. He'd drink at the bar."

I recalled passing the Julien, a grand if faded-looking hostelry, as I drove through downtown. Until I heard of Scarface Capone's connection, I hadn't really been sure if I was staying in Dubuque for the night.

Given this discovery, I decided another walking tour was in order, tempted as I was to drive back to explore the dive bars I'd seen on the way in. So I checked in to the Holiday Inn a couple of blocks from the Julien and struck out after dark. My first stop was the Blackwater Grill and Bricktown Brewery just a couple of blocks away. A brochure I'd picked up someplace said it was Dubuque's "only authentic brewpub restaurant," and "food first" was still my beer quest motto.

The Blackwater was a visually arresting place—soaring ceilings, floor-to-ceiling windows, hardwood floors, and richly paneled walls. Gleaming copper brew kettles sat encased in a glass-paneled room right in the middle of the main dining room, so you could watch the brewing in action. I sat near one of the tall windows and quickly picked the dinner special—a fried walleyed perch sandwich—from the menu and ordered a pint of the pub's seasonal Oktoberfest, described as a medium-hopped amber ale. Food and beer were delicious but, with tables stuffed with families, couples, and clusters of tourists all chowing down and chatting away, I paid up and headed for the Julien, where I hoped the bar setup would be more conducive to talking to people.

I was soon in animated conversation with Krissy Hogue, a young New York transplant who had moved to Dubuque about a year earlier to be closer to her mother. She was holding down bartending chores at the Julien's Riverboat Lounge. The 144-room hotel had been built in Victorian style over the shell of an existing hotel in 1854 and had been called the Julien Dubuque (after the city's founder) for most of its life until a fairly recent name change had made it the Julien Inn. It used to be the most elegant place in town; it was when Capone controlled it during the Prohibition years of the 1920s. These days it seemed a bit like parts of Dubuque itself—faded but proud. The cheap rooms went for $49, a bargain even in Dubuque.

Capone's Riverboat Lounge was a large, airy space that had a 1970s feel about it. It had clearly been built big enough to handle sold-out hotel crowds and partying local swells, too, but neither was present on this night. The long bar that Krissy waited on was busy, but the rest of the cavernous space was mostly empty, though she assured me that the regular Tuesday night karaoke crowd would fill up some of the tables soon. This wasn't a craft beer place; it served Bud Light, Miller Lite, and Old Style (one of Pabst's resurrected beers, remember?) on tap. A hand-lettered sign on the wall behind the bar announced a recent innovation: "We Now Have Bottled Beer."

I asked Krissy about the Al Capone connection; she knew the bare bones of the story but, being a conscientious bartender, was preoccupied helping to resolve the anxieties of an Asian businessman who was sitting a few stools to the left of me, nervously sipping a beer. He was a Julien guest and had just gotten a cell phone call from his wife in Chicago telling him that she had gone into labor with their first child. He'd explained to Krissy in halting English that he had flown into Dubuque from Chicago earlier in the day and was wondering whether there might still be flights out tonight. She couldn't find him a flight but within ten minutes she'd arranged a $210 cab ride.

He got up to leave and then announced, "It's going to be a girl!"

By this time, pretty much everyone within earshot had been following this mini-drama. The bar erupted in well wishes and the clank of beer glasses, and off he went.

Krissy got busy serving up $1.25 glasses of Old Style draft when, as promised, the karaoke crowd and their audiences filtered in, mostly groups of youngish women and a few kids. They arranged themselves at separate tables and took tightly scripted turns singing songs by Madonna, ABBA, Cher, and the like, with a break now and then for some solitary male who would barge up, as if on cue, and break out into some hard-rock anthem by ZZ Top or that ilk. It was all delightfully wretched— I think that's what karaoke actually means in Japanese—until a very pale, thin, prim, and grandmotherly-looking woman in a dress better suited for church than for the bar walked slowly to the mike. I was expecting a hymn but she grabbed the mike and sang the hell out of Patsy Cline's "I Fall to Pieces," then segued into a killer version of "Crazy." She sounded so much like Patsy she even quieted the blabbermouths at the bar.

When the wannabe Madonnas returned to the mike, I turned to the guy to my right and spoke up in admiration at his drinking style—I'd noticed he'd ordered two beers at a time and was drinking them in a two-fisted manner.

"Oh, that," he said. "That's the tradition here among regulars."

His name was Jimmy and he was a cook at the hotel. Usually, he said, he gulped down four beers this way after knocking off work; then he went home to help his third-grade kid with his homework. Tonight he was on his way to a wedding reception in the Julien's ballroom upstairs. (In fact, the Julien, he told me, had the only official ballroom in all of Dubuque.)

"Who's getting married?" I wanted to know.

"Hell, I dunno," he said. "But I cooked all their food so I'm going anyway. They've ordered twenty kegs of beer. That's a lot of beer, pal."

I told Jimmy about my beer book and asked if he had any advice.

"Take your notes early in the evening," he suggested.

I laughed, and Jimmy, clearly a wise man, went off to party in the ballroom.

I turned to my left and met another Jim a few stools down: "Jim Massey," he said, offering his full name. We struck up a conversation. He was a longtime Dubuque resident and knew the Capone connection.

"Yeah, Dubuque was a wild place back then," Massey told me. "Capone would hang out in East Dubuque, which is just across the river in Illinois, but he spent a lot of time over here, too. He'd hide his car at what used to be a Skelly station [a gas station chain long out of business] at fourth and Locust, down in the basement. The building is just down from my house and I've been in it many times. That basement is big enough to hold several cars."

I'd always been under the impression that Prohibition and

speakeasies were all about illegal whisky and bathtub gin. But, in fact, the Capone gang made tens of millions of dollars annually illegally brewing and bootlegging beer and making underground tavern owners offers they couldn't refuse to sell it. Capone's brand was Sieben's, an old established Chicago brewery founded and owned by a respectable family of that name. Some Capone histories have him owning the brewery outright, but the real story seems to be that Capone and his henchmen controlled it through a lease to some third party who had promised the Siebens they intended to make nonalcoholic beer. One thing was clear: whenever illicit tavern keepers tactlessly turned down Capone's generous suggestion that they start carrying Sieben's beer, they were viciously beaten and their places trashed. Word got around, and Sieben's became a very popular brew. (A grudge involving Capone's beer operations, it turns out, was ultimately responsible for the so-called St. Valentine's Day Massacre in which Capone thugs gunned down seven rival thugs by posing as cops and shooting their victims in the back. The February 1929 executions shocked even jaded Chicagoans and marked the beginning of the end of the Capone era.)

Sieben's went on to brew beer legally until 1967, when it, too, became a casualty of the Lager Wars; it has since been torn down. About all that remains is a recipe, floating around among home brewers on the Internet, called "Al Capone's Prohibition Beer." It purports to be an actual lager brewed at the time Capone controlled Sieben's; Beer Geeks have taken to it because it's a lager made not just with malt but with rice and soybeans.

As far as Massey knew, Capone behaved, comparatively speaking, like a gentleman when in Dubuque, though he was awfully fond of the strip joints in East Dubuque. Massey said both Dubuques were relatively tame today compared with even thirty-five years ago, when he worked as a Dubuque cop before signing up with John Deere & Co., the farm machinery maker. He'd spent twenty-nine years as a security guard at Deere before retiring in September 2001. But back when he walked a beat, Dubuque as a beer town and all-around drinking town was hard to beat. "You realize Dubuque didn't get liquor by the drink until 1963," Massey told me. "The bar owners didn't want it—there was a lot more money in it if you didn't have to buy a license. [Licenses, as an aside, are strictly limited in numbers and often have to be acquired from existing license holders for tens of thousands of dollars.] The state would come in now and then and knock down an illegal tavern and they'd have to pay a $300 fine. But they'd be back in business the next day."

Massey stopped to sip his beer, then went on: "Dubuque was a factory town, very blue collar, and you wouldn't believe the number of bars. There was one just across the street from here, and just around the corner within one block between Main and Locust there were five taverns. It was unbelievable.... But then, you know what they say about Dubuque. It's half Irish, half German, and all Catholic." (One other thing I heard Dubuquers say about Dubuque: that as a city it ranked second *in the world* behind Munich in per capita beer consumption. But I was never able to independently confirm that accolade.)

Dubuque had at one time or another supported at least twenty-two breweries, Massey said, but all had eventually folded, the last one, Dubuque Brewing and Bottling Co., closing in 1998. It was a decent-sized regional brewer—100,000 barrels annually—famous for its Dubuque Star label. The brewhouse still sat over on the riverfront, not that far from the Mississippi River Museum. It was shuttered now and had been picked over by the breweriana people, but "years ago," Massey told me, "you could go down there and go in and have a beer they called Big Star."

The more I talked with Massey the more I liked him. He was a self-confessed barfly with a keen sense of humor, a thinking man's drinking man who liked history and understood that all history is local, in a way. He was a youthful sixty, but had seen enough in his time to make connections to the global events that were crashing like slow waves on his own town and his own life.

Of Dubuque's up-and-down economic fortunes, he said, "Look, John Deere, where I worked all those years, at one time had 16,000 people here. Now there are about 3,000. They used to be a manufacturer. They used to make their own motors. Now John Deere is an assembly plant. They buy all the components and parts from all over the world and put them together here."

Does that mean that Dubuque jobs have gone overseas? "Yeah," said Massey, "but that's the way everybody does it now."

Jim had a lot to say on beer, too, and his views reflected one strain of thought I heard often on the River of Beer among thinking lager people, who drank from the taps of the Bud juggernaut and even accepted its inevitability, yet lamented Big Beer's slaughter of the regional brewers of a kind that used to spice up the beer-drinking landscape. "I used to drink Blue Ribbon way back when," Massey said. "I finally came around to Bud. I drink Bud Light and Coors Light, mostly—face it, Bud, Coors, and Miller are all that's left pretty much. For years I wouldn't drink Bud because they were too big. But everybody carries the beer. Now, as you can see, I'm drinking Coors tonight, not Bud, because tonight I'm mad at Bud again—for putting all the little breweries out of business. But, what the hell, you can't beat 'em."

On a personal level, Massey told me he had been single for many years, had seven adult children and fourteen grandkids. He now lived downtown just a few blocks from here in a renovated 1880s house with a woman quite his junior. He called her Sweetie; they'd been together eight years. She collected antique baby dishes and toys, and he collected "Dubuque stuff and antique beer advertisements." Said Massey, "Our house looks like a museum." Sweetie's other preoccupations, he said, were "baking cookies and drinking pop" and going for daily 3:00 A.M., seven-mile runs with her three dogs, then walking another six or seven miles in the afternoon. Massey himself far preferred bar hopping and beer drinking to pop sipping and jogging. The Julien, he said, was often his first stop on his more or less daily route.

Jim, I noticed, seemed to be able to put away prodigious

amounts of beer with impunity. I was trying—whether out of pride or politeness, and maybe some of both—to keep up, but realized I wasn't much of a match. Of course, I had to remind myself that I *was* in the Midwest and thus a place, by reputation at least, that had me drinking with the big dogs. (It was only later, checking per capita consumption by state, that I learned Iowa actually ranked a disappointing sixteenth in the nation, with a 35.5 gallon per capita average. On the other hand, Wisconsin, which I'd just left, at least was in the top five—fourth to be precise, at 39.7 gallons per capita. A state I'd have never guessed—New Hampshire—ranked first at 44.8 gallons per capita.)

Jim announced there were other places he wanted to take me, Paul's Tavern especially. At some point, after resolving most of the problems of the world (and spending a sobering moment contemplating how we would spend the first anniversary of 9/11, which in a jolt I realized was tomorrow), we barged out into the night and into Paul's, just a couple of blocks away.

Massey was right; no serious beer-joint hunter should miss Paul's. It was loud, boisterous, and crowded with a literal boat-load of revelers who had come by excursion boat from the Quad Cities downriver (the Quad Cities being two Iowa and two Illinois towns clustered together on opposite banks of the Mississippi—Davenport, Iowa, perhaps being the best known). Paul's had the extra benefit of having kept some lucky taxidermist in work for a long, long time, since the heads of almost every big-game animal known to man were stuck up on plaques along the walls, glassy eyes staring from all directions. It also had 85-cent "scoops"—pint-plus-sized drafts of Old Style—and, boy, the Quad Cities gang was knocking them back like returning marathoners swarming a Dixie Cup water cooler.

Paul's also had Maria. She was a willowy blond bartender with a big smile, a skimpy halter top, and a very short skirt, who waved us over as soon as she saw Jim.

"Hey, Jimmy," she yelled, "I got something to show you!"

We pushed our way through the crowd and up to the bar.

Maria smiled, then giggled. "It's nothing weird or anything—not really," she said.

Then—tah-dah!—Maria reached down to her splendidly bare midriff and pressed on her navel.

Well, actually, she pressed on her brand-new navel ring.

Well, actually, see, what it was...was this small, glittering, uh, metal penis that snapped up to the ready position each time she pressed down on some mechanism to which it was quite cleverly attached.

For full effect, Maria pressed down.

Many, many times.

The Quad Cities bunch was falling down in uproarious laughter at this, and I would've, too, had I been able to close my mouth.

Maria poured us scoops, even though I don't think we asked for them, and I sprang for the buck-seventy, plus a big tip, being on expenses and all. Then Jim and I fought our way into a semi-quiet corner to contemplate Maria's adornment. We sipped our beers, and I couldn't say yet whether Paul's was the Perfect Beer Joint. But I had to admit that I'd just had a near Perfect Beer Joint Moment.

Massey and I did make it to one other place, the Busted Lift. It was quiet and civilized. It had about one million beers, all of them craft beers. It had an extremely beer-knowledgeable bartender, and it had beer-savvy owners who came over to greet us and lavish us with information. I later looked it up on the Web, and every Beer Geek who had ever visited it seemed to give it five stars.

Alas, we had been there but a bit when Jim looked at me and I looked at him and he said an astonishing thing. He said, "I'm full. No more beer. I'm going home."

Off he went, and I realized Jim was a wise, wise man. I headed for the Holiday Inn shortly thereafter.

A Side Trip Deep into the Lair of Extreme Beer

Strong beer is the milk of the old.
—Henry Miller

Milton, Del.—Michael Jackson, a normally voluble man with the enviable job of roaming the globe tasting this and that beer and who, to date, has sampled, who knows, thousands of them, is temporarily speechless. Machinery hums and clanks in the background, and the earthy-warm aromas of hops and beer permeate the air. Jackson stands, beer mug in hand, in the high-ceilinged brewhouse of the Dogfish Head Craft Brewery contemplating one of the biggest beers he's ever had.

Beer Geeks will forgive me while I explain to everyone else that I don't mean the size of his beer mug. Jackson, the legendary British beer writer who has come to the brewery at the invitation of its owner and founder, Sam Calagione, is cogitating his sampling of Dogfish Head's 120 Minute IPA, drawn directly from a tap on its finishing tank. The beer is still about three weeks away from bottling but, brewed in the hoppy India Pale Ale style, has already achieved an astonishing alcohol level of about 19 percent alcohol by volume (ABV). And on one major spectrum on the flavor meter—a hops-measuring indicator called International Bittering Units, or IBUs—it stands at 125 IBUs.

Think about it this way: a middle-of-the-range IPA is about 6 percent to 8 percent ABV and maybe 30 IBUs; most mass-produced American lager is about 5.5 percent ABV, with IBUs ranging from 8 to 22; Michelob Ultra, Anheuser-Busch's recent low-carb light beer that it has pitched to women, rings in at 4.1 percent alcohol and only 4 IBUs.

In beer taste terms, 120 Minute IPA is nuclear fission in a glass, yet here's the kicker: it still tastes like beer and not booze, as some high-alcohol beers have a tendency to do. It is but one example of a growing phenomenon at the outer edges of the craft beer industry: Extreme Beer.

We have diverted once again from our narrative to enter one of the inner sanctums of the Extreme Beer movement.

"It's very drinkable," Jackson, after a long pause, says to Calagione, 120 Minute IPA's creator and, in the words of his employees, the brewery's mad wizard. A few minutes later, Jackson, sampling another Dogfish offering out of a tank—a dark, raisin-based ale improbably named Raison D'Etre that comes in at a mere 8 percent ABV—shakes his head and laughs.

"This is outrageous," he says in the measured, cheerful way he often speaks. "It's outrageous that these beers are that good and that drinkable—and strong enough to remove everybody's socks."

He turns to Calagione and says, "You'll finish up in jail, you know. They will erect stocks all up and down the eastern seaboard. They'll get you for doing this."

Calagione, laughing, says, "I hope you're right."

A man of restless energy, insatiable curiosity, and quirkily ambitious brewing goals, Samuel Anthony Calagione III, thirty-four years old, is unquestionably among the Young Turks pushing the boundaries of beer in the Extreme Beer movement, which isn't merely about making ultra-strong beer but about redefining what beer could be. As for Jackson's comments, Calagione is—temporarily—flattered, since resting on laurels isn't a Calagione trait. He is the great-grandson of Italian immigrants; his grandfather worked in a shoe factory before starting a small vending-machine business in Boston that paid the way for Sam's father to go to college and on to medical school. His father is an oral surgeon and entrepreneur, adding a scientific bent to the blue-collar pluckiness he got from his grandfather.

Calagione points out that the 120 Minute IPA, continuously hopped during a 120-minute boil by a proprietary robotic gizmo he invented called Sir Hops Alot, isn't done fermenting and was conceived with loftier ambitions than the 19 percent ABV already achieved. "We were thinking 24 percent or 25 percent would be nice," Calagione says, but he expresses doubt, despite resorting to brewing voodoo that he won't fully reveal, that it will get that high. He's used several pitches of proprietary yeast strains, and though he won't say what the strains are, he quips, "If you looked at the yeast under a microscope, you'd see lots of leather skirts, whips, and chains." He then turns to his lead brewer, Bryan Selders, and says, "What do you think it'll come in at, Bryan?"

Selders guesses it'll be closer to 20 percent than 24 percent. (It will actually get bottled at 21 percent—and sell for $8.99 retail for a 12-ounce bottle.)

No matter that 120 Minute IPA is already the strongest beer of its *style* ever measured on the River of Beer since science gave Beer Geeks the ability to track such things as alcohol level and IBUs. Calagione knows that one beer stands between him and one of brewing's more peculiar but nonetheless coveted trophies—bragging rights to having made the strongest beer in the world.

That beer is Jim Koch's Samuel Adams Utopias MMII, a fact that can't be doubted because it is enshrined in *The Guinness Book of World Records*. Released by Koch's Boston Beer Co. in November 2001, it shocked the beer world by coming in at 48 proof—24 percent ABV. All the more remarkable is that only a decade ago, most beer experts believed that 15 percent

ABV, given that brewers for decades had relentlessly pushed existing strains of beer yeast to their limits, was a brewing wall that couldn't be surmounted without, say, throwing beer into a pot still or perhaps freezing it in finishing tanks. The Germans, among others, make an 80 proof beverage that is distilled from beer, but it survives with little semblance of beer taste. And distilling beer in the U.S. is technically illegal without a permit, as is freezing, which is considered simply another form of distillation. In that process, water and alcohol separate into ice and liquid respectively. By drawing off some of the ice and leaving the alcohol intact, a brewer could greatly boost ABV levels. But, legalities aside, both would amount to an uncricket way to achieve an ABV record.

In 1994, Koch, working with his own proprietary strains of yeast over multiple fermentations, fired the first shot in the ABV wars by blasting through the 15 percent brewing mark with a dark ale called Triple Bock at 17.5 percent, which had been three years in the planning and making. As if that weren't enough, Koch threw down a gauntlet to other craft brewers by declaring that he had brewed a beer that consciously crossed the line between beer, wine, and spirits; a beer that, after brewing, he had aged for eighteen months in used oak whisky barrels before bottling; a beer that he said had "the complexity of a fine cognac, vintage port, or an old sherry" and that "should be sipped from a small snifter in a two-ounce serving."

Calagione was barely out of Pennsylvania's Muhlenberg College then and didn't enter the craft brew fray until the summer of 1995, when he and his wife, Mariah—his high school sweetheart—opened a brewpub near the beach in Lewes, Delaware, twenty miles from Milford, Delaware, where Mariah grew up. But in a few short years, the pub would prove so successful that the Calagiones would find themselves expanding into the full-fledged, fast-growing craft brewer that Dogfish Head has become. Sam was already drawing crowds to the pub by putting together adventurous seasonal concoctions like Punkin'

Ale (brewed from real pumpkin) and style-bending offerings like Chicory Stout (an ale with touches of chicory and Mexican coffee) when in the fall of 2000 he made his first major public splash in the beer world. That's when he undertook the brewing of Midas Touch from the 2,700-year-old recipe (recall the history chapter) that Dr. Patrick McGovern, the University of Pennsylvania Museum archaeological chemist, had roughly figured out from intricate biochemical analyses of residue found in the tomb in central Turkey thought to be King Midas's.

McGovern had already heard of the small Delaware brewery whose motto is "off-centered ales for off-centered people." So he approached Calagione with the recipe, hoping that he would make a small batch for a funerary feast that researchers had planned to honor Midas. McGovern was certain that his concoction, sorted out using things like mass spectrometers and gas chromatographs, was an elixir of beer, wine, and mead made with numerous exotic ingredients, but he had no clue as to the proportion of each.

This was exactly the kind of challenge that motivates Calagione, who spent weeks trying to sort out the ancient brewing mind, the ancient brewing climate, and the appropriate modern equivalents of ancient brewing ingredients. The test batch caused such a stir that by 2001 Dogfish Head was commercially brewing Midas Touch Golden Elixir, which included very unbeerlike portions of white muscat grapes, honey, and saffron. Calagione decided to put it in a 750-milliliter wine bottle, complete with a cork, with a suggested retail price of $14.

Midas Touch—at 9 percent ABV a strong ale and, like Koch's Triple Bock, a decided hybrid on the beer spectrum—wasn't a direct riposte to Koch. But in 2002, after Koch had wowed the beer-drinking world with his 24 percent Utopias (which he sold in 3,000 numbered and signed 24-ounce mini copper brew kettles for $100 a bottle), Calagione jumped into the strong-beer ring, first by pushing his raisin ale, Raison D'Etre, to a whopping 21 percent (and renaming it Raison D'Extra). Then he popped out a brew called WorldWide Stout that came close to dethroning Millennium with an ABV reading of 23.04 percent. (Calagione, in fact, could claim WorldWide was the strongest beer in *production* since Millennium was a one-off product.)

Imitation is certainly a form of flattery here, for Calagione admires Koch on one level, particularly the way he publicly stirred up the craft brew movement and helped precipitate an unprecedented round of research among yeast makers aimed at developing strains that may one day push the ABV limit even further. But Calagione also climbs into the strong-beer ring like an underrated boxer who believes he has a good chance to deck the champ. This is all a more formidable challenge, since Boston Beer is the undeniable behemoth of craft brewers, with annual revenues of more than $230 million; Dogfish Head is still of a size to be classified as a true microbrewery.

This rivalry (mostly good-natured, with a few barbs thrown here and there about whose concoctions are more faithful to beer) has gotten little attention in the wider world. But among the Beer Geeks this is juicy stuff. In May 2003, *Beverage Business,* a trade magazine, devoted a four-page spread to the ABV jousting titled "The Race for the *Überbeer* Is upon Us." It quoted one admiring but worried craft brewer who feared the craft segment of the industry was sliding into "strong beer hysteria" given the number of copycats that Koch and Calagione had spurred. Meanwhile, among the Beer Geeks, the homebrewers, and the Yeast People, debate swirls: How have Koch and Calagione gotten so much more kick out of beer yeast than brewers in the past? Are they pushing exotics like champagne, wine, or even distiller's yeasts to get to these staggering alcohol levels?

Koch, for his part, demurs, saying only that the imputed 15 percent wall of yore was always more "of a mental issue than a technical one" and allowing as how he'll probably take the 24 percent ABV to 26 percent or 27 percent one day soon. (Indeed, Koch's 2007 Utopias reached a record 25.6% ABV.) And both Koch and Calagione took pains to tell me that their goals weren't merely to dazzle by proving yeast could be pushed to produce unbelievably high ABV levels. "We've learned a lot about high-alcohol fermentation but, more important, about creating wonderful flavors in high-alcohol malt fermentations," Koch wrote in an e-mail. "If the beverage is unpalatable, who cares how high the alcohol level is."

I went to see Calagione for the first time well before I began my trip down the Mississippi after learning of his connection to the King Midas project. At that point, I hadn't actually fixated on the concept of Extreme Beer, which turned out to be a kind of stealth phenomenon kicking around the craft brew world that was just beginning to be articulated as a movement. (As this was being written, the world's second-ever annual Extreme Beer festival had just been convened in Boston.) It's impossible to say who invented the term, but the first reference I could find to it in this context was by Koch in a 1994 interview with *Management Review* magazine to describe his Triple Bock.

As noted, microbreweries had sprung to life with the original goal of rescuing America's early brewing legacy, with its zesty ales and throngs of rival regional brewers, from a lager-soaked and vastly consolidated beer landscape. Now, after putting some 1,500 new breweries or brewpubs into business and pumping at least 10,000 individual new beers onto the market, some brewers had grown bored with that original mission and decided that it was time to take beer to the next level. Others saw the seeds of counterrevolution—craft beer itself, in the view of some craft brew rebels, had begun to move too far toward the mainstream with lighter styles (Samuel Adams now has a light beer, for example) that craft beer revolutionaries once mocked.

And it was clear that ultra-strong beer was itself just one manifestation. Midas Touch was but one of scores of examples of how beer was growing so startlingly bold and exotic that it was, in fact, beginning to make early craft brew seem mainstream. Fritz Maytag at Anchor Brewing could say without hesitation that his original ales, given that almost all beer back then was pale lager, could be considered extreme for those times. But certainly not now; when I interviewed Maytag at his San Francisco brewery in the summer of 2003, he marveled at the creativity and audacity sweeping the craft brew movement today and said, given such competition, "it's not easy to be amazingly creative anymore."

Calagione was certainly doing his best to push the beer envelope. Of the dozen beers he made, only one, Shelter Pale Ale, at 5 percent ABV, could be considered a "session beer"—beerspeak for a beer like Bud, Miller, or Coors that you'd consider adopting as your everyday beer and could reasonably drink a lot of. His best-selling brew was Raison D'Etre, his audacious 8 percent ABV raisin ale. And what was to be made of his Immort Ale, an 11 percent ABV beer that undergoes a secondary fermentation with champagne yeast and whose ingredients include organic juniper berries, vanilla, and maple syrup?

This clearly wasn't a guy who had much interest in converting die-hard Bud drinkers. "Nah," he said in an early interview, "I'm not really so much about trying to sell 'better beer' to beer drinkers as I am about trying to win over the cognac and wine crowd."

Other brewers were crowding into the Extreme Beer niche. I'd sampled a beer made by a New Jersey beer maker, Heavyweight Brewing Co., that was a knockoff only in the sense that Extreme Brewers could envision a knockoff: it was called Two Druids' Gruit Ale and was described as "an assertive pale ale brewed with yarrow, sweet gale and wild rosemary [in lieu of hops] in this unique interpretation" of a medieval beer style called gruit ales. Heavyweight noted that original gruits were thought to have psychotropic properties. (LSD beer, anyone?)

I attended a beer tasting at D.B.A., one of Manhattan's top craft beer bars, and had a beer called "Train Wreck O' Flavors." I admired it so much that I tracked down the brewmaster, Todd Ashman, at a small brewery and brewpub outside Chicago called Flossmoor Station. (Ashman has since relocated.) He told me the beer was made by actually blending beer styles (in this case Flossmoor Station Barley Wine and a beer called TOMBA, short for Toasted Oats Molasses Brown Ale). Ashman had even upped the blending ante by putting out another brew called Born Cross-Eyed, which combined the barley wine (so called because it is beer made with an alcohol strength close to wine), TOMBA, and a beer style called imperial stout. This isn't dissimilar to the way scotch makers blend several whiskies to make, for example, Dewar's or Chivas Regal.

And forget about the mass market lager mantra that the only good beer is a fresh beer. Ashman was also making a lot of barrel-aged beers—strong, dark beers such as stouts and porters that he was "putting to sleep" for up to three years in used Jack Daniel's whisky barrels before bottling. This was beer, he insisted, that would age well and was "made to be drunk in a brandy snifter and enjoyed with a good cigar."

I'd heard about a brewery in Vermont called Magic Hat that was also making outrageously strong and esoteric stouts— called the Humdinger Series of Magical Elixirs—that were also meant to be aged and, in another measure of the Extreme Beer movement, were selling for $20-plus a bottle. Alan Newman, the brewery's co-founder, described his brewing philosophy as essentially guerrilla war against mass market lager. "We work hard to expel the American myth that all beer is corn lager and that all beer should be $1 a bottle," he said when I talked to him by phone. "Beer is liquid food," and in his opinion, Extreme Beer was merely the gourmet end of it.

Newman insisted that after he toted up his costs for packaging (for which craft brewers, not having economies of scale, pay a premium) and the vast amount of malt and other ingredients that went into making his huge beers, "Honest, I don't know if we make any money at $20 a bottle."

Whatever the case, all this was a far cry from even $6.99 per six-pack craft ales, and light-years away from six-packs of Bud, Miller, or Coors on sale for $3.99 at the local supermarket. I'd found at least a half dozen other breweries—Washington State's Fish Brewing Co. and New York State's Brewery Ommegang among them—plus a number of beer makers in Belgium, the European heart of Extreme Beer, that were making beers that retailed in the $20-to-$35-a-bottle range. When I wrote a feature about Extreme Beer for the *Wall Street Journal* and arranged a tasting of the stuff at Manhattan's Blind Tiger, a third of the seventeen beers we sampled retailed for $20 or more. Collectors had even driven up Koch's Millennium offerings to as much as $300 a bottle on eBay.

One way of looking at this is to see Extreme Beer as part of a broader American trend over the past two decades to take simple and beloved commodities—coffee and blue jeans, for example—and move them to a more sophisticated plane. Hence, the $5 cup of Starbucks with a twelve-syllable name and the $100 pair of Calvin Kleins. Why not beer?

You can add to that the restless experimentation that the craft brewers (most of whom, like Calagione, started out as restlessly experimental homebrewers) have brought to beer—a creativeness that, in the long Lager Wars, the major beer companies decided was best spent on marketing. Thus, everywhere I went among the craft beer makers, people were working on beers or brewing techniques that were worthy of Jim Koch's efforts at developing Triple Bock and Utopias.

Of course, none were quite making a claim as extreme as did Koch when he put out his MMM Millennium stout in celebration of the real millennium. He stuck it in a bottle whose color, chemistry, and space-aged sealing mechanism are designed to last, he says, to the year 3000.

* * *

I arrived at Calagione's Dogfish Head brewery on a day when things were a mess. He had just a few weeks before moved out of a cramped 5,000-square-foot space nearby and into a cavernous

27,000-square-foot building that had once been the refrigerator for a huge cannery that had closed down in the 1960s, taking a big chunk of Milton's economy with it. This quaint southern Delaware town of about 1,700, on an inland waterway leading to the coast, had first come to prominence as a nineteenth-century shipbuilding power, a legacy still apparent in the oddly canted Victorian houses crafted from lumber scraps from the shipyards. The cannery, Sam said, had "basically been a boil on the ass of Milton for the past decade," when a real estate syndicate that included his father-in-law bought the building and a big parcel around it in the year 2000. Plans were afoot to eventually turn the plot into a mixed residential-commercial hub that would include 530 condos and houses and could double the town's population. Calagione was offered a long-term lease on the cannery space under what he said were "extremely favorable" terms and jumped at it. At the moment he was surrounded by fallow land scraped up by bulldozers and backhoes as they carved out streets and put in utilities. The brewery, though, which he'd fitted-out with barely used equipment bought at 20 cents on the dollar from a failed Philadelphia microbrewer, was up and running and capable "of making 100 barrels every time we fire it up," he told me. That's still small—as of this writing Dogfish Head's output was about 14,000 barrels a year. But that was double the 2002 production and phenomenal considering that when Calagione opened the brewpub just seven years before, its output—for the entire year—was 380 barrels.

And if others could only see rubble in the jumbled parking lot out the front door, Calagione looked out and saw the green lawns of a boccie ball court he planned to install, busy streets and sidewalks, and the brewery, with a forty-eight-seat restaurant and bar sprouting in its lobby, as the hub of it all. Construction on the nautically themed bar and restaurant had just begun but Sam, a literature major prone to dragging Emerson and Thoreau into beer discussions, had managed to get the Dogfish Head credo (by his hero, Emerson) up on the lobby walls:

Who so would be a man must be a nonconformist. He who would gather immortal palms must not be hindered by the name of goodness, but must explore if it be goodness. Nothing is at last sacred but the integrity of your own mind.

We went into the brewery office, a glassed-off fishbowl with a half-dozen Dilbert-like cubicles holding cluttered desks topped with PCs, where Calagione began to lay out the basics of his and Dogfish Head's history. He and Mariah had gone to high school together in Massachusetts—they met when he was seventeen and she was fifteen. Interest blossomed, though the relationship suffered a temporary hiatus when Sam got bounced out of school a couple of months before graduation. He cited "accumulated mischief," though the final straw was when he was caught skating naked at night in the school's ice hockey arena. Muhlenberg College in Allentown, Pennsylvania, looked past nude hockey escapades to see a promising student, and Sam steeped himself in literature and writing, while admitting that he didn't totally abandon some of his wilder high school impulses and often stayed in the dock with the behavior police.

Mariah finished high school and enrolled in Brown University in Providence, Rhode Island, majoring in public policy. Sam, after graduating from Muhlenberg, went off to tend bar in New York, where he discovered a love and talent for homebrewing. Despite the distances over those years, the couple saw each other pretty much every weekend and summered together, renting a house in Rehoboth Beach, Delaware, very close to where the brewpub is now. Sam's beer tastes were definitely a work in progress—Mariah recalls him getting a bartending job during one of their Rehoboth college summers and dressing up as Bud Man, in a big blow-up Bud outfit, as part of a promotion.

By the time Mariah finished Brown, Sam had put his lit degree to work by doing some serious writing—a business plan. They had toyed with the notion of opening a brewpub in Providence but decided on the Delaware beach region because they knew the lay of the land. And, at the time, Delaware was one of only a handful of states that didn't have either a brewpub or a microbrewery, and Sam said, "we wanted to be the first." It wasn't quite as simple as raising the capital and hiring a cook, however; Sam and Mariah also had to write enabling legislation to change a Prohibition-era Delaware law that prevented beer from being sold where it was brewed.

The brewery got its name, Calagione told me, not from some local landmark but from a promontory off the Maine coast near Boothbay Harbor, where his parents have a rustic summer cottage. He described the early going: "When we first opened, I was a twenty-five-year-old English major with no business experience and no money. You can imagine how receptive the banks were to my situation. So we had the dubious distinction of being the smallest commercial brewery in the country. I'm pretty sure our brewing system was the only one ever delivered by a UPS truck. We ripped the tops off of three kegs, slapped propane burners beneath them, and went to work brewing ten gallons at a time. While it truly sucked from a labor perspective, since I was brewing two or three times a day, five days a week, it was great from an experimental perspective. I brewed so often that I would get bored brewing the same recipes. So I would wander into the kitchen of our brewpub and grab some raisins or maple syrup or apricots. I would change one variable each time I brewed and follow the changes through to see how it affected people's opinions of the beers once they were on tap out at our bar. Our tiny stature proved to be a huge advantage in the long run. We took risks with nontraditional ingredients, and the worst-case scenario was ten gallons of horrible beer. Thankfully this didn't happen too often."

While Sam is the beermeister and handles the "look and feel" of the brewery and brewpub, the operation is very much a joint venture, with Mariah, thirty-three, handling back office chores, advertising and marketing, and a more esoteric job that she described as "keeping us out of trouble." She offered one common scenario in which they collaborate: Sam will come up with an idea for a new beer. "I'll say to Sam, I wonder if we do more brands, will we undercut our existing brands? And Sam will say, well, you've got to be innovative to move ahead. We'll go round and round like this for a while and out of it will come something like Punkin' Ale. It's my job to drive him crazy—in a good way."

Calagione had to interrupt our initial interview to take care of a few pressing matters, so we met later at his brewpub near the beach, where I sampled his one "normal" beer, Shelter Pale Ale. I liked it (and I would like all of his IPAs even better). I realized what a relentlessly experimental mind Sam had when I quipped of Shelter, "So this is the closest you come to plain vanilla lager, right?"

He looked at me, serious for just a moment, and mused, "Hmm, plain vanilla lager. Now that's an idea." (He hasn't made it yet.)

I would end up visiting Dogfish Head and the brewpub several times, and I caught Sam on a number of beer occasions in Manhattan, often in the company of his employees. One of the things that struck me about his operation was how it could seem relaxed and casual and utterly determined, all at the same time; if you didn't see the brew kettles you could easily mistake it for one of those blue-jeans-mandatory PC start-ups in the early Silicon Valley, where everyone had a very good time while they fomented the digital revolution. At Dogfish, the fun seemed clearly tied to the notion that they were all gonzo fighters in the name of Extreme Beer, and the only thing you were allowed to take seriously was the beer itself.

Calagione runs the place with a management style that his workers describe as a mix of absentminded professor, mad genius, great delegator, and prankster. His most consistent traits, besides reliably inventing ever-more-adventurous beers, are being notoriously late for meetings and fond of dropping whatever he's doing to have a beer with his employees. He also seems to have the knack of surrounding himself with able people and trusting them to carry out the work. "Sam will present us with a beer idea," says lead brewer Bryan Selders, "and then let us have at it. He values our experience and abilities and doesn't squelch that with any sort of visions of self-grandeur."

On the other hand, if you go to work for Dogfish, you can expect an expansive view of your job duties. Fred Mazzeo, the brewery's general manager, says that on his first day on the job he was whisked away into a cow pasture, where he was required to interact with very large bovines while Sam choreographed a photo shoot as part of an advertising wordplay on the term "pasteurize." Mazzeo's job was to don false cow teeth and one of those helmets with beer holders attached to a drinking tube, and mug, cowlike, for the camera.

Of course, Mazzeo might have seen this coming given the way Calagione hired him in 1997. Mazzeo had been working for a Wilmington brewpub chain and had pitched up at a beer tasting at the Wilmington train station on behalf of his pub. "There I was in my starched logo shirt and crisply ironed, corporate-obligatory khaki pants and here comes some sweaty, unshaven guy dragging a homemade beer cooler through the crowd. Murmurs of 'That's Sam' flutter through the throng. I had no idea who he was. He begins to set up in the cubicle next to me. His first words were 'Can I borrow a wrench?' followed by 'Do you have pliers?' and finally, 'Got any cups?'"

Mazzeo debated whether he ought to help this obviously unprepared lout but out of pity came up with the wrench and pliers. As he turned away, distracted by something else, he heard a pop nearby and figured Calagione had tapped into his keg. He sure had, for when Mazzeo turned back to look, he got a faceful of beer from the fulminating keg that had already drenched Calagione himself.

Mazzeo says he was a flash away from anger when he tasted the beer that "dripped down my face and head and into my mouth. It was Chicory Stout, and I realized it was far better than anything I was pouring."

Out of this wet and sticky encounter came a job offer.

Selders has gotten the most unusual Sam assignment to date. Calagione, who does things like trying to convince the Ralph Lauren people that Dogfish should be designing an official RL beer for them, decided the River of Beer had fallen woefully behind in its adoption of hip-hop. On a business flight with Selders one day, he saw Bryan fiddling with a small battery-operated gadget that turned out to be a drum sequencer; Selders brews up music as a hobby. He explained the machine to Sam and then forgot all about it.

A few months later, though, Sam, realizing there was a beer conference coming up that involved a battle of the beer bands, decided he wanted to rap. So he coaxed Selders into helping him put together and record a five-song CD under the pseudonym the Pain Relievaz. The title is *Check Your Gravity*, gravity being a technical term that essentially describes the progress of fermentation. The CD's theme is essentially the tension between Big Beer and the Beer Geeks.

Of course, putting out this CD was not quite enough for Calagione, who is also known for his movie-star good looks and true flair for another Calagionean concept that he describes as "beer as theater." One night, at an event I attended, he dragged Selders to the Blind Tiger in Manhattan, where, with the help of the very same battery-operated drum machine, they actually performed the album before a packed audience of delirious Ale Heads who—perhaps aided by Calagione's 120 Minute IPA that was on tap that night—went wild. The hit of the night was a song called "I Once Got Crazy with an A-B Salesgirl!"—a send-up of a bar encounter between an opportunistic ale drinker and a comely saleswoman for Budweiser. Never mind that the batteries on the drum machine died in the middle of the song. Sam, as Funkmaster IBU and doing a reasonable imitation of Vanilla Ice, stopped, started over, and carried on a cappella, hitting lines like: "I said what do you want? / She said a Budweiser / I said girl, you must be on more drugs / than my homeys down at Pfizer."

"We are, no doubt," Selders told me, "the finest Beer Geek hip-hop group of our generation."

The evening of my first trip to Dogfish Head, Calagione and I later left the brewpub for a ten-mile drive down to Dewey Beach, a kind of raucous party enclave of the Delaware Shore, where stood a lager bar called the Rusty Rudder, frequented by the kind of people who populate Coors Light commercials. Sam steered us there because the bar nonetheless sold his Shelter Pale Ale and because a favorite regional band of his called Love Seed Mamma Jump was playing. Calagione, as he would in our numerous other meetings, showed a relentless curiosity about everything he heard, and he spent about as much time peppering me with questions about how I'd come up with the notion of this book and pitched it to editors as I peppered him with beer questions. I was particularly curious about the brewing creative process and how he got ideas for new beers.

He told me about a new concoction that he was making that would be called Pangaea; its signature would be that it would include at least one ingredient from every continent on earth. The Calagiones have two children, Sam IV, who is four, and Grier, one, and Sam said he first got the idea when he was watching a dinosaur movie with his son.

"The movie depicted the original landmass, Pangaea, that existed before the earth broke apart into continents. This is right around the time of the bombing of Iraq, and France and Germany were calling us out on it. I'm not all that political but I thought it would be fun to make a beer that brought all of the continents back together." The ingredients: Australian ginger, African sugar, Asian basmati rice, a South American grain, American hops, French barley, and bottled water from Antarctica. (A few months later, before Pangaea had actually gone into production, I got an e-mail from Sam jokingly bemoaning the fact that Anheuser-Busch had just announced it was putting out a new high-end lager in the pilsner style called Anheuser World Select that was being brewed with ingredients from four continents. "Can you believe that?" he wrote jokingly. "The bastards are copping my idea!")

Calagione, though, seemed most proud of his experimental work with hops, especially the notion of continuously hopping beer. He had a theory that if you added a small, constant stream of hops to the boil, instead of big dramatic doses at the beginning and the end, you might be able to ratchet up hop levels without raising bitterness. One issue was that there was no existing machinery to automate continuous hopping; either it would have to be done laboriously by hand, or machinery would have to be improvised.

"The first time we tried continual hopping," he said, "was with the first batch of 60 Minute IPA that I brewed back in 2000. I used one of those goofy circa 1978 electrified vibrating football games, canted at an angle and rigged up with a five-gallon bucket of pelletized hops over our boil kettle. The hops would vibrate down the angled football game and into the kettle in a single-file stream."

The improvised football hopper worked well enough to get them through the first batch; then the football game got wet and shorted out. But the taste of the beer convinced Sam he was on to something and sent him scurrying to design the pneumatic hops feeder that he dubbed Sir Hops Alot. The 120 Minute IPA that Michael Jackson sampled from the Dogfish tanks is certainly an example of Extreme Hopping. Not only is it continuously hopped but "we go a step further by adding a pound of pellet hops to the primary fermenter every day for a month," he told me.

This is kind of like a pizza maker taking the pie out of the oven every four minutes and throwing on another layer of mozzarella and pepperoni. But Calagione defends the hyperhopping, "because, you know, life is short and all."

Later that night at the Rusty Rudder, Calagione and I sat at an open-air table with a couple of his buddies we'd bumped into, sipping Shelter Pale Ale and just getting acquainted. And I knew Sam was a real Beer Guy, and not just a Beer Geek, when, toward the end of the evening, with our cash rapidly depleting and an ATM nowhere in sight, we decided to extend the night by one more beer. So we pooled our pitiful reserves of pocket-crumpled dollar bills and loose change and ordered—what else?—two pints of the really cheap Miller Lite on tap.

And drank them, I must report, with great pleasure.

Back on the River of Beer

Beer and Remembrance: Slouching Toward Hannibal by Way of Nauvoo, Illinois

The tavern will compare favorably with the church.
—Henry David Thoreau

On the first anniversary of 9/11 I found myself, foam cup of coffee in hand, back on the Great River Road a full 100 miles south of Dubuque, motoring through towns with names like Blue Grass, Muscatine, Fruitland, and Wapello.

It was a pristine morning, the sky a pale blue, the sun dappling treetops painted in a serendipitous cloak of light and fog. The river was nowhere visible here, obscured by an elongated distant green line that marked the levee. But I'd seen it at sunrise from the decks of the *Diamond Jo*, the Twain-styled riverboat and casino that docked next to the Mississippi River Museum.

Despite my late night with Jim Massey, I'd pried myself awake in time to catch the *Diamond Jo*'s two-hour early morning cruise in hopes of catching up with some early morning beer drinkers.

But as I watched the boat fill with busloads of pensioners swarming for nickel slot machines and keno games, I realized this was probably a poor reporting bet. And it was—nary an ounce of beer touched a single lip, though I patrolled the *Diamond Jo's* various bars like a sentry in a war zone. ("Are you kidding?" one bartender told me when I plaintively wondered about the possible existence of a breakfast beer club. "This is the sarsaparilla cruise.")

The *Diamond Jo* docked, and I lit out for parts unknown.

The country I now traveled through was a mix of plains to the west and hardwood river bottoms to the east, and a road sign I stopped to read told me this was once prime Plains Indian country, Wapello, for example, being named for a great Fox Tribe chieftain who died in the 1840s. In the long, wide-open stretches between the towns grew great rolling rivers of corn and soybeans just beginning to yellow under an insistent late summer sun. Now and then some white clapboard farmhouse, a truck or tractor or combine parked in the yard, tumbled from the fields to break the immense folds of green and gold.

The weather held fair, and where the road ran up in sight of the river, which was not often along this stretch, the Mississippi fanned out as dark and wild and sun-dappled as Mark Twain himself must've seen it. In fact, the river here had historically proved a little too wild and unpredictable for the locals. Louisa County, Iowa, of which Wapello is the county seat, lost more than 200 homes to flood mitigation efforts after the Great Flood of 1993.

I'd switched on the car radio and a National Public Radio station drifted in and out. All the programming was 9/11-anniversary related, but being NPR, it was delivered in calm, modulated tones by speakers of serious purpose and was reflective and informative in a way that didn't seem sensationalistic or lurid. And there were no pictures. I hadn't consciously timed my beer quest to this distracting stroke of the calendar, though I wondered now if I'd done so subconsciously. When I'd briefly discussed the anniversary the night before with Jim Massey, we'd both agreed that the last place we wanted to spend the anniversary was in front of a TV, where the horror of that day would no doubt be replayed endlessly. The planes had struck the Twin Towers while I was in the air, flying from La Guardia to Atlanta. The *Wall Street Journal*'s offices across the West Side Highway had been severely damaged, and we would instantly be uprooted to joyless temporary quarters in South Brunswick, New Jersey; friends and colleagues had seen and experienced terrible things. A neighbor in the New Jersey village where I lived had been killed, leaving behind his kindly wife and three children. A dozen others in my town perished.

There was no chance I would ever forget any of that. Out here, at least, I could be plugged in without being overwhelmed. And it was reassuring, as the day wore on, that the day had gone uneventfully—that the chronic, low-grade, unspoken fear that the Bad Guys would try something else on the anniversary hadn't materialized.

When I'd lose NPR, I would switch over to a country music station or just switch off the radio and drive through the countryside in silence. The combination was mysteriously calming, and I drove on and on, at the languid pace of a tourist, still with no particular destination in mind.

At Burlington, Iowa, a pretty town of 30,000, I passed houses with American flags at half staff and a gas station with one of those portable signs out front that said, in plastic black lettering, "Never forget." I saw people gathering on lawn chairs in front of a church. About a dozen miles below Burlington I saw a sign for a toll bridge across the Mississippi. This seemed like a good excuse to duck into Illinois.

I was glad I did when I saw the signs for Nauvoo, Illinois, about ten miles south. I'd never been there, but I knew a bit about the place.

In the late '80s, as a reporter in the *Journal*'s San Francisco bureau writing stories about the West, I did a major piece on the Mormon church, whose world headquarters are in Salt Lake City, Utah. I recalled that Nauvoo had once been Mormonism's capital and sacred center until the church's founder, Joseph Smith, got into a fracas with locals and wound up murdered by a mob that broke into the jail where he was being held under protective custody. Such hostility drove Brigham Young in 1846 to lead the remaining church members to Utah on a 1,300-mile odyssey by ox-drawn and hand-pulled covered wagons. Two years after that, a massive temple that Smith had overseen the building of in Nauvoo was torched by arsonists, and Nauvoo's Mormon presence was all but eradicated. Still, the place loomed large in the church's colorful and often controversial history.

I'd expected to find a little town, and it was; the population was 1,200, and for the most part it was an unostentatious, low-rise hamlet perched on a slow bend in the river, with a number of turn-of-the-century buildings along its main drag. But two unexpected things caught my eye as I drove through. One was a humongous Mormon temple, so gleaming white that it had to be new, and that by an order of magnitude dwarfed everything else in town. The other was a small bar, looking as scruffy and friendly as a good-natured yard dog. It was just up the street from the temple and sported a conspicuous sign in the window that said, in part: "Nauvoo's House of Sin."

I smelled a whiff of controversy and did a U-turn, parking near the bar, which was called the Draft House. I got out and walked over and read the sign in full:

> *Please Enter Nauvoo's House of Sin*
> *Know You're Welcome, Come On In*
> *Heaven Knows We're All Swingers*
> *'Cause Even Jesus Hung Out with Sinners*
> —With Love from Everyone Inside

Being both sinner and journalist, I felt compelled to go in. It was about 3:30 in the afternoon, and the only life in the place was a cluster of guys gathered at a long bar at the back of the joint. The front, in fact, looked more like a restaurant than a bar, and that's pretty much what it was. I'd arrived, according to a sign inside, on Chicken Night. For five bucks you could get half a fried chicken, all white meat if you wanted it, plus the fixings.

I made my way back and settled in at the bar, where I met Don, Dan, and Jimmy, who were partaking in an afternoon lager break before heading back to various trades. This used to be a very American thing to do. Before World War II, beer was as much a part of the blue-collar workplace as coffee is today. Brewery workers in particular drank throughout the day and got free beer as part of their pay package. Liability and tort lawyers, not to mention changing views about workplace safety and comportment, have put an end to this practice.

It didn't take long to get the gist of what had prompted the Draft House sign. A Mormon in the town's planning department had reportedly denounced the Draft House in a public forum as a house of sin deserving of being closed down. (Mormons, at least the devout ones, don't drink or even partake of coffee, tea, or caffeinated soft drinks.) Sonja Bush, the woman who owned the bar, took grave exception and complained in the press, and things had been frosty ever since, though the Mormon who had uttered the reputed slur had since left town (and, I would learn later, had denied saying quite that). As I sat and listened, though, it was clear that this wasn't just a spat over errant words.

The gleaming white temple I'd seen down the block, the men at the bar told me, had just opened in June after three years and $25 million in the making. It was 54,000 square feet and an exact replica of the temple that burned in 1848. Its construction had pumped a huge amount of money into the town but not without a number of conflicts, its size being only one of them. Local construction folk often bridled over Mormon overseers demanding everything be done in a "Utah way." And since completion, about 250,000 devout Mormons had flooded into Nauvoo to see the temple and to visit the Joseph Smith Historic Site, a rambling compound sitting at the north edge of town. For the Mormons this was holy ground, the place of their prophet's martyrdom. But for the two-thirds of the local residents who aren't Mormon (they are mostly Catholic), this was a matter of some ambivalence. True, all those visitors had been an economic boon, but some of them had come to town "acting like they owned the place," Jimmy at the bar told me. "They think they do, but they don't."

Mormons refer to members of all other religions, including Jews, as gentiles. And the guys at the bar had all heard stories of gentile Nauvoo shopkeepers being snubbed by Mormon visitors when they answered no to the question "Are you LDS?" (This is an abbreviation of Latter-day Saints, which is what the Mormons call themselves.) The subtext of the temple was a local worry that it might encourage large numbers of Mormons to move to Nauvoo, thus changing the character of the place (and not necessarily for the better, if you're a beer-drinking Christian or a bar owner).

To be fair, though, many religions inveigh against alcohol, have a clannish streak, and declare themselves to be the one true faith. And I'd spent a lot of time in Salt Lake City, which is dominated by Temple Square and, by population, is about half Mormon. I'd always found it reasonably open and cosmopolitan—not exactly New York or L.A., but on par with, say, comparable-sized towns in the Midwest. The Mormons hadn't exactly turned Salt Lake into Squaresville, and many Mormons I'd come to know had no interest in doing so.

Some of the local consternation, I learned, was tinged by a fair amount of skepticism about Mormon piety over Nauvoo. Non-Mormons generally read the history of Joseph Smith's sojourn here slightly differently than do the flock. Smith, in their most jaded view, was a charismatic megalomaniac who'd come from the East (New York State, actually) touting a fantastical, essentially occult religion that he said had been revealed to him in gold tablets, by either an angel named Moroni or, based on more recent interpretations, a white salamander. The tablets formed the basis of the Book of Mormon, which teaches that modern-day Mormonism descends from lost tribes of Israel who wandered into America in ancient times, keeping the true word of God alive.

The Book of Mormon foreshadowed that a prophet would come forward one day to restore the "Kingdom of God to earth," and unsurprisingly, according to Smith critics, Smith took that job for himself. Before he ever got to Nauvoo, he had tried to set up theocracies in Ohio and Missouri and had been run out of both places. Nauvoo, critical historians say, was his third attempt, and he had raised a militia of 1,500 well-armed men to see it through—a development greatly unsettling to the local non-Mormon population. When a non-Mormon newspaper wrote a story critical of him and Mormonism, the Smith-controlled city council ordered the paper sacked and the presses destroyed. That Smith was later murdered by a mob enraged by this act is as incontrovertible as it is unconscionable. But in the view of some non-Mormons, Smith was hardly a saintly man plunking for religious freedom; he was a religious tyrant with an army. In the non-Mormon view, this all makes the new Nauvoo temple a curious monument indeed.

I was contemplating all this when Sonja Bush herself, the Draft House's owner, came in to get things squared away for Chicken Night, which she told me was their busiest night of the week. About two-thirds of the crowd would be families with kids, though, true, there would be some beer drinkers among the lot. But she had worked at the bar for ten years and owned it (but not the building that holds it) for five and could recall no particularly sinful behavior, other than alcohol consumption and the occasional live performance of rock music, that might have set the Mormon city official off.

Now, as a good reporter, I'd already pumped the guys at the

bar for any history of sordid misbehavior. And one of them did confess that once, perhaps one beer over the line, he'd gotten accidentally bumped into a big open garbage can in the joint but had been recovered with no injury save to his pride. And they did tell me that Chicken Night used to be All-You-Can-Eat Chicken Night until some guy gobbled down ten chickens while barely sipping the one beer he'd bought from the bar, thus putting an end to All-You-Can-Eat Chicken Night. But whether he was guilty of the sin of gluttony or simply exploiting a weakness in the interface of capitalism was a matter of perception.

"If the cops do come in here," Dan told me, "they're looking for potato chips."

For Sonja Bush, the issue was simply being the object of an affront that she felt stemmed from religious narrow-mindedness. "At first, I just went along with it," she said. "But then I got so mad.... This is a farming community and the people who come in here are good, honest, hardworking people. We have fun and there's no real sin that goes on."

With the temple open three months now and the summer crowds having thinned out, I asked her if things had calmed down. "There's still tensions," she said, "though not as much because I think they've come to accept for now that we're here."

Then she dropped a bombshell: "I lease the place and my landlord just sold the building to a Mormon in Utah. I'm sure he's using my lease money to turn it into a little nest egg and will convert this into anything he wants to one day."

Then she laughed: "Yeah, I think they're going to get me."

I thanked her and the guys at the bar for their time and went seeking a counterpoint to this. But there were no tourists (Mormon or otherwise) milling about the temple, and I couldn't just go in: temples are closed to nonbelievers. So I drove back to the Joseph Smith Historic Site, where I inquired of a kindly woman at an information desk in the Historic Nauvoo Visitors Center—a rambling, modern building—if she knew anything of this controversy. She said she didn't, but she did offer me a number of Historic Nauvoo pamphlets and suggested I take in the "inspiring film" interpreting "the early developments of Historic Nauvoo." I accepted the pamphlets but passed on the movie, opting instead to walk over to see the Historic Smith Family Graveyard where Smith's remains lie. I wondered what Smith himself would make of all of this.

And I wondered if I would make an odder stop along the River of Beer.

* * *

An hour before dark, I drove toward another shrine, this one to a most secular man and a most secular faith, if literature can be called a faith. I'd entered Hannibal, Missouri, about seventy miles south of Nauvoo, and was heading in the direction of the childhood home of my literary hero, Samuel Langhorne Clemens, better known as Mark Twain. I'd decided that this odd day ought to be capped with something personally inspiring, whether Hannibal mustered even a single candidate for the Perfect Beer Joint.

Hannibal—"America's Hometown," a sign told me—seemed to lay out quiet and drowsy in the late afternoon sun. I followed Mark Twain historical markers and desultory traffic down into the city center and then farther down toward the riverfront, where most of the town's considerable Twainabilia can be found. I'd decided Hannibal was as far as I was going, and I immediately faced a lodging conundrum: the old and faded (but perhaps character-filled) Mark Twain Hotel or the Hotel Clemens Best Western. (Coming in, I'd also noticed the Comfort Inn on Huckleberry Drive, not to mention the Super 7 Motel and a Travelodge, both on Mark Twain Avenue.) My problem was solved when I realized, upon closer inspection, that the old Mark Twain Hotel was closed to lodgers and that the Hotel Clemens Best Western sat right across the street from the Mark Twain Dinette & Family Restaurant. It was also within walking distance of both the Jumping Frog Café and Becky's Old Fashioned Ice Cream Parlor and Emporium, not to mention things I really wanted to see, like the Mark Twain Boyhood Home and Museum, Becky Thatcher's House, the Tom and Huck Statue, and the Adventures of Tom Sawyer Dioramas.

Hannibal is a town of about 18,000, and it made me wonder how many jobs here were tied to the Twain industry and how many things named Twain, or named for Twain characters, there were. Later, flipping through the Yellow Pages, I learned that even the Miller Beer wholesaler in town called itself Mark Twain Distributing Co. Twain, a lager man, probably would've appreciated the beer connection. It's hard to know what he would have made of the Sawyer's Creek Fun Park, Café and Christmas Shop, with its bumper boats, miniature golf course, and Tom Sawyer and Becky Thatcher dolls—looking like mutant cousins to the Cabbage Patch Kids—at $22.95 a pair, mail order.

All the Twain sites were locked up tight by the time I parked the car on a steep grade and checked into the hotel behind a bus-load of elderly tourists who seemed to be in a contest over who could register the slowest, and several biker couples whose for-midable tattoos at least gave me a number of worlds to visit while I waited in line. Still, before dark, I was able to wander around and peek in windows of Twain's home, and Grant's Drug Store, the handsome clapboard business and house where Twain's fam-ily lived for a couple of years when they fell on hard times.

There was enough signage about that I was able to refresh my memory that Twain was actually born in Florida, Missouri (not to be confused with Louisiana, Missouri, or Mexico, Mis-souri), and moved to Hannibal in 1839 as a four-year-old. He moved away in 1853, having worked briefly as a printer and a journalist, packing with him the boyhood memories that would turn into *The Adventures of Tom Sawyer* and *The Adventures of Huckleberry Finn*, and salt numerous other of the thirty-odd literary works he would produce in his lifetime. When Twain revisited Hannibal in 1882 to complete his seminal memoir of his river pilot days, called *Life on the Mississippi*, he wrote of it:

The whole town lay spread out below me then, and I could mark and fix every locality, every detail. Naturally, I was a good deal moved....From this vantage ground the extensive view up and down the river and wide over the wood expanses of Illinois, is very beautiful; one of the most beautiful on the Mississippi, I think.

The town still posed handsomely from the bluffs above, though in character it didn't much resemble historical descriptions of Twain's old Hannibal with its rowdy port full of flatboaters and river rats, its slaughterhouses and port-packing plants, its lumber mills, barrel makers, and odoriferous hide-tanning factories. I strolled well beyond the few square blocks holding Twain's renovated Hannibal and, in the fading light, on a street of somewhat faded houses, experienced a kind of Tom-and-Huck moment when I was accosted by a large and menacing dog of uncertain breed—I was guessing a Great Dane–shepherd mix, with the moderating influence of maybe a bull mastiff someplace in the gene pool. The lads no doubt, with Twain's acquiescence, would have beaned the monster with a handy rock, fed it something ghastly but not fatal, or found some other clever way to throw it off their tracks. I could merely stand and back away and yell at the beast, hoping the owner might appear and be more hospitable than the dog. (On the other hand, I have a theory that dogs often look and act like their owners, which, in this case, would have exacerbated my problem.) This stalemate ended only when a car came up the street and the pooch happily went snarling after it, gnashing at a rear tire, as I sprinted in the opposite direction.

On the late side of the dinner hour, I found my way to Bubba's, a restaurant tucked into a handsome old warehouse on the "wet side" of the Mississippi River levee (what locals call the Flood Wall) not far from the hotel. I chose it by name alone. I'd lived in Columbia, Missouri, for three years as a graduate student and always found that Missouri, outside of St. Louis and

Kansas City, felt more like the South than the Midwest. And when in the South, you are required, every time you encounter a place named Bubba's, to stop and eat there. It was a good choice. I opted for the pit-smoked barbecue ribs and they were terrific.

It was there that I allowed myself the idle thought of what it would have been like to go beer drinking with Sam Clemens, perhaps before the time, late in his life, when he had become so exasperated by the chronic tragedy and folly of the world that a pint or two could no longer comfort him. Though I hadn't plotted ahead in search of beer joints, I had bothered to do some beer research on Twain and found a number of references that made me think he had once been a committed beer pilgrim himself. In Albert Bigelow Paine's 1912 biography of Twain, Paine writes of Twain as a San Francisco reporter, living in a flat above the tin roofs of Chinatown. There, he and his companions, after late night beer-drinking sessions, would sometimes toss their empties down upon those very same roofs, then duck for cover behind the blinds when bleary-eyed residents came stumbling from their houses, shaking their fists at all the clattering. Paine described the beer-drinking outings, and Twain's fondness for the barleyed beverage, this way:

> He was hard at work on the [San Francisco] *Call,* living modestly with Steve Gillis in the quietest place they could find, never quiet enough, but as far as possible from dogs and cats and chickens and pianos, which seemed determined to make the mornings hideous, when a weary night reporter and compositor wanted to rest. They went out socially, on occasion, arrayed in considerable elegance; but their recreations were more likely to consist of private midnight orgies, after the paper had gone to press—mild dissipations in whatever they could find to eat at that hour, with a few glasses of beer, and perhaps a game of billiards or pool in some all-night resort. A printer by the name of Ward—"Little Ward," they called him—often went with

them for these refreshments. Ward and Gillis were both bantam gamecocks, and sometimes would stir up trouble for the very joy of combat. Clemens never cared for that sort of thing and discouraged it, but Ward and Gillis were for war....

In those days Twain was troubled with sleeplessness...and he had various specifics for promoting it. At first it had been champagne just before going to bed, and we provided that, but later he appeared from Boston with four bottles of lager-beer under his arms; lager-beer, he said now, was the only thing to make you go to sleep, and we provided that.

And I decided that Twain himself might have weighed in on the controversy back in Nauvoo after reading a letter he had written, while on hiatus in New York in 1867, to his old newspaper back in San Francisco:

You are aware that in New York, after twelve at night on weekdays, you cannot buy a glass of wine or liquor for love or money, and you cannot buy it on Sunday at any time. It is a great thing for the morals of New York, but it is demoralizing to the vicinage. It inflicts twenty thousand beer-swillers upon Hoboken every Sabbath. You remember the pious girl who said, "I found that my ribbons and gewgaws were dragging me down to hell, and so I took them off and gave them to my sister." Well that is the way we are doing for Hoboken. We found that beer drinkers were debauching our morals, and so we concluded to turn them over to our neighbor. The ferry-boats go over packed and crammed with people all day Sunday, and the beer and such stuff drank in Hoboken on these occasions amounts to oceans, to speak liberally. They say that they are going to inaugurate an excise law over there, next Sunday, and then what will thirsty New York do?

Alas, Bubba's was a pleasant enough place to ruminate these matters, but it was mostly empty and, though it served beer, it didn't qualify as a beer joint. So I wandered back along quiet, darkened streets, fairly beat from more than six hours in the car, thinking that maybe on this Wednesday night all of Hannibal had already gone to bed and so I would, too. But as I crossed Main Street I noticed lights a couple of blocks away and what looked like the orangey glow of a neon sign. As I got closer I realized it was a bar and that there were actually people drinking beer in it. It was about nine o'clock; I wandered in.

The place was called Sid's National Bar & Grill, and whether it was a biker bar or not, it was at this moment about half filled with bikers, with biker girlfriends, and with a few people who looked like they could be bikers-in-training. Loud biker rock pounded from the jukebox and the bikers themselves were engaged in a rather raucous and competitive game of darts involving one of the larger dart players—well, human beings, actually—that I'd ever seen in person, a guy reminiscent of that late-'50s soap commercial character Mr. Clean, but tattooed as thoroughly as Dennis Rodman. I threaded my way to the bar and, remembering where I was, ordered a Bud. Since I lacked tattoos, an earring, a muscle shirt or muscle jacket, a black leather jacket, a proper pirate's head scarf, and the proper frayed denim jeans hung with chains and held up with studded belts, and since I did not have on what bikers might consider manly footwear (having dressed for dinner in chinos and penny loafers), I didn't want to stick out any more than I already did. I tried striking up a conversation with my bartender, but between the music and the dart-related exhortations it was so loud that I could barely manage to find out how much I owed for the beer, much less plumb the deeper meaning of Sid's National Bar & Grill. So I sat on a bar stool sipping my Bud and watching the darts match unfold, the air filled with smoke, music, chatter, and occasional outbursts of cheering and cheerful profanities. Thus, I was hardly prepared for what happened next.

A man in a ball cap suddenly stood up from a table, yelled "Quiet!" at the top of his lungs, and then said, "It's 9:10 on

9/11. In a minute, at 9:11, I want everyone to stand in a minute of silence for the people who died in the World Trade Center and their families."

The place hushed. Darts ceased flying. Somebody pulled the plug on the music.

And as the clock struck 9:11, the bikers, some still clutching beers and some taking off caps, bowed their heads in a deep and enveloping silence.

And this position they held, for well more than a minute, until someone moved toward the jukebox and plugged it back in.

9

We Divert West to Sleuth Amongst the Yeast Rustlers

Let me tell you the secret that has led me to my goal.
My strength lies solely in my tenacity.
—Louis Pasteur

Woodland Hills, Calif.—Perhaps you have lived your life, as I had, unaware of international beer yeast smuggling rings. You probably didn't know, either, that beer yeast rustlers were ubiquitously afoot in the land.

But they're out there all right, and all yeast is fair game. They have kits and they have knowledge—and they know how to clone. Actually, the correct term is clone-purify. But we'll get to that later.

Now, that beer yeast is the object of any intrigue whatsoever seems, on the face of it, curious considering that it is a microscopic, single-cell, potato-shaped fungus that sells, in dry form, for as little as 50 cents per half-ounce packet. With five of those you can make five gallons of homebrew (about fifty-three 12-ounce bottles). For that $2.50 investment, you get a slurry of powdery yeast composed of about 250 *billion* individual cells, making a single cell of beer yeast one of the great bargains on the planet.

However, the intrigue over such a seemingly lowly thing seems less curious when you spend time among the Yeast People. Among the Yeast People, there is nothing simple or ordinary about beer yeast. It is beautiful, glorious, mysterious, magical, sexy, and, of course, to them, the single most important ingredient in beer. Its historical and mystical name is God Is Good. For without beer yeast—a voracious feeder and a feral and potent multiplier—beer would not ferment and thus would lack that salutary taste- and mood-enhancer called alcohol.

But what really drives the passion of the Yeast People, whose ranks are formed by madly passionate homebrewers and madly passionate craft brewers, is the incalculable prospect that different strains of beer yeast bring to beer's flavor. That yeast affects beer flavor and character in a macro way has long been known. *Saccharomyces cerevisiae*, more commonly known as ale yeast, and *Saccharomyces uvarum*, more commonly known as lager yeast, form the microbiological fault line of the world's great beer taste divide. One produces the earthy-warm flavor of ale, the other the smooth-cool flavor of lager. This more or less comes down to a function of how, and how effectively, the two strains feed.

This macro knowledge, however, has been supplemented of late with a vast cache of micro knowledge of how the lowly yeast does its thing, and to what effect. Yeast dances through thirteen steps en route to devouring malt sugars and throwing off alcohol (and carbon dioxide) as a by-product. In between, a lot can (and does) happen. Only recently, for example, scientists, using gas chromatographs attached to sniff ports manned by trained human nosers, discovered that yeast reactions account for dozens of flavors and odors, some previously unknown, some that were thought to be the result of other beer components. They have isolated these in such intricate ways that you can, if you care to, brew to achieve these flavors and odors, assuming you observe certain intricacies of application.

If you are a lager maker like Dixie Brewing Co., a New

Orleans brewer that has used the same yeast strain since it opened in 1907, this doesn't concern you except, perhaps, as a matter of interesting arcana. If, however, you are a craft brewer seeking to make new beers with distinctive signatures, this interests you greatly. Likewise, you care if you are a homebrewer out to make a beer that tastes like, for example, Sierra Nevada Pale Ale; or out to make some exotic beer style like a Baltic porter; or out to make a beer that crosses so many beer style boundaries that you're certain it has never been made before on earth.

What else interests you, especially if you are that kind of homebrewer, is the fact that of a few hundred recognized beer yeast strains in the world, only about 100 are available commercially in the U.S., principally through two for-profit yeast labs, Wyeast Laboratories in Odell, Oregon, and White Labs in San Diego. That number in reality may be somewhat less; the two companies offer about fifty strains each, but some may be the same yeast sold under different names. Still, that's a lot more than were available when President Jimmy Carter, homebrewers' all-time favorite politician, signed a law back in 1979 legalizing homebrewing at the federal level and opening the way for the states to do the same. Back then, homebrewers were pretty much stuck brewing with baker's yeast unless they were willing to write off to England to mail-order a few measly strains of ale yeast.

But if you *are* one of those madly passionate homebrewers among the nation's estimated two million beer-making hobbyists, the ability to get your hands on close to 100 beer yeast strains—strains that anybody else can buy—is simply not good enough. Propelled by the maddening theory that if you just had the yeast, you could make Sam Adams as well as Boston Beer does, or you could make some highly exotic beer that could change your brewing life, you want them *all*.

And this, if you believe the committed among the yeast-rustling community, can pretty much be done.

Upon the advice of Randy Mosher, the affable Chicago Beer Geek I'd met at a homebrew contest in Houston, I took time from the quest to find the Perfect Beer Joint and flew out to Los Angeles to meet Maribeth Raines-Casselman. Mosher told me that not only was Maribeth one of the nation's acknowledged beer yeast experts but that she had probably done more to advance the odd science of yeast rustling than any other person in America.

Yeast rustling, unlike the variety practiced on cattle, is not to anyone's knowledge illegal, and thus far nobody has sued anybody over it. Modern beer yeasts have evolved from wild, naturally occurring strains; they are not genetically engineered, so they are not strictly speaking patentable (though people have patented industrial *processes* that involve yeast, but not thus far in the brewing industry).

But that's not the same as saying the issue isn't of concern. Most commercial breweries have yeast they consider to be proprietary, and they don't (usually) hand it out or want it falling into outside hands. The big lager makers like Anheuser-Busch have made significant investments in high-tech labs and spend millions of dollars a year to propagate their yeast and keep it pure. (As a cost per bottle of beer, yeast is practically nothing; the brewing cycle spins off five to six times more yeast than brewers ever need to make future beer, and brewers face a disposal problem with the excess.)

Many big breweries like Anheuser-Busch, SABMiller, and Coors have used the same yeast strains forever—strains, they say, brought to America by their founders. They refresh them regularly by recloning from pure cultures they have set aside in what are called slants—sealed test tubes, stored in freezers, with a sterile medium that guards against contaminants. But most of the hundreds of new craft brew and brewpub start-ups of the past two decades had no yeast to call their own, nor the money or space to run internal yeast labs. Hence both Wyeast and White Labs sprang to life to help them develop, perfect, push, and preserve their yeast strains. Some small brewers who did have their own yeast admitted their murky origins. I had at least two craft brewers tell me that they got their yeast strains from people inside other breweries who smuggled them out. I had craft brewers tell me they obtained samples of another brewery's yeast and allowed it to mutate into a strain that they now call proprietary. (Yeast can mutate in as few as ten generations.) Now and then a craft brewer will openly share its yeast, only asking that those who use it give the original owner some credit in the marketing fine print. But most craft brew strains managed by the yeast labs are protected by "no sharing" agreements that prohibit the labs from selling them, say, into the homebrew market, or giving them to other commercial brewers.

This is where the yeast rustlers come in.

I caught up with Maribeth and her husband, Steve Casselman, in their modest ranch house in Woodland Hills, one of those sprawling, homogenized suburbs just northeast of Los Angeles. "House" might be a bit of a misnomer. Maribeth and Steve are ardent homebrewers who own a popular commercial beer, which they send out to be contract-brewed, called Hollywood Blonde (it's an exotic, award-winning American Kölsch, which is a type of ale known for its clean, lagerlike qualities). Their house and garage are totally given over to these pursuits. Seven refrigerators hold beer in various stages of production; beer kegs are everywhere, including one, with tap, out by the swimming pool; an enormous 50-gallon homebrewing apparatus stands in the driveway (the average amateur brews in a 5-gallon crock); a utility closet holds a beer-fermenting room; and boxes of beer bottles waiting to be filled and bottling equipment crowd various nooks and crannies. In addition, spare bedrooms have been commandeered and turned into labs full of test tubes, beakers, flasks, and microscopes, where Maribeth conducts most of her yeast work.

You don't exactly have to have a Ph.D. to perfect the art of rustling up yeast cultures from other people's beers, or actual samples of their yeast, but Maribeth happens to have one anyway. A friendly, big-boned Midwesterner with a quick wit and a hearty laugh, she got a doctorate in biochemistry from Michigan State University back in the 1980s, where among her favorite memories was being able to buy Wiedemann's lager longnecks for five bucks a case. "That was the bomb," she told me. (Now-defunct Wiedemann was a Kentucky brewer and another 1980s Lager Wars casualty.) After spending time on the faculty at UCLA doing cancer research, Maribeth moved to the private sector, where she runs a research group for a nearby biotechnology concern called Biosource. There she helps genetically engineer synthetic hormones and detection reagents that big pharmaceutical companies use in drug testing. There is a clear beer benefit to this job, since it gives Maribeth access to a high-tech liquid nitrogen refrigerator in which she can cryogenically store captured yeast (forever, in theory) in slants under mineral oil at minus 80 degrees Celsius.

I arrived on a late summer afternoon and it was 112 degrees Fahrenheit outside, a detail I learned from Steve Casselman as he came in from the garage, where some of the seven refrigerators reside, bearing big unmarked bottles of cold beer. Steve, a mirthful man with a boyish grin and huge enthusiasms, runs a business from home in the esoteric niche of reconfigurable computing (which Steve, if he were writing this, could explain to you). We sat at their dining room table, and while Steve poured the homebrew, Maribeth began to tell me about yeast. But first she diverted to the beer we were going to drink.

"This is Dougweiser," she said. "It's essentially a really strong Budweiser at 9 percent alcohol by volume. We made it with rice like they do. It's a pain in the ass unless you can get somebody to build you a $100 million plant. You boil up the rice till it gelatinizes and essentially becomes liquid starch. It's a mess to make." (They named it for a friend and fellow homebrewer named Doug, who was killed in an automobile accident on the way to a homebrew competition.)

I took a sip and it was potent and good—though not very much like Bud.

Maribeth also told me we would later be trying their take on a tripel, which is a Belgian-Dutch ale style that traditionally designated the strongest beer in the house. "Ours is a super-strong Belgian, probably 15 percent ABV," she said. "So we call it Sex-Tipel." This, she explained, was a play on "sextuple" because "it's stronger than a tripel. And after you drink it you'll want to have sex but you'll probably tip over instead."

This brought a howl of laughter from Steve, though he'd no doubt heard this before. One thing I would learn about Maribeth and Steve, who are both forty-five years old: they really liked their beer, and they really liked to laugh.

She then started to fill me in on why and whither the obsession with yeast.

In the beginning, Maribeth said, it was the dearth of authentic beer yeast that drove homebrewers in the early 1980s to take matters into their own hands. They could do this because of yeast's biology. As a single-cell organism, it does not need a mate to propagate; it divides when it is fed and happy, as many as twenty times in its life cycle, spinning off buds that grow into identical daughter cells. Under the right conditions, the beer forms of *Saccharomyces* (a term literally meaning "sugar fungus") do this rather rapidly and exponentially. Thus, even though you might need billions of yeast cells to ferment a 5-gallon bucket of wort into beer, you could start by isolating a single healthy yeast cell, throwing it into a sugar-rich, commercially available medium known as starter, and letting it do its thing. In three days or so, you can be riding herd on your own yeast ranch with billions and billions of cells. In the easiest of all worlds, somebody would actually give you an active, healthy sample of the yeast—people have passed on sourdough bread yeast like this and kept the recultured yeast alive for decades. But, absent a gift of yeast, there are other ways to get it.

One way is to simply find what are known as bottle-conditioned or cask-conditioned beers—usually, but not always, ales. Again, these are unpasteurized beers to which yeast has been added to the bottle or barrel after primary fermentation to boost both alcohol and carbonation levels. These beers thus contain live yeast. If you go down to the supermarket or the craft brew emporium and buy such a beer, whether a bottle or a whole kegful, it isn't particularly hard to swab a sample of this beer onto a slide, put it under a microscope, and find yeast—probably clusters of them. Maribeth said there is a mild amount of experience required in selecting the appropriate cell. She then showed me what she meant. On a slide under a microscope with various yeast blobs floating about, she looked for uniformity. "You probably wouldn't want that big fat one you see there. It might be bacteria or a mutation. And you wouldn't want those small ones either for the same reason."

Once you find the cell you like, you pluck it out with a device called an inoculation loop, put it in starter, and off you go. The technical term for culturing up yeast like this is "clone-purifying."

Maribeth started homebrewing about thirteen years ago after meeting Steve, who had taken it up seven years earlier. (They married* in 1995 outside the Anchor Steam Brewery in San Francisco and brewed a stout from the emulsified remains of their chocolate wedding cake.) She began looking around the yeast landscape and found it rather bare. And most homebrewers were not yet that yeast-savvy and didn't appreciate the significant connection between the taste and character of their beers and the yeast they used. A few people did, and some of them were even starting to clone-purify. "But they acted like it was voodoo magic," Maribeth said. "You had to have a glove box (a small clean chamber) and autoclave (essentially a pressure-cooker) and all this special equipment. I said, 'No, we do this all the time in the lab without such things.'" Her lab skills told

---

* During a subsequent fact-checking interview, Maribeth Raines-Casselman told me she and her husband Steve had separated.

her that after ordinary sterilization techniques, like submerging vessels in boiling water, you could keep vials, test tubes, beakers, and the like sterile by simply draping them with a common household item: aluminum foil.

She began teaching her techniques and preaching her yeast gospel at homebrew club meetings and conventions, including her hometown club, the Maltose Falcons (which happens to be the oldest homebrew club in the nation). "You were trying to tell them yeast was making an impact," she said. "I would brew from the same wort and pitch four or five different ale yeasts just to demonstrate that point. I had one yeast that made a beer that tasted just like Jack Daniel's. The yeast was the only explanation. I could show them that the Bass Ale yeast makes an ale that tastes like Bass."

She dove into clone-purifying after a fellow homebrewer, who needed a lot of yeast for some 50- and 100-gallon batches of beer he planned to make, asked her to produce enough to do that from a tiny sample of a yeast strain he already had. (Though yeast is cheap to buy, it's still even cheaper to clone.) Word soon got around that MB, as her friends often call her, was seriously on to the yeast thing.

Traveling homebrewing friends started bringing back yeast samples from places as far away as England and Belgium, though with varying degrees of success. They would go into pubs, ask for some cask-conditioned ale, and, usually surreptitiously, pour a sample of it into a jar. (Imagine having to explain to airport security what you were doing with all those jars with beer dregs sloshing around in them.) Often, though, these friends visited breweries and got the samples simply by asking for them—a practice that most breweries have since wised up to and have mostly stopped. But the pub samples and gifts of yeast didn't always make it back in good shape.

"We had this friend who was going to Austria and he was going to visit all these breweries," Maribeth said. "So I made up this yeast hunter's kit, just some small vials with stoppers on them and some pipettes. You could pop them open, pop in your beer sample or your yeast sample, and stick it in your shirt pocket, no hassles."

The kit worked so well that two things happened. One: Maribeth started to accumulate a lot of yeast. "One guy alone brought back three separate strains of Pilsner Urquell [the Czech pilsner that was the world's first golden, clear beer] and a bunch of Belgian strains," she said. She would clone-purify the samples, test-brew with the clones, and, if they made good beer, store the samples in her lab's nitrogen refrigerator for future use and propagation. Soon, she had so much yeast that she found herself with a small mail-order yeast business. Two: the kit became so popular that she developed a cheap commercial version of both a capture kit and a cultivating kit, which she started selling through a third-party vendor. She only recently got out of the mail-order yeast business to turn her attention to making a commercial success of Hollywood Blonde, but by then "I felt like I'd gotten rid of a lot of the misconceptions about how this all worked," she said. And indeed, these days a number of online and corner store homebrew shops carry yeast capture kits starting at about $7.50. For about $300, including microscope, would-be yeast rustlers can outfit an entire yeast-culturing lab.

And just how common is it for people to actually invest in these things? "It's not at all unusual," Bev Blackwood, a member of the Houston-based Foam Rangers homebrew club whom I'd gotten to know, told me when I queried him. "It's not for the casual brewer. You really need to be lab-oriented since you're talking agar plates, microscopes, stir plates, and the like. But several Houston-area homebrewers culture their own yeasts and I know of at least one who maintains his own private yeast bank on slants."

Blackwood, in fact, said he had a yeast-rustling project of his own underway. He'd brewed a batch of beer that seemed to have picked up an infection in one of his bottling lines—meaning that some spoiler bacteria had intermingled with the yeast and given the beer a sour flavor. Blackwood turns out to be fond of a Belgian style of purposely made sour ale called gueuze (sometimes spelled geuze) that is originally fermented with wild yeast but that gets its predominant flavors from various microflora—i.e., bacteria—that Belgian brewers introduce into the fermentation cycle by exposing their fermenting beer to the open air. He had some bottles of gueuze at home, and so, said Blackwood, "what I did was to drink the gueuze and then save the crud at the bottom of the bottle, which is composed of the various microflora that have been working on the beer. I used this stuff to dose my new bottles. My theory was that if I was going to have to deal with an infection, it might as well be one that I'd enjoy drinking." (The beer turned out swell.)

Maribeth, meanwhile, still undertakes special yeast projects: she'd just finished clone-purifying "on a large scale" some Chimay yeast for BJ's, a large brewpub chain that has an outlet near her. Chimay, a brand of bottle-conditioned Belgian ales brewed by Trappist monks, is one of the world's most beloved beers among the Beer Geeks; both American craft and homebrewers have gone wild for the style. Getting Chimay's yeast, however, isn't as easy as it used to be. "Ten years ago, when I was doing this," Maribeth explained, "Chimay yeast in the bottle was *the* Chimay fermentation yeast. Then they found out these wacky American homebrewers were cloning the yeast and making beer with it—and the American brewers were getting it. So then they started using a special carbonation yeast for bottle conditioning. Now it's hard to get good Chimay yeast."

So where did she get hers?

Maribeth smiled. "I can't give you all my secrets," she said.

However, this much is known: both Wyeast and White Labs do in fact sell yeast that the Yeast People will tell you are *the* actual strains used by many big-name commercial breweries both here and abroad. For a variety of reasons they just can't be called that. For one, the yeast labs don't want to rile up the breweries; second, they don't want to imply that a homebrewer, having acquired a commercial beer yeast, will automatically be able to brew a beer that tastes exactly like the commercial beer in question.

It was this situation that provided my first inkling that beer yeast was the object of such passion, desire, and speculation. I'd introduced myself by e-mail to members of the Foam Rangers club, Blackwood among them, and was directed to their informative website. Browsing it, I was intrigued by an essay by Ranger Steve Moore, who had gone to the rather elaborate trouble of putting together a list of eighteen yeast strains sold by the commercial yeast purveyors and, drawing on the collective knowledge of the Yeast People, articulating whose yeast they actually were. One example was a yeast sold under the moniker "1056/American ale yeast" and nicknamed "Chico."

"Everyone knows it's the Sierra Nevada yeast," Moore wrote.

Another, called "Irish ale yeast," was clearly the Guinness yeast, he stated. And then there was another dubbed "Pilsen lager yeast" from "a classic American pilsner strain."

"Yeah," Moore wrote, "from the largest brewery company in America…and the world…somewhere around St. Louis. Throws a green apple/acetaldehyde flavor that is characteristic of Bud, if you aren't careful."

When I later talked in person to Moore and Blackwood about this, they said that assiduously mining the yeast grapevine to try to figure out exactly whose commercial yeast was finding its way into the homebrew market was considered one of the great side sports in homebrewing. For the record, the Yeast People will say they could be wrong about such correlations. But when you talk to them in private, these things are considered to be so well known as to be beyond debate. Maribeth, when I asked her what yeast she used in her Dougweiser, said matter-of-factly, "That's the Rolling Rock yeast."

Rolling Rock, of course, is one of the remaining surviving regional lagers, brewed by Latrobe Brewing Co. of Latrobe, Pennsylvania.

As to the theories of the availability of Bud yeast, the prevailing speculation is that it had long ago fallen into the hands of homebrewers, who traded it around under the moniker "Amateur Brewer's Yeast"—or "AB Yeast," for short, the AB being a wink and a nudge that really meant Anheuser-Busch. It's a matter of historical fact that Anheuser-Busch was in the baker's yeast business until 1988; one of the Yeast People told me that for a while the baker's yeast strain it sold was actually the same as its Bud beer yeast strain. True or not, AB Yeast ended up in the yeast labs where it is sold under guises such as the one that Steve Moore described.

Beyond that, there are other ways the Bud yeast could have made its way into this quasi-public domain. Bud is pasteurized and filtered before bottling to kill any existing organisms, including yeast, so there's little chance that yeast could have been cloned directly from the beer itself. But given the tons of yeast that Anheuser-Busch uses annually and the number of people with access to it over the decades, it's hardly unimaginable that a thimbleful walked out of a brewery someplace one day and into the test tube of a yeast rustler. And, as we'll see, the possibilities don't end there. The official Anheuser-Busch position is that the yeast it uses today is from the original strain acquired by founder Adolphus Busch and is indeed proprietary. The company had no comment on whether people have or haven't cloned it.

* * *

It's hard to imagine that brewing had carried on for thousands of years, till the mid-nineteenth century, before it gained hard knowledge of yeast's role, but it did. Thanks to Antoni Leeuwenhoek, the Dutchman credited with inventing the first useful compound microscope in the late 1600s, scientists had long been able to see microorganisms, even yeast. But the prevailing wisdom had been that yeast and other microorganisms were the products of spontaneous generation; in the case of yeast, scientists believed yeast to be a by-product of alcohol, not alcohol a by-product of yeast. Thus, as noted earlier, it was left to Louis Pasteur, in his groundbreaking 1876 book *Studies on Beer*, to unwind and unlock the science of zymurgy—how yeast does the work of fermentation—and convincingly prove his statement that "fermentation is the consequence of life without air."

Brewers (and modern-day yeast rustlers) also owe a huge debt to Emil Christian Hansen, a part-time novelist and full-time chemist at the Carlsberg Brewery in Copenhagen, who in 1883 first isolated a single cell of beer yeast and showed that yeast could be propagated and "banked." Inspired by the work of Pasteur, Hansen had been asked by his superiors to tackle the question of why beer batches often spoiled in the summer. What he discovered was that beer yeast colonies of the time contained good and bad actors; the bad ones were cells that were dormant in the cool weather but sprung to life in the summer heat, throwing off flavors that spoiled beer. The good ones were what would become known as lager yeast—indeed, *Saccharomyces uvarum* is still sometimes known as *Saccharomyces carlsbergensis* in honor of Hansen's work. Until that moment, knowledge of yeast hadn't meant brewers were in full control of it. Hansen essentially "tamed" the beast and made possible the reliable replication of pure yeast strains (thus giving a huge boost to the unfolding lager revolution).

By one estimate, beer yeast is one of about 600 species of yeast in the world, and they exist in every climate on earth. Most are harmless or, like *Saccharomyces*, beneficial, though some are linked to food spoilage. A few, like *Candida albicans*, the strain responsible for common yeast infections in humans, can cause minor health problems (and major ones in people with seriously depressed immune systems).

Yeast may be single-cell organisms but they possess somewhat complicated DNA; they have about 6,000 separate genes (compared with about 66,000 for humans) and sixteen chromosomes (compared with our twenty three). They also have their equivalent of the Human Genome Project, called the

Comprehensive Yeast Genome Database, which is an amplification of work completed in 1996 by a consortium of more than 100 worldwide research labs. That year, scientists finished the DNA sequence mapping of *Saccharomyces cerevisiae* and came to the startling conclusion that a goodly number of the 6,000-plus yeast genes have considerable similarities to human genes and perform many of the same functions. The import of this? It gives scientists a potent new tool to comparatively study human gene functions—the vital role certain genes play in switching on or off other genes, for example—with implications for pinpointing the causes and perhaps cures for more than forty diseases, including cancer and cystic fibrosis.

None of this is particularly surprising to the Yeast People, who constantly marvel at yeast's adaptability across many environments, including beer fermentation tanks, and the elegantly efficient way that fermenting species do their work. *S. cerevisiae*, or ale yeast, is known as a top-fermenting yeast because of the propensity of its colonies to clump together and, aided by the surface tension of wort, to float near the top of fermentation tanks, where its work is evident by a frothy, brown head created by the carbon dioxide it gives off. It typically ferments at 55 to 75 degrees F.

For reasons not fully understood, *S. uvarum*, or lager yeast, doesn't congregate and clump as well. It therefore floats in suspension far deeper in the wort column (wort, again, being the sweet, amber liquid extracted from the barley mash). When its fermentation stage is done, it goes dormant (as all yeast eventually does) and settles out far more readily at the bottom of the fermentation tank. This is one explanation, absent filtering, why lagers clear more easily than ales. Lager yeast also ferments at much lower temperatures—from 34 to 55 degrees F—explaining why it was discovered so late in beer's history and why, until reliable mechanical refrigeration came along, it was so much harder to deploy and control.

But the major difference between ale yeast and lager yeast is what they dine on. Wort, the amber extract produced by mixing cooked barley malt mash with hot water, is rich in sugars, notably monosaccharides, disaccharides, and trisaccharides. It's a slight oversimplification but essentially lager yeast metabolizes these sugars more efficiently, leaving fewer by-products than does ale yeast, giving lager a taste that, to most palates, is drier, crisper, and cleaner than ale. Conversely, it's the residual sugars and by-products that ale yeast leaves behind that account, in part, for its earthy, fruity, more complex taste profile.

Another person with an informed opinion of these matters is Joseph Owades, founder of the Center for Brewing Studies, a brewery consulting concern in Sonoma, California. The craft brew revolution is an ale yeast revolution and most Yeast People are Ale Heads. Owades most certainly isn't. Now in his eighties and still a beer consultant, he is the man credited with inventing that contemporary lager juggernaut, light beer, back in the early 1960s while working for the Rheingold Brewing Co. (Rheingold, a big Brooklyn lager maker, went bust in 1976 but has been brought back on a much smaller scale by a descendant of the founders.) Owades's brewing breakthrough—totally unheralded at the time—came from his extensive knowledge of yeast and its synergistic relationship with barley malt. Owades noticed that barley lacked an enzyme that would allow it to release *all* of its sugars for yeast to feed upon; by introducing a chemical enzyme to complete that process, he was able to engineer a beer that, when it was finished, contained zero fermentable sugars (and thus far fewer calories than regular beer). The yeast to do that job was the highly efficient lager yeast, Owades told me, not that picky ale variety. (If the yeast strains were music, Owades would tell you that lager yeast is elegant, melodic jazz while ale yeast is all funk and blues.)

Rheingold put out this beer, called Gablinger's, as a diet beer for men, and it flopped. Meanwhile, Rheingold literally gave the formula to Chicago's Peter Hand Brewing Co., which brewed its own version called Meister Brau Lite. It didn't go anywhere, either. But in the early 1970s, Miller Brewing Co. bought Meister Brau Lite from Peter Hand, renamed it Miller Lite—and the rest is history.

"What did we know?" Owades said by telephone during an interview from his home in Sonoma. "We were in Brooklyn, they were in Chicago. The beer didn't seem to be going anywhere. So we gave the recipe away." (Owades is still in the light beer game, however, recently collaborating with Jim Koch's Boston Beer on its first ever Samuel Adams Light.)

Owades doesn't dispute the basic science of yeast rustling but he thinks there are too many variables in what different strains of yeast do during fermentation to make cloning an effective way to actually replicate somebody else's beer. Besides the differences in the way ale and lager yeast ferment sugars, yeast also produces a staggering 1,300 other compounds loosely known as congeners. These include esters, which can throw off flavors that approximate things like green apples, bananas, or vanilla, and sulfur compounds, which can give off earthier, barnyard-like aromas.

"All these companies, Bud, Coors, and Miller, have their yeast from way back and they all are a little different in the congeners they produce," according to Owades. Moreover, he said, congener production can vary within a yeast strain itself, depending on a number of variables, fermentation temperature and available sugar among them. So even if someone had Bud's yeast and knew exactly how much rice, malt, and water to use, they still might miss badly on cloning Bud if they get these other variables wrong.

On the other hand, Owades said yeast security is a real issue since all breweries make more yeast than they need and have to dispose of it some way. "The little guys dump it down the sewer when nobody's looking," he said. Middle-sized brewers throw it out with the spent grains from the mash tank (the grains often become cattle feed). But such grains leave the brewery at about 160 to 170 degrees, making it likely any yeast mixed in would die. Some big brewers sell surplus yeast to food companies. "Campbell's Soup buys a lot of surplus yeast from breweries on the East Coast," Owades told me. Still, with all that yeast floating around, it's not implausible that some viable yeast ends up in foreign hands.

One afternoon over beers in Manhattan, I ran all this by Boston Beer's Jim Koch to get the brewer's perspective.

"Yeast does certainly matter," he told me. "If you look at the flavor profile of Bud, Miller, and Coors, I'd say the major difference is the yeast. That little green apple factor in Bud? That's a yeast deal. As for our beer, it's pivotal. Our yeast is proprietary. We consider it a secret. I literally don't know its exact origins. I don't know whether it was cultured from some unusual German brewer. I know you just don't find these things lying around."

As to yeast rustling: "It's technically possible. With our beer, you could get it from a keg of unpasteurized beer. Now, is that easy? No. Our kegs go through one or two filtrations and then a trap filter that is scaled down below the size of a yeast cell. So any yeast that you found would be a little weird—the cells would have to be extremely small. I don't think those would be the ones you'd want to clone to try to duplicate the character of Sam Adams. Beyond that, there's a lot of liquid in a keg. I think it's a fool's errand to go fishing around in there for a few microscopic cells of yeast. They say there's an atom of Jesus' spit in every glass of water—but go find it."

Koch gave slightly more credence to recovering viable yeast from discarded spent grains and admitted that theft could always be a possibility. But even that has caveats. "Let's just say somebody swiped some Sam Adams yeast ten years ago and it's been swapped around. It may not be the same yeast anymore. One of the tricky things for a brewer is that yeast mutates, and if it mutates very much, there is a good chance it will change the character of the beer." (Brewers, in fact, every so often run a DNA analysis of their yeast to make sure it's the same yeast.) Beyond that, Koch said, many beers—including his strong beers, Triple Bock and Utopias—use multiple strains of yeast. So it wouldn't do yeast rustlers much good if they got only one strain and not the others.

I decided to take the matter of yeast rustling into the heart of a yeast lab, and flew out to Portland to visit David Logsdon, founder and president of Wyeast, the older of America's two commercial yeast purveyors. I found him in new lodgings in a compact, austere two-story building anchoring a small office park in Odell, an abundantly scenic town of 1,800 about seventy miles east of Portland.

Logsdon is a dapper man with a professorial demeanor and a mustache to match. He was a food science major and microbiologist who was earning a living in the coffee- and food-import business in his hometown of Portland in the early 1980s when he felt the coming sea change of the craft brew revolution. A homebrewer, he'd been dabbling in yeast rustling himself and ended up with a fairly sizable collection, which he began to share with fellow amateur beer makers. His wife, Jeanette, was also a lab microbiologist doing work for a company that produced animal feed supplements.

"We saw there were lots of brewers waiting to start breweries and we felt we could do things for them," Logsdon told me. "We were already getting good feedback from the homebrewers so we just threw in the towel of our day jobs and started Wyeast." (The name, it turns out, has nothing to do with yeast. It's the name of a mythical Indian chief whom the gods, to punish for his part in a destructive love triangle, turned into the nearby natural monument known as Mount Hood.)

What started as a small family affair is now a bustling business with fifteen full- and part-time employees. Wyeast banks "a few hundred" beer yeast strains, Logsdon said. It regularly serves about 500 craft and brewpub customers, a base that may swell by another 500 depending on the time of year. Beer is a somewhat seasonal industry—Oktoberfest and Christmas are prime times for breweries to bring out occasional beers—

and Wyeast does a brisk business helping such brewers match yeast strains to their ambitions. The company also ships about 10,000 homebrew yeast packages (most of it these days liquid yeast, which has begun to push dry yeast out of the market) to homebrew stores every week, making it the largest customer of FedEx out of the Portland airport. It now has customers, both homebrewers and breweries, in twenty foreign countries.

Logsdon was so enthusiastic about yeast and beer that in 1987 he even helped found a craft brewer called Full Sail in nearby Hood River, Oregon; the brewery is still thriving, though Logsdon and partners sold their holdings to employees in 1999. Logsdon then began to redevote himself full time to yeast, inspired in part by the knowledge that the developing science of microanalytics was bringing to the field.

It was Wyeast that in the fall of 2002 contracted with an outside laboratory to run gas chromatograph/sniff-port tests on beers to try to get an analytical reading on precisely what flavors and aromas the yeast used imparted to beer. To do this, they brewed up thirteen separate batches using identical wort and fermenting each with a different yeast strain. "There were compounds that were never identified with beer before that they found for us," Logsdon said. Wyeast will continue such tests, the import being that they open the possibility that existing yeast strains can be pushed and utilized in ways that were unimaginable before.

As for yeast rustling, the more Logsdon explained the yeast business, the more it began to dawn on me that lots of new brewers and perhaps not a small number of old brewers had gotten their yeast that way. Joe Owades had told me that most of the early lager barons came from Germany bearing yeast of sometimes murky origins. "Did they get it from their father or grandfather?" he said. "Maybe. Maybe not. Everyone thinks they have their own particular strain, and maybe they do. But nobody knows for sure."

Thus, veiled as it is in a certain amount of mystery, the Yeast

World operates in a state of plausible deniability—a kind of "don't ask, don't tell" mentality—that gives cover to yeast rustlers. Moreover, it's not that easy to tell yeast apart: you can't just peer into a microscope and say, "that one is Bud's yeast, that one is Rolling Rock's."

"It's extremely complicated," Maribeth Raines-Casselman told me. "The old way to identify the two different beer strains was to throw yeast in wort and see what it made—an ale or a lager. But to tell Bud's from Rolling Rock's you need a high-tech DNA lab."

Logsdon agreed, noting there is a technique called electrophoresis—using an electric current to separate molecules such as DNA fragments from similar molecules—that allows scientists to precisely fingerprint, say, the Bud yeast and tell it from another. But that would only be half of the battle. "As with most trade secrets or even patented or trademarked material," Logsdon said, "it's up to the owner to sleuth out predatory practices by others. A difficult task—particularly when the yeast can be removed from the product before ever reaching the public. So in reality, it's become a bit of a game of who has whose yeast and what's being done with it and what it's being called."

Indeed, David Wendell,* Wyeast's technical director, told me while I was there that he'd been approached by a homebrewer not long ago who gleefully announced, "I've cloned some of your yeast!"

Logsdon had a slightly better story. "It becomes more of an issue to us when we sell yeast to a commercial brewery—one that eventually buys more and more yeast because they are successful. They become so successful, they eventually build their own lab, hire a microbiologist—and reculture *our* yeast themselves. Now, how is that for helping put someone on the map only to be eliminated once you have?"

---

* Author's note: David Wendell no longer works at Wyeast.

Before I left, I asked Logsdon about the homebrewer speculation that the commercial yeast labs were selling the Budweiser
yeast under another name. He demurred but did say Wyeast and
the Bud folks had collaborated on yeast research not that long
ago and that his lab had sent Anheuser-Busch clones of all of its
yeast samples—save one.

When I checked back with Maribeth Raines-Casselman several months after I'd first interviewed her to see if she could
impart any knowledge on this matter, she told me, "Oh, yeah.
We got it twice. Once from a guy in a Bud plant who gave us
some. And once from scrounging some discarded beechwood
chips."

10

Questing Onward

Bud Land and Vicinity:
In the Castle of the King

When the beer bubbles the masses forget their troubles.
—*The People's Daily* of China

St. Louis, Mo.—"Hello, My name is Bethany, and I'll be your tour guide today."

And a winsome tour guide Bethany is: young, fresh-faced, smiling, articulate; attractive in her uniform of knee-length jean shorts and red polo shirt, but not so alarmingly attractive that she would draw attention from her purpose. If you've been to Disney World and been greeted by the scrubbed, buttoned-down, and rigidly polite ticket takers, you've met Bethany before. This is how some of the flower of American youth helps pay its way through college. (In fact, Bethany later told me she was a public relations major at a school in neighboring Illinois.)

But this isn't the Magic Kingdom with Mickey patrolling the litter-free ramparts, though there is something Disneyesque about the place, what with its spacious mall-styled gift shop, its posh horse stables holding imposing show horses, its cutesy trolleys, and its razzmatazz video displays in various media-wired lobbies. Having executed the two-and-a-half-hour drive from Hannibal to St. Louis, I am standing at the portal of the Kingdom of Budweiser, by trademark "the King of Beers."

Bethany's job is to take about 100 other visitors and me on the 2:30 P.M. tour of the massive Bud brewery on the banks of the Mississippi River. This gathering point is reached by way of the aforementioned gift shop, where almost every conceivable item that could be inscribed with Bud or Bud Light or Michelob or other Anheuser-Busch brands or trademarks, including the famous Clydesdale horses, is on display and for sale. The $161.95 Bud Light golf bag caught my eye, as did the $14 Clydesdale flannel boxer shorts, as did the $15 Budweiser workout T-shirt and the $75 Budweiser hammock. (The boxer shorts were tempting but there was nary a horse on them—just the Clydesdale name stitched into the waistband.) More than 300,000 visitors annually wander through this shopping opportunity en route to the tour, which is free.

And the bonus at the end of the one-hour walk-through, Bethany tells us up front, is "two free Anheuser-Busch products of your choosing"—that's tour-speak for two free beers. (This is a judicious limit designed to keep Bud pilgrims out of trouble with St. Louis's Finest, who staff a handsome brick police substation just across from the brewery.) Bethany also admonishes us to "stay with me at all times. There are no hidden six-packs along the tour, so if you go wandering off from me you won't find any."

This, plus Bethany's other warning that we not reach over into the bottling line to snatch a Bud clattering by, as this would have the deleterious effect of shutting down the line while rewarding us with an unrewardingly warm beer, brings gleeful laughter from a fair number of the tourists-in-waiting. Judging from the proliferation of Bud T-shirts and ball caps adorning the attendees, this isn't a gathering of dubious Beer Geeks come to snoop and ask tricky questions of the King's minions. These are mostly Budweiser groupies eager to get an inside look at the machinery that produces their favorite beer.

Without even having peeked inside the plant, I've already recognized that this is beer on a scale I hadn't yet encountered. Looming up from the freeway approach, the redbrick facade of the brewery was seriously imposing, especially after the mom-and-pop breweries I'd seen so far on the River of Beer. Page Brewing's entire operation in Minneapolis wouldn't have filled the Bud gift shop. The whole enterprise straddles 100 acres; it is the biggest of Anheuser-Busch's twelve regional brewing plants, not to mention the location of the original Bud plant, not to mention Anheuser-Busch's world headquarters, where August Busch III, great-grandson of the founder, Adolphus Busch, plots daily to keep the King of Beers the king of beers while preparing to hand the company over to his son, August Busch IV, currently president of domestic beer operations. It thus amounts to both the historical and the beating heart of what can be persuasively argued is the most successful commercial brewing enterprise of all time.

And much of the company's success and growth to a position of utter dominance in the world's second-biggest beer market has been won in the past forty to fifty years, as it set out single-mindedly, against many worthy, well-financed, and like-sized competitors such as Schlitz, Falstaff, and Pabst, to win the Lager Wars. "People find it hard to believe now, but back when my father took on the Budweiser distributorship down here, nobody particularly wanted it," I recalled Herbert Schilling, a longtime Bud distributor in Lafayette, Louisiana, telling me during an early interview for this book. "In 1950, Budweiser wasn't a substantial player where we were—Falstaff, Schlitz, and Regal, those were the big players. I recall my father telling me, 'People can't even pronounce Budweiser, much less me sell it.' In fact, a lot of people hadn't heard of it."

Nowadays, it might be hard to find someone, save in one of the shrinking number of unwired outposts of the planet—

perhaps among the bushmen of the deep Kalahari desert in Namibia—who *hasn't* heard of Bud. Along with brands such as Coca-Cola, Microsoft, and Mercedes, it is considered one of the most valuable trademarks on earth. Weighed against year-end 2006 results—U.S. market share (51 percent), wholesale beer revenues ($18 billion), annual volume of beer produced (157 million barrels worldwide in 2006), number of employees (more than 30,000)—almost any way you wish to measure commercial success, Anheuser-Busch sits atop the U.S. and global brewing world. Its advertising spending in 2002—$413.4 million—was about $180 million *more* than the annual *revenues* of craft brewing giant Boston Beer. It sold 22.7 million barrels of its own beer abroad in 2006 (Budweiser is the bestselling lager in Ireland), and owing to equity stakes in Mexico's Grupo Modelo (Corona), Tsingtao of China, and Compañía Cervecerías Unidas of Chile and Argentina, it racked up another 31.6 million barrels of foreign sales in 2006. And again, with Corona soaring ahead as the leading U.S. import, the Grupo Modelo/Corona investment (a 50 percent nonvoting stake) has proved a valuable hedge against imports, which now claim almost 11 percent of the U.S. market.

And it wasn't lost on Bud watchers that the company in the spring of 2003 unveiled with much fanfare a new beer called Anheuser World Select—a kind of malty pilsner in a green bottle that some see as a belated direct riposte to Heineken, which also happens to be a malty pilsner in a green bottle. So, let's see: not so long after Corona surpasses Heineken as America's leading import (and Anheuser-Busch benefits from this with its 50 percent stake), Anheuser-Busch introduces a beer it hopes will further erode Heineken sales.

Not for nothing has Anheuser-Busch been compared with a certain software company that is often accused of seeking nothing less than total world domination of its particular market: Microsoft.

In fact, as I traveled down the River of Beer, I found Bud to be a kind of obsession, a kind of spectral elephant in the room. Homebrewers would deride it one moment, then spend an hour talking among themselves about what brewing alchemy was responsible for that "little green apple bite" that is part of Bud's taste profile. (Yeast, recall, was Jim Koch's answer.) Several homebrewers even told me they made Bud—from recipes floating around in homebrewing circles and on the Internet (and, of course, as explained earlier, using what is considered to be the real Bud yeast). In fact, I was able to find at least two purported Bud recipes with a quick Google search.

Well, actually, what some homebrewers told me was that they usually didn't make Bud as it is today, but Bud as it used to be, before, as they put it, the company "diluted" the beer with ever more rice and other adjuncts and greatly reduced its hoppiness (which had the effect of lowering its IBUs). Now, whether in fact pre-Prohibition Budweiser or even 1950s Bud was actually a fuller-bodied lager than modern Budweiser; whether Bud went to adjuncts to shave brewing costs (as some homebrewers claim) or because Adolphus Busch simply thought rice made better—and easier drinking—beer, or both, remains a matter of debate and conjecture. Anheuser-Busch won't comment on such matters beyond insisting that rice has always been part of the master taste plan that makes Bud so popular, adding that as "one of the world's most coveted recipes, we jealously guard it and consider this information confidential and proprietary."

Indeed, no matter where I went, questions about Bud seemed always to generate a lot of heat and passion and debate, not unlike the heat and passion and debate you get when you toss Microsoft into a dinner party conversation. I'd get fierce adulation from the committed Bud Heads who would lash Bud critics as snobs and elitists; I'd get scorn of a kind that was pretty much summed up by Ian Baumann's critique of Bud back in Minneapolis and the anti-Bud manifesto I'd read at the Casino bar in La Crosse. I'd get wary admiration from freethinkers like Jim

Massey in Dubuque, and among Bud's competitors—the craft beer people in particular—I'd pick up a mixture of fear and disdain, sometimes bordering on loathing, and all usually anchored by grudging admiration. Brewmasters, especially, would tell me that lack of consistency is the hobgoblin of all brewers and breweries. Thus, what Bud is able to do—make beer in twelve gigantic, far-flung breweries that comes out so consistent in taste, color, and aroma that only an expert palate or two, or an extremely sensitive machine, can measure the difference—is a brewing feat of the highest order.

Of course, some couldn't resist throwing in: "But considering the beer they make, why would they bother?" This would usually be followed by a lecture on how, given that all mass market lager tastes pretty much the same, Bud really is a triumph of mass marketing, not mass brewing. And its hard to argue that the billions of dollars that Bud, Miller, and Coors have thrown into advertising in the past decade alone haven't had a profound impact: they have.

But the underlying thesis of the anti-Buds is that beer consumers in general are unsophisticates who can be gulled into drinking swill and vinegar if the drumbeat of advertising is steady enough and clever enough. I'm simply not convinced of that. Recall that high-flying Schlitz lost the farm when it chemically shortened its brewing cycle to hasten production and as a result changed the taste of its product. Schlitz drinkers could *certainly* tell the difference and abandoned it en masse almost overnight; all the advertising in the world couldn't bring the label back to its perch. It seems more likely to me that Bud, like Coca-Cola, has found a seam into mass tastes—among its qualities is that it is inarguably inoffensive to most palates—and has expertly exploited that seam through a variety of methods. Shrewd and heavy marketing is certainly one. But the company has built an aggressive distribution network and spent heavily and passionately on quality control, making huge investments in things like regional breweries and refrigerated warehouses. And let's not forget its application of bare-knuckled business practices, which I deal with in a moment.

The flip side of this, of course, is Budweiser's riposte to the craft beer crowd: if your beer is so good, then why can you only manage just over 3 percent of the market? Putting aside for the moment Bud's ability to outspend every other beer company on the planet, the most candid assessment I got of that was from Fritz Maytag at Anchor Brewing. Maytag is an articulate, plain-speaking man who could never be mistaken for a fan of Anheuser-Busch or middle-of-the-road lagers (or even most British ales or supposedly hearty German lagers). But he told me bluntly: "Look, the truth is most people *don't like* hoppy, malty beer," and lagers like Bud predominate because "most people want a light, refreshing drink," and lager can certainly be that. Maytag went on: "Ninety percent of the beer drinkers want that all of the time. Ten percent of beer drinkers want that some of the time, and they want the beer we make some of the time. To get that 10 percent to drink what we make all the time is probably not realistic now, though things do change."

The other Bud undercurrent I was picking up from its rivals, big and small, was that it wasn't so much the company's size and spending power per se that rankled but its style—the words "bully" and "arrogant" were often used, together or just a few sentences apart, to describe the company's rough-and-tumble business attitude. To be fair, the very size and nature of certain big corporations make them lightning rods for all kinds of critics. Go ask the antiglobalists about Nike and they will do their best to convince you that Nike is a corporate Satan out to exploit vulnerable Third World workers in sweatshops; Nike prefers to think of itself as a shrewd and successful purveyor of high-quality athletic gear, doing the Third World a favor by putting its people to work. Similarly, when I asked some Bud distributors and other Bud folk about their corporate critics, they would parry pejoratives such as "arrogant bully" with "hard-nosed business opportunist."

Whatever the case, Anheuser-Busch's response to the microbrew-craft-beer incursion is certainly illustrative of the Bud Way. Lest you think that the Bud people have let the craft beer movement go unnoticed—after all, what's a measly 5 percent (based on 2006 dollar sales) of the market to the 900-pound gorilla?—think again. Anheuser-Busch has rolled out its own version of craft brews. Currently, under the Michelob label, it makes an American interpretation of a Hefeweizen—a German wheat beer—plus three other craft-styled beers: Michelob Amber Bock, Michelob Black and Tan, and Michelob Honey Lager. It makes and distributes out West, where craft brewer Sierra Nevada Brewing Co. has won legions of fans with a hot-selling pale ale, a beer called Pacific Ridge Pale Ale. And it has bought minority interests in two respected craft brewers, Redhook Ale Brewery in Seattle (a 30 percent stake) and Widmer Brothers in Portland, Oregon (a 36 percent stake), in exchange for agreements to give those beers access to Bud's vaunted distribution network.

These moves caused both hand-wringing and a fair amount of hooting among craft brewers (some of whom began to refer to Bud's strategy as microbrewphobia, and to Redhook as Deadhook). But all but the most ardent Bud haters conceded these were perfectly legitimate and inevitable responses from a company that didn't get to be the King of Beers by playing slow-pitch softball. (And, by the way, SABMiller and Coors also have entered the craft beer fray, though with less zeal than Anheuser-Busch.)

However, these measures were but the prelude to an all-out war that Bud declared in 1996 when two things happened. The first was that August III visited Anheuser-Busch's Hawaiian distributorships that year and came away appalled that far too many of his Bud floggers were letting Anheuser-Busch products sit too long in warehouses and store shelves (thereby risking the prospect of them becoming skunked). Worse, from his view-point, far too many were carrying rival products—including some successful local craft brews that had sprung up in Hawaii. Out of that came a Bud program called "100% Share of Mind" in which Anheuser-Busch started offering its distributors juicy financial incentives to essentially kick all but Anheuser-Busch products off their beer trucks.

Now, the Bud view was that considering that these distributor-ships had been built on Bud money and Bud incentives, why the hell should they carry other beers on their back? The counterview was that America's Three-Tier System of beer distribution—beer makers selling to distributors selling in turn to retailers—has been the law since the repeal of Prohibition. It was put in place specifically so that big beer companies *couldn't* own or lock up the distribution channels to the detriment of their competitors. And, under the law, it could be decidedly illegal for Bud to *order* its distributors not to carry other brands.

But offering them incentives to do so? Well, that's another matter. In fact, the Justice Department launched a probe of that practice in 1997 but concluded a year later that there was no reason to intervene. That didn't stop four Northern California microbreweries in 1998 from filing an antitrust lawsuit against Anheuser-Busch in federal court in San Jose, claiming precisely that the program violated antitrust laws because it was coercive to nominally independent distributors and designed to squeeze the little guys out of business.

Anheuser-Busch, as part of its vigorous defense, began subpoe-naing owners of other Northern California microbreweries in a bid to show that well-managed craft breweries were still raking in good profits despite the Anheuser-Busch program. The case, according to a spokesman for Anderson Valley Brewing Co., one of the plaintiffs, was settled out of court in 2003; neither Anheuser-Busch nor the plaintiffs would discuss terms of the settlement.

Still, it wasn't lost on people—distributors in particular—that Anheuser-Busch would play hardball with franchisees it felt were not carrying the freight. In 1997, the company unilaterally canceled a twenty-nine-year-old Florida distributorship held by the family of the late baseball legend Roger Maris on the grounds that the Marises had ignored customers, repackaged outdated beer, and falsified documents to conceal mismanagement. (Maris had been given the franchise in 1968 by then Anheuser-Busch chairman August A. Busch Jr. when Maris was playing for the St. Louis Cardinals, which the beer company then owned.) The Maris family sued, saying the accusations were false and that Anheuser-Busch wanted to transfer the franchise to friends of the company. A Florida state court jury sided with the Marises in August 2001 and awarded them $50 million in damages; the family then upped the stakes a month later by filing a $1 billion defamation suit against Anheuser-Busch. The company appealed the $50 million verdict and said there was "no merit" to the defamation matter. But the parties reached an undisclosed settlement in August 2005 as the defamation suit was being tried.

All this legal drama is interesting but it doesn't particularly articulate the moral case that the craft brewers think they have. That case was made when Fred Eckhardt, a Portland, Oregon, elder statesman of the craft brew movement who had also written a seminal book on homebrewing, took up the quill and aimed a sharp public blast at Anheuser-Busch in an essay in *All About Beer* magazine. It was titled "The Budweiser Menace." Wrote Eckhardt:

> I had always thought of "Bud" as a friendly beer produced by friendly people. That illusion was totally shattered when the management of your company began to shut out small brewers, starting in Hawaii, after the visit of August A. Busch III. His childish tirade and even more childish actions at that time were a disgrace to a great company's name. Worse, it is a reflection of what's gone wrong with corporate America. It is not necessary to attack one's small competitors and dominate the marketplace to dominate the market.

Such dominance does not have to be destructive. Microbrewers, craft brewers, and homebrewers have made American beer the best on the planet. Your company should bow down to these wonderful people and be eternally grateful for their prescience.

Anheuser-Busch would answer this in time but, meanwhile, it had opened a second front aimed mostly against craft beer, filing a complaint with the federal Bureau of Alcohol, Tobacco and Firearms accusing a number of craft brewers of misleading consumers as to the content and nature of their beer. That's because some craft beer makers—Jim Koch's thriving Boston Beer Co., for one, and Pete's Brewing Co., the Palo Alto, California, makers of the popular Pete's Wicked Ale, for another—had opted to contract-brew their beer, using the excess capacity of the growing number of empty lager breweries instead of building breweries from scratch. Bud also went after Miller, claiming Miller's Plank Road craft operation was a "phantom brewery" whose Miller affiliation was not adequately acknowledged in its consumer marketing.

But Koch, who had built his Samuel Adams label into a $200-million-a-year business by this time, appeared to be the prime target. No matter that it was well known in the industry that Koch—and Pete's, for that matter—had concocted their own recipes in their own test breweries, bought their own ingredients, and sent their own brewmasters into the contract breweries to oversee such operations. The Bud folk cried foul, noting (correctly) that neither Sam Adams nor Pete's disclosed this contract-brewing information on their bottles. (They do now.) Bud even sent August IV out to spar in the press with Koch after Koch and some of his allies fired back, accusing Anheuser-Busch of petty jealousy over craft brewing's success, trying to use regulation to stifle competition, and failing to make a few disclosures of its own. Koch, for example, argued that there was little difference between what he did and what Anheuser-Busch does, farming its beer operations out to eleven regional breweries instead of making everything in St. Louis, the brewery that most consumers identify with Bud (and not disclosing that information on the bottle). Beyond that, Koch replied, "When competitors malign contract brewing, I say it's the same thing as if Julia Child came over to my house to cook dinner. It may be my kitchen, but it's her dinner."

A couple of months later, in a question-and-answer session with the trade publication *Brandweek*, August IV and David English, Anheuser-Busch's manager for specialty brands, weighed in again to explain why their actions shouldn't be considered hypocritical:

BRANDWEEK: With the labeling complaint you filed with the Bureau of Alcohol, Tobacco and Firearms, you came down pretty hard on brewers who're only a fraction your size. Why bother?

BUSCH IV: All of our brands say "Anheuser-Busch." We're not afraid—in fact, we're very, very proud—to put that statement on our beers. Because we brew the best beers in the world. And while we applaud the effort of small brewers in raising the posture of the industry...these are created in contrived ways by our competitors to try and get their foot in the door in these categories. We're taking exception.

BRANDWEEK: Well, take your Texas-only ZiegenBock beer: you have to really squint to spot "Anheuser-Busch" on the label. Is that much different than what companies like Miller are doing with Plank Road in trying to intrigue consumers enough for them just to try the beer?

The answer, from English, the specialty-brands manager, was that minuscule or not, the Anheuser-Busch label was on the beer, thus Bud was being "very, very up front."

But the low point, according to Jim Koch and the craft beer people, came in October 1996, when NBC's *Dateline* picked up the controversy and basically came down on Bud's side. It treated the revelation of Koch's contract-brewing as a scandal worthy of prime-time television while, according to a transcript of the broadcast, allowing an Anheuser-Busch marketing executive to fret about "honesty and truth in labeling." Toward the end of the broadcast, the show's co-host told his viewers that Budweiser's recipe is "the same as it's always been; it just uses modern brewing technology now."

Eckhardt, in his seminal 1989 book, *The Essentials of Beer Style*, had cited annual German brewing profiles that showed that Budweiser's IBU profile (again, a measure of its hops contents) had been lowered by a third between 1985 and 1987. He waxed indignant: "I was amused by that information. I had always assumed that A-B was a progressive corporation, and that they regularly updated their recipes as well as their methods. Sadly, this isn't the case, I guess. They've made no attempt in over 100 years to save money by using less expensive ingredients. . . . They've always used the same grain and the same amount of the same hops. Oops, the same hops? The same amount of them? The same bitterness level? Goodness, gracious, I had the crazy idea that A-B had been steadily reducing the hop and bitterness level in Budweiser for quite some time. But I guess that's just my jaded taste buds, and the various analyses I've seen over the years were all prevarications."

Eckhardt also took aim at Bud's own truth-in-labeling by arguing that a Bud icon—a label assertion that Bud is "Beechwood Aged"—is patently false, since the use of the chips, which are boiled and sanitized to rid them of any flavor, is actually part of a clarifying process that helps free beer of cloudy yeast. "Beechwood aging is not aging at all. It's not done in barrels either, as the word 'aging' implies from its association with wine in oak casks." Indeed, he noted that in the past, some brewers have used aluminum chips to clarify beer, "but they've always had the good sense not to label such beer 'aluminum aged.' "

This brought an icy Anheuser-Busch response, this time

from its brewmaster Mitch Steele, who accused Eckhardt of spreading "false information....We never have claimed that beechwood aging takes place in beechwood barrels. Our beer is aged in stainless steel vessels....Beechwood aging is a traditional European brewing process." And "Budweiser is aged, or lagered, with beechwood chips for approximately three weeks, a longer period than used by many brewers."

Eckhardt shot back: "Whatever else it is, 'aging' it ain't, even if the beer does stay in chips for three weeks....Mr. Steele, aging in wood is one thing, clarifying beer (by whatever means including aluminum chips, beechwood or maple chips, and isinglass or egg whites) is another....We all know that your job would be in jeopardy if any of that beechwood flavor escaped into your Budweiser beer."

Call it a tempest in a beer mug if you will. But this went on for about a year. Bud actually took out negative print and radio ads in Koch's home territory of Boston; Koch countered with a satirical ad of his own and threatened to run ads questioning the quality of ingredients Anheuser-Busch used in its products. It ended, finally, when Koch's lawyers brought a complaint to the National Advertising Division of the Council of Better Business Bureaus—a mediation group—and the group ruled that in fact the Anheuser-Busch ads contained "contextually inaccurate" statements implying that Boston Beer was deliberately misleading consumers about the origins of its beer. Bud then pulled the ads, and the tempest died down.

* * *

None of this, unsurprisingly, finds its way into Bethany's well-rehearsed, fast-paced presentation as we make our way around the humongous Bud plant. She first gives us a brief history of the early beginnings of Anheuser-Busch: how Eberhard Anheuser, a German immigrant, came to America in 1843. After settling in Cincinnati, he went on to St. Louis, where he opened a soap-and candle-making company. In 1852, though he had no brewing experience, he invested with partners in a year-old beer-making enterprise called the Bavarian Brewery; in 1860 he bought out his partners and changed the name of the brewery to E. Anheuser & Co. Around that time, twenty-one-year-old Adolphus Busch, who had moved to St. Louis in 1857 via New Orleans and had bought a small interest in a brewing supply company, met Eberhard.

Adolphus, Bethany told us, was "the second youngest of—can you believe it—twenty-two children!" and Eberhard "liked him so much that he introduced him to his daughter.... A year later, they were married. That's how we get our Anheuser-Busch connection."

It was a good move; within a few months, Adolphus was working for his father-in-law, and a few years later he bought a half interest in the brewery. During this time, beer was a commodity made and sold locally, but according to Bethany, Adolphus "had a vision of transcending this and creating a national brand that catered to all tastes across the nation." So, in 1876, "with his good friend Carl Conrad, he invented what lager? There you go: Budweiser!" She added that Adolphus "coined the name Budweiser because it had a slightly Germanic sound and would appeal to German immigrants and Americans alike."

In 1879, the brewery changed its name to Anheuser-Busch Brewing Association and a year later, after Eberhard died, Adolphus became president. "He stayed in this position for thirty-three years and is considered the founder of our company," Bethany tells us, adding, "today, August Busch III is the chairman of the board and he's also credited with transforming our company into an international corporation with business and marketing activities throughout the world."

She then prefaces Bud's enviable perch atop the U.S. beer world—citing the fact that one of two beers purchased in America is an Anheuser-Busch product—by saying, "Now we've come a long way from 1852. This year we celebrate the 150th anniversary of our company."

Now, as a scribe of some seasoning, I knew Bethany didn't write this script that she had so ably recited. But I did wonder, as she tugged us toward a meeting with the Clydesdales, about a few things. If Bud was dating its history from the time that Eberhard bought into the Bavarian brewery, why isn't Eberhard considered the founder of the company, since Adolphus didn't come aboard until years later? And as for how Adolphus "coined" the term Budweiser because of its Germanic sound, I knew that simply wasn't true. Anheuser-Busch, in fact, has been locked in a running 100-year legal dispute with a brewer in the Czech Republic, Budejovicky Budvar, over the right to use the Budweiser name in Europe and other countries around the world where the Budvar beer has long been called and marketed as Budweiser. The name comes from Budweis—essentially the German appellation for the Czech town Ceské Budejovice, where the Budvar brewery was founded and where beers similar to Budvar have been brewed since the Middle Ages. The style came to be called Budweiser the same way beers brewed near Pilsen came to be called pilsners.

Beyond that, a 1991 book by two *St. Louis Post-Dispatch* reporters called *Under the Influence: The Unauthorized Story of the Anheuser-Busch Dynasty* suggested it was most likely that Carl Conrad, not Adolphus Busch, invented or acquired the Bud recipe, noting that the beer was contract-brewed by Anheuser-Busch until Adolphus bought the recipe from Conrad, a wine merchant, after he went bankrupt in 1882. (That book, the reporting of which was bitterly contested by the Busch family, portrayed the Busches as an autocracy of controlling and ambitious German bluebloods, whose stewardship over Anheuser-Busch for over a century was a tale of "opportunism, unbridled power, family conflicts, sex scandals and violent death." The Busches, unsurprisingly, were said to hate it.)

At any rate, I wasn't going to quiz poor Bethany over these trifles. Not when we had horses to meet.

The Clydesdales, in their stunningly beautiful, arched stable, perfumed with a curiously mixed aroma of hay, horse manure, and beer, are impressive. And among the fun details Bethany tells us is that the first Bud Clydesdales, a Scottish draft horse breed, were hitched up to the Bud wagon just after the repeal of Prohibition to deliver beers of thanks to politicians who had supported repeal, among them President Franklin Roosevelt. We also learn that Clydesdales at birth are already three feet high at the shoulders and weigh 125 pounds (poor Mom!) and that grown ones in the Bud stables grow to six feet high at the shoulders and weigh a ton. And boy, do they eat: twenty-five quarts of mixed feed, fifty to sixty pounds of hay, and thirty gallons of water *a day*.

Bethany also reveals that it is not easy for a Clydesdale to make the grade at Bud, since every horse with ambitions to pull the ornate, fire-engine-red Budweiser beer wagon must be at least four years old and *must* have the following four attributes: four white feet, a white blaze on the forehead, a black mane and tail, and a dark brown bay color. Furthermore, females need not apply: only males can pull the hitch.

We then move on to the brewhouse and beer making, where, among other things, we get a gander at those (infamous) beech-wood chips, which we are told come primarily from trees grown in Kentucky and Tennessee. (This, after one baffled tourist brings laughter by asking how on earth Bud collected so much "beachwood.")

Though Bethany refers to the brewery's "Beechwood Aging Cellars," she offers an explanation that might have satisfied Fred Eckhardt. She tells us the chips, once boiled and sanitized, are layered at the bottom of the lagering tanks and that "the chips don't have any flavor or taste to them. They don't give the beer anything" but merely aid in fermentation. Once the beer is drawn off, the chips are mulched and spread by Bud maintenance people around various nearby parks, "which is the main reason," Bethany tells us, "you'll find the happiest squirrels in the region in this area."

Since I've already taken the reader on one brewery tour, I won't belabor the entire process again. But I will say that the Bud plant is a place of grand scale and superlatives, a veritable Goliath of a brewery: eighteen gleaming mash tanks, each holding 18,900 gallons and bathed in the light of what's known as the Hop Vine Chandelier, a massive, ornate fixture that was part of the Belgian exhibit at the 1904 St. Louis World's Fair; six imposing copper brew kettles, each capable of brewing 19,215 gallons of beer at a time; a clamorous twenty-five-*mile*-long bottling line, filling 980 bottles a minute; a clattering canning line, running at 2,000 cans a minute (all under the roof of a building covering twenty-seven acres); a warehouse holding 500,000 cases of beer, which seems like a massive amount but which Bethany tells us "only keeps our Midwestern distributors happy for eighteen hours."

Before our tour is over, Bethany drops a few other tidbits that I find interesting. Among the "all natural ingredients" used to brew Bud and its cousins is "drinking water." Bethany also tells me that spent mash (used-up malt or other grains) recovered from the bottom of mash tuns makes good cattle feed, and that the brewery produces enough spent mash each year—1.5 million tons, to be precise—to feed an estimated 4 percent of the nation's cattle.

I ask where all that grain comes from in the first place, and Bethany says, "Oh, we grow a lot of it ourselves." She then goes on to explain that Anheuser-Busch's economies of scale are such, and its need to obtain highly consistent ingredients so important, that it had some time ago formed the beer world's only agricultural division devoted solely to growing, processing, acquiring, and researching hops and beer-useful grains. I puzzle over this and realize that somewhere in Anheuser-Busch is a high-ranking executive who runs this operation and who, for lack of a better term, might be the world's chief beer farmer.

I decide that a visit to the world's chief beer farmer would be a highly worthy stop along the River of Beer, assuming it could be arranged.

Then we're off to the hospitality suite, where we queue up to claim the two free Anheuser-Busch beverages of our choice. (As a matter of full disclosure, I stop at one: a Michelob Amber Bock.) I ask the guy in line just ahead of me what he thought of the tour. He smiles and says, "Hey, that Bethany—she's all right!"

He introduces himself as Kent. He's a lanky guy in sneakers, jeans, a Garth Brooks T-shirt, and a Bud Light cap. He says he works in lawn maintenance and comes by now and then when things are slow.

He points to his cap and says, "That's my beer. I've been here before, and actually, seeing how it's kind of noisy and all, I don't really pay that much attention to the tour anymore. Honest? I just come for the beer."

* * *

St. Louis may be defined by the giant presence of Anheuser-Busch, but it's hardly the only beer play in town. The city has a reasonably robust craft brew scene—as of this writing it supported about a half dozen brew pubs—and I would eventually find my way to the Schlafly Tap Room, where the brewery's version of a hefeweizen, an unfiltered American wheat ale, was awfully tasty. (If the Schlafly name is familiar, it should be. The founder and owner is Tom Schlafly, nephew of conservative icon Phyllis Schlafly.)

But I had a pressing mission, so I headed for the city's historic Soulard neighborhood.

The Bud plant sits on the edge of Soulard, a charmingly funky neighborhood on St. Louis's near south side. Named for a Frenchman who surveyed the area for the king of Spain, its original boundaries date to the 1790s, making it one of the oldest neighborhoods in the city. As I walked around, it reminded me vaguely of certain precincts of New Orleans, with its period row houses, Victorian town houses, and the occasional mansion undergoing (or in need of) renovation, as well as its gorgeous, turn-of-the-century churches, lively public spaces, corner grocery stores, and ethnic restaurants.

There are reasons the Bud plant is here. One is geology: numerous natural caves run beneath Soulard, and caves, nature's own temperature-controlled refrigerators, made ideal places for early German lager makers to store their temperature-temperamental beer. Another is real estate. In the mid-1800s, Soulard, with its affordable housing and central location, became the portal neighborhood for large numbers of Germans—like Eberhard Anheuser and Adolphus Busch—who had been steaming to the U.S. Recall that beer was local then, and breweries were basically neighborhood affairs; Eberhard invested in the original Bavarian Brewery because it was where the drinkers were. (One footnote, which I credit solely to *Under the Influence*, the unauthorized Busch family biography, was that the pre-Budweiser that Eberhard made was so dreadful that bar patrons would occasionally spit it back over the counter to show their disgust. But Eberhard's energetic and talented son-in-law, Adolphus Busch, was such a gifted marketing man that he sold barrels and barrels of it anyway.) Many of the Germans moved on, to be followed by several ethnic waves of working-class newcomers: Lebanese, Slovaks, Croatians, and Bohemians, to name a few. People I met told me that these days Soulard was slowly being gentrified, but it still had a diverse, energetic, blue-collar feel about it.

I was walking around not to sightsee, pleasant as it was, but in hopes of finding a bar—well, actually, what I wanted to find was *the* bar closest to the Anheuser-Busch brewery. I was curious whether the castle of the King of Beers cast a particular spell on a place so near it; at the very least, I thought I might run into some Bud workers taking a break from making beer to drink some. (Not that I expected to find them drinking Miller

Lite or anything.) So I'd walked north and, well, about a block later, there was a bar: the Cat's Meow.

It sat in a pleasant, brick-front two-story building and it had not one but *two* Bud signs: one hanging from brackets above the door and, in the window, a bright and clever neon sign depicting a green-glowing cat lounging atop the red-glowing word "Budweiser," his tail curling around the "r." I must also report that a lighted Pabst Blue Ribbon sign, not nearly as clever, hung in the top of the window. I didn't enter immediately; it was 4:00 P.M. and the place looked empty, so I decided to take my exploratory walkabout and return later.

Later I found Deanna Springer, a cheerful twenty-something, pouring $1 glasses of Bud draft for a gathering crowd of happy-hour regulars. The Meow inside pretty much matched the outside: a long bar to the right and clusters of tables to the left and rear. This was all stuffed into a relatively compact and austere space, with the usual bar clutter about: beer signs, bric-a-brac, photographs of regular customers, promos for the frozen pizza you could order, and a bumper sticker on the wall that read, "I Love Cats." Deanna told me she was a former customer who'd crossed over to the serving side about a month before to help pay her expenses at a college she attended in Illinois. She'd admired the Meow as a customer because it was friendly, cheap, and a nice mix of neighborhood folk, young and old, working people, and drinking-age college students who swarmed into Soulard on the weekends to visit its plentiful bars and thriving live-music scene.

When I told her about my mission and why I'd specifically picked the Meow—its prospect in the shadow of the King of Beers—she laughed and said she couldn't think of any particular advantage to being the King's neighbor. "It's not like we get the beer from the back door of the plant or anything. It goes to a distributor before it gets back to us." Then, she did think of one advantage: "We do get a lot of brewery guys in here." She looked around and said, "Hmm, I don't see anybody. Maybe later tonight."

I, of course, had to ask what they drank. She laughed again and rolled her eyes: "Bud, what else!"

But the Meow, I noticed, wasn't a Bud monopoly: among the beer taps I saw Miller Lite poking its head up among the Bud brands. Deanna told me she also served Heineken in bottles, along with Labatt Blue, a Canadian lager. "Actually," she said, "we sell a lot of Miller Lite."

I wondered whether this might be a revelation that would alarm August III and August IV.

I was sorry that the Bud guys were a no-show but I struck up a conversation with a woman on the bar stool next to me who, from the snippets of conversation I'd overheard, seemed to know every person who entered the door. The place was now about three-quarters full and getting noisy.

Her name was Brenda Kreitz. Dressed in black and, I'd guess, in her middle forties, she knew a lot about Soulard and a great deal about the bar, which had been in business at least since 1945. Soulard, at the moment, she said, was a good real estate play, having come from being "one of the poorest places in the city" to being one of those up-and-coming neighborhoods that the press likes to write about and say it discovered.

Brenda and her husband, Paul Kreitz, were, in fact, in real estate themselves, having just moved into a renovated four-bedroom house a block from the Meow that they'd snagged for $100,000. Lots of Soulard places were selling now for $300,000, and they were looking for other houses to buy, rehab, and sell. Paul did the finding; Brenda did the back office work. One dynamic in the Soulard market, Brenda told me, were persistent rumors that Bud was always on the prowl for certain kinds of properties and might be looking one day "to buy out this entire street."

When I broached the subject of the Perfect Beer Joint, Brenda practically jumped up and down for the Meow. After I heard her story, I could see her point.

"We just got married—one month and two days ago," she

said. "We met on the Internet. Can you believe it? It's the third time for both of us. Third time's the charm, right? Yeah, we were down here at the Meow one Friday night and I needed a change so I said, 'Hey, why don't we go to Vegas?' And Paul said, 'Yeah, why don't we? Let's get married. Let's go right now!'"

Brenda stopped to catch her breath, then said: "Well, there were all these people in the bar around us and they said, 'Yeah, that's a great idea. Go do it now!' So off we went to the airport. We got to the airport and there were no flights out."

Paul chimed in: "That's the way we make decisions—we just say, 'Right now, let's go! Let's do it!'"

They stayed with friends out by the airport that night and, not losing courage, flew out to Vegas the next day. It was a Saturday but "the courthouse is open 24/7, so there was no problem there," Brenda explained.

They spent three blissful days in Vegas—well, after a kind of rough start. They ended up in the most expensive hotel in town the first night and "boy, did they skin us," as Brenda said.

"Oh, man. We were living downtown, ba-by!" Paul said, doing a remarkable imitation of the goofy movie spy, Austin Powers.

They checked into a slightly more modest bed-and-breakfast the next night, breakfast including $1 bottles of St. Pauli Girl, a nice German lager. "Basically, the way I look at it," Paul said, looking at Brenda in admiration, "3,000 miles and $3,000 later, we were married."

"And, yeah, the plot was hatched right here at the Meow," Brenda said.

After a while I left the Kreitzes to their numerous Meow buddies to meet an old Missouri journalism school classmate and her husband for dinner. I circled back later, still hoping to catch some Bud workers, but the Meow was mobbed instead with college kids doing their best to make the Busches richer than they already were. I called it a night; it had been a long day on the River of Beer.

For complicated reasons, I decided to hang around St. Louis the next day and around 5:00 P.M. found myself back at the bar. Surely, beer workers drank beer to start the weekend? But after essentially canvassing every person in the joint, there still wasn't a Bud worker to be found. Curious.

I did, though, make the happy acquaintance of the Grassers, Chris and Mary, who were seated at the bar, Mary sipping $1.50 screwdrivers, Chris drinking $1 Bud Lights. They were a retired couple living in a downtown high-rise apartment and they were exactly the kind of mirthful people you hoped you'd meet in beer joints. They'd been married for thirty-four years and had no children, so a lot of their social life revolved around what they called "making the rounds" in Soulard, which was their favorite neighborhood.

In fact, they told me that they made the rounds pretty much every night and had been coming to the Meow at least two nights a week for the past ten or fifteen years. They had clearly scouted out the lay of the drinking land hereabouts and seemed to have intricate knowledge of which bars had what drinks on special at any given time. They ticked off six or seven that were part of their regular circuit, but the Meow was a constant because, as Chris told me, "it's the cheapest place in town."

"Look at this screwdriver," Mary said, tapping her tall glass. "It's a big strong drink."

I asked Mary if she would nominate any of her regular places as the Perfect Beer Joint. She laughed and said, "Well, I don't know, Ken. I like them *all!*"

Mary went on to tell me that to some extent she was fond of bars because in her younger days she had spent many years working as a cocktail waitress in the Jefferson Hotel downtown at a time when the Jefferson, which is no longer a hotel but a retirement home, was one of the top hotels in St. Louis. "And, let me tell you, I made tons of money—just tons of money. I was getting $100 a night just in tips. Of course, I looked a little better then than I do now."

I looked at Mary and she looked all right to me: slender, well dressed, one of those women of indeterminate age. Chris, too, looked like the fit golfer he would later tell me he was. ("I play golf," he'd confided, "so I can go to the nineteenth hole.")

Mary said, "Now, guess how old I am?"

I cringed, then blurted out fifty-five.

She threw her head back and laughed. "Seventy. I'm seventy years old, can you believe it? And I don't color my hair, either!"

Mary told Chris she was ready for another screwdriver and he ordered one.

She turned to me and said, "You know, when we first started talking I didn't mind talking to you. But now I'm more interested 'cause we're talking about me!"

The Grassers seemed keen to help me on my quest and they began going over the bar prospects nearby when it suddenly dawned on them that they hadn't told me about Pam.

"Oh," Mary said. "You've gotta go see Pam. She works over at Gladstone's and everybody in Gladstone's loves Pam."

"A lot of the guys are in Gladstone's *because* of Pam," Chris said.

For about the next ten minutes, the Grassers filled me in on Pam's charms—her friendliness, her way with customers, her sense of humor, how she never forgets anybody's name. As they talked, I realized that they were articulating a phenomenon on the River of Beer that I'd witnessed many times over and was loosely beginning to think of as the Beer Goddess phenomenon. It was hardly rocket science, but there was an undeniable connection between the healthy and robust sale of beer (and liquor) and the presence of friendly and winsome young women.

As to almost make my point for me, a younger, somewhat disheveled acquaintance of the Grassers sidled up next to them at the bar to say hello. I didn't catch his name, but when I posed my Perfect Beer Joint question to him, he blurted out, "Girls, girls, girls!"

About that time, Mary looked at her watch and consulted

with Chris. They both realized that Pam was working at Gladstone's this very day at this very minute, but that she was likely getting off soon and, really, it would be a tragedy if I missed her, and thus we should run over there right away. So we quickly settled up at the Meow and went barging out into the street, where we collected our separate cars and drove to Gladstone's just a few blocks away.

The Grassers found parking and were getting out of their car. I circled the block, unsuccessfully trying to find a space of my own, and as I came around in front of Gladstone's again, I saw a woman leaning into a double-parked pickup truck talking to a man with a ponytail. And there were the Grassers on the sidewalk, animatedly pointing at me and then pointing at her and, well, I knew in an instant that was Pam.

Pam!

Now, let it be recorded that Pam from a distance, even to my dispassionate journalistic eye, did seem to be an exceedingly handsome and imposing woman. So I pulled up somewhat sheepishly and rolled down the passenger-side window and Pam, smiling, came over to say hello and to apologize for the fact that, worthy beer scribe that she was sure I was, she was late to pick up her five-year-old son and couldn't hang around to talk.

But, leaning into my window and looking at me with great seriousness, she said that if beer was what I was interested in, well, "You come back and I'll show you what I've got. I'll give you a sample."

Boy, did she smile.

And then she walked away into the sunset.

And I knew I'd just had another nearly Perfect Beer Joint moment. And I wasn't even in a beer joint.

11

Prowling Among the Beer Suits

In my opinion, most of the great men of the past
were only there for the beer.
—A. J. P. Taylor

Boston, Mass.—Dennis Buettner, a late-blooming student of beer culture and a would-be beer entrepreneur, has come with a laptop loaded with a video pilot of an idea whose time he's sure has arrived: Beer TV. An earnest, energetic, sandy-haired man with the demeanor of a natural salesman, he is walking around with the laptop on and open, showing the pilot to almost anyone he can buttonhole. The short segment features a comely interviewer following around a handsome and cheerful beer truck driver discussing the joys of beer delivery.

Buettner's beer claim to fame thus far has been to set up a Web site for another quixotic idea of his, the United States Beer Drinking Team, which he admits he started as a lark when thinking about how much he loved beer during a slow night shift at work. Now he envisions the USBDT as beer's premier consumer representative, not to mention a hugely marketable list of beer drinkers and enthusiasts that every beer company and bar owner in America would love to tap. And he is convinced, in an era when cable TV can support multiple programs about house makeovers, that Beer TV is a no-brainer.

"Wouldn't America's 90 million beer drinkers all be potential viewers?" asks Buettner, who works on his beer aspirations while working three evenings a week for NASA. He just needs backers.

So Buettner (pronounced Bitner) has come here, to an upscale Marriott Hotel in downtown Boston this weekend, because he correctly divines that beer money and beer power and beer influence will be present in abundance—potentially a good thing for a beer entrepreneur seeking exposure and funding. The people who want to get distribution and exposure for Three Stooges Beer are here, too, along with a gaggle of others peddling things like the Icefloe system, a series of chemically activated beer chillers that ostensibly let you serve cold draft beer out of a keg in, say, the Sahara Desert without the need for ice. About 3,000 people will attend this event, many of them in positions to bankroll Dennis Buettner, take a flyer on Three Stooges lager, or buy up large numbers of Icefloe instant beer chillers.

I've diverted from our narrative to attend the 2002 annual meeting of the National Beer Wholesalers Association, a besuited gathering of that influential beer tribe that serves as the broker between the beer makers and the beer retailers. As noted earlier, the nation's 2,700-odd beer wholesalers are the middle rung of the Three-Tier System, created in the wake of the Twenty-first Amendment as a way to curb the pre-Prohibition excesses of the big beer companies by taking the distribution of beer (and wine and spirits as well) out of the hands of the makers and putting it into the hands of broker-distributors heavily regulated by the states.

The distributors gather at these meetings to talk about political, economic, and technical issues vital to them. But they also attract the company of the high-powered members of the other two tiers, most notably the upper echelons of the management of Anheuser-Busch, SABMiller, and Coors, off whom the vast

majority of beer distributors make their money. August Busch
IV and Pete Coors will be in attendance as will be John D. Bowlin, president and CEO of SABMiller. The wholesalers will also
get their first close look at the corporate types from London-
based South African Breweries, who engineered the $3.6 bil-
lion acquisition of Miller in May of 2002 (and perhaps intend
to remake it; indeed, Bowlin, since the reporting of this event,
has left the company). Beer moguls from the clutch of remaining
regional lager makers like Yuengling, Latrobe, and Pabst will
be around; even Jim Koch of Boston Beer will come to hobnob,
though the craft beer presence will be small. This is Big Beer's
stage, and under the NBWA's direction, it is determined to put
on a sophisticated, useful, and glittering extravaganza for its
hardworking, moneyed, and well-connected throngs.

Thus, it has gathered various beer economists, prognostica-
tors, and consultants on arcane matters such as beer warehouse
design to parse beer's economic, technical, and political climate
at daily seminars. Tucker Carlson, the political commentator,
has been brought in to supply the big-name speaker. Workshops
by day will give way to lavish schmooze-fests by night, when the
beer makers take over various Marriott ballrooms and trans-
form them into stage sets meant to resemble speakeasies or
elegant supper clubs. For if the craft beer segment of the industry lays claim to being the creative heart of American beer, the
NBWA's annual powwow makes clear where the true center of
beer money and beer power lies.

According to 2007 NBWA statistics, beer wholesaling alone
is a $15 billion annual business in America, employing more
than 91,000 workers with a payroll of $5.6 billion. But that in
itself is but a fraction of the beer economic pie. The beer industry as a whole, beyond generating almost $86 billion in retail
sales and $36 billion in annual taxes, directly employs about
946,000 workers in breweries, warehouses, and retail operations; it pays them annual wages of $25 billion. Most brewery
jobs in the United States are union jobs, making beer industry

workers among the best-paid factory laborers in the nation. Big Beer marshals these statistics as one way of saying to its perceived enemies that when you mess with beer, you're messing with a vital and deeply American industry. And beer, unlike, say, textiles, computer chips, and running shoes, doesn't outsource its beer making to India so that it can ship ever-cheaper lager back to America; it has kept most of its jobs, and spends most of its money, at home.

But one of the true indicators of Big Beer's clout is the socioeconomic position of its 2,700 licensed distributors. As the NBWA likes to point out, beer wholesalers reside in almost every congressional district in the United States, and they run locally owned small businesses that on average generate $11.8 million in annual sales and employ about three dozen people. Or put another way: they are a well-informed, well-organized collective of grassroots millionaires of the type who sit on local chamber of commerce and hospital boards, and who tend to know and have the ear of their elected politicians. They can be mobilized with breathtaking speed through the NBWA's e-mail and fax channels. And they are armed with up-to-date data and political intelligence by the NBWA, which was formed in 1938 and carries water for the industry on issues like its perennial "drink responsibly" campaigns, and extraneous matters that crop up from time to time—recall the NBWA's co-sponsorship of the beer-and-health seminar.

But the NBWA's real job is to plump for beer-friendly legislation in Washington—the recent, if only temporary, repeal of the estate or death tax was in part an NBWA victory on an issue vital to the family-dominated beer wholesaling business—while guarding the industry's flank against onerous legislation and what it considers to be its two major perils. The first is new taxes; the industry feels it has never fully recovered from the sales wallop it suffered in 1991 because of a doubling of the beer excise tax from $9 to $18 a barrel (about 32 cents a six-pack)—an act that set off the greatest beer sales slump in thirty years. With beer now back on something of a roll—2003 was the eighth consecutive year that shipments from brewers and importers to wholesalers had increased—new taxes are considered anathema. Indeed, the NBWA has lobbied vigorously for *repeal* every year of the 1991 excise tax increase, though so far without success (mostly because it hasn't been able to get the sixty votes it needs in the Senate).

Big Beer views as its second major peril the multiheaded specter of what it calls the neo-prohibitionists, a loose collection of think tanks and advocacy groups that are perennially battling beer over issues such as underage drinking, beer advertising (especially its impact on underage drinkers), and drunk driving laws. These groups—Mothers Against Drunk Driving, the National Center on Addiction and Substance Abuse at Columbia University (CASA), the Center for Science in the Public Interest (CSPI), among them—don't consider *themselves* neo-prohibitionists; they prefer the term public watchdogs. MADD, as reported earlier, has been the force behind a federal mandate, shored up by a congressional threat to withhold federal highway funds to states, to lower the threshold for driving-under-the-influence from a blood alcohol level of .10 to a level of .08—a change that the National Highway Transportation Safety Board says could statistically save 500 lives a year. The highway funds pressure has worked: as of this writing, only five states—Colorado, Delaware, Minnesota, New Jersey, and West Virginia—were holding on to the higher limit.

But that hasn't stopped the NBWA from relentlessly pressing its contrarian's message—that the federal "blackmail" of the states to gain .08 standards by withholding highway funds is a violation of the Twenty-first Amendment, which cedes such matters to the states; furthermore, that even MADD knows that it's the high-blood-alcohol-level drivers who cause the preponderance of *fatal* traffic accidents, not the .08 crowd, and thus the move diverts attention and enforcement resources away from the core problem.

Even in what seems like a losing cause, the NBWA's pugnacious president, David Rehr, has publicly challenged MADD,
accusing the group of playing footsy with the liquor industry—
gaining hard liquor's acquiescence on the .08 issue in exchange
for hard liquor's support of a MADD push on Congress to
increase the excise tax on beer. And Rehr, who has a Ph.D. in
economics from George Mason University, wasn't content simply to verbally joust. The NBWA in both 2002 and 2003 would
get more than 220 members of the House of Representatives
to cosponsor a bill to *roll back* the federal excise tax—a bill
that it knew it had little chance of passing in the Senate, where
beer's clout is somewhat more tenuous. But the idea was to put
groups like MADD on notice that they faced a daunting challenge of passing a new excise tax hike in the House. Indeed, not
for nothing these days is the NBWA—especially when it acts in
tandem with its sister group, the Beer Institute, whose members
are mainly the big and middle-sized beer makers—consistently
ranked among the top ten most powerful lobbying groups in
Washington. (When I ran this by Dean Wilkerson, MADD's
executive director, he told me Rehr's reasoning on the .08 issue
was flawed, since statistics have shown that *any* stiffening of
drunk driving laws has a trickle-down effect on the number
of heavy drinkers on the road because such laws make people
"think about taking that next drink." Furthermore, he denied
any tit-for-tat deal with the spirits people on taxes, saying what
Rehr described as collusion was merely the liquor industry's
pragmatic interest "in talking to us about an issue [the .08 legis-
lation] of mutual concern." A spokesman for the Distilled Spirits Council of the United States, the lobby group for the nation's
liquor makers, echoed that view. And as for taxes, he added
that while liquor excise taxes are already substantially higher
than excise taxes on beer, "we nonetheless don't favor increased
excise taxes on spirits, wine *or* beer.")

Still, the NBWA's clout and aggressive persona are a matter
of great pride to Rehr, forty-four years old as of this writing,

who came to its helm in 2000 after having served as the organization's vice president of government affairs starting in 1992. He'd been recruited from the National Federation of Independent Businesses, a small-business, anti-big-government lobby group, after the 1991 beer excise tax hike—a development that had caught the NBWA flat-footed and with a sense that it had little clout in Congress. Rehr had cut his lobbying teeth fighting (and defeating) people like Dan Rostenkowski and the Democratic leadership over efforts by the Clinton administration to impose new health-care regulations on small businesses, which Rehr's constituents considered punitively expensive. He arrived in the corridors of Big Beer with the belief that the excise tax looked an awful lot like the kind of sin-tax battering that the tobacco industry was taking and, if left unanswered, might soon result in a landslide of unfavorable taxes and regulations punishing beer.

"But we *aren't* tobacco," says Rehr, who despite his often combative rhetoric exudes a kind of boyish charm. "Our product is something we're proud of, something that millions of Americans enjoy responsibly, and something that studies show that if consumed in moderation actually is good for you. Tobacco was always out there hiding in the weeds. We are determined not to hide at all—and not to let our product become 'denormalized' and equated with tobacco or drugs." (Or, Rehr would add later, liquor.)

Indeed, long before Rehr joined the NBWA, Big Beer, as well as the liquor and wine industries, had publicly acknowledged that their products could be abused, and all had launched expensive public service campaigns aimed at curbing excessive drinking, underage drinking, and drunk driving. Beer's most strident critics see these campaigns as self-serving and ineffectual. (And, indeed, as this book was going to press, tort lawyers filed a multibillion-dollar lawsuit against the big beer makers that, like a similar suit filed against tobacco companies, accuses them of willfully trying to lure underage drinkers to beer with cynical advertising campaigns.) Still, the beer industry estimates it spends tens of millions of dollars a year on responsibility programs that do things like remind its customers of the value of a designated driver or admonish high school kids to "make the right choices and enjoy after-prom celebrations without alcohol." That's in sharp contrast to the tobacco industry's decades of obfuscation and denial in the face of mounting evidence that smoking posed enormous and predictable health risks. Beyond that, Big Tobacco's political power center always lay in three Southern states—the Carolinas and Virginia. Contrast that to the NBWA's claims that its member-distributors inhabit almost every congressional district in America.

One of the first things Rehr helped the NBWA do was beef up its PAC, or political action committee, nicknaming it Six-PAC. He also hastened to beat a path for beer back to the mainstream, coming up with a slogan: "Family Businesses Distributing America's Beverage." (That certainly makes a less tempting target than the anti-alcohol lobby's view of beer as Beer Tycoons Profiting from Underaged and Problem Drinkers.) Soon the slogan was both an advertising campaign and a rallying cry emblazoned on every fax or letter the NBWA sent to Capitol Hill. In 2002, the NBWA and the Beer Institute, led by Jeff Becker, embarked on an even more ambitious campaign called "Beer Serves America." The two groups financed copious and serious historical and economic research that tied beer to America's earliest roots and produced the figures, based on complicated mathematical models, that put beer's GDP at a whopping $144 billion. The point that Rehr hammers over and over again is that "we *are* mainstream, we contribute deeply to America's economic fortunes, we have nothing to hide, and we will not cede the moral high ground to the neo-prohibitionists."

Rehr has taken to enforcing the latter point by being one of the most aggressive lobbyists around—indeed, he clearly takes delight in mixing it up with those he sees in the neo-prohibitionist camp. Besides his public jousting with MADD, Rehr in the fall of 2003 preemptively blasted a National Academy of Sciences report on underage drinking, accusing the federal agency of ignoring its congressional mandate to review the effectiveness of existing prevention programs while pushing "junk science" solutions that he contended were simply more neo-prohibitionist posturing.

"What was meant to be a thorough review of programs to fight underage drinking has turned into an opportunity for panelists to dictate to Congress their views on taxation and advertising, and vilify a legal industry," he fumed in a statement he fired off to the Senate Subcommittee on Substance Abuse and Mental Health before the report even hit the press. He and the NBWA were particularly incensed that the committee refused to include beer industry nominees on the panel, instead loading it up, in their view, with well-known anti-alcohol advocates who then pressed for the perennial chestnuts of the anti-alcohol lobby: higher beer taxes, an anti-alcohol advertising campaign financed by beer but controlled by the government, and a curb on beer advertising.

The outcry drew an equally outraged response from George Hacker, director of the Alcohol Policies Project of the Center for Science in the Public Interest—a guy who'd been in the ring with Rehr many times before. "We're not surprised by this thuggish behavior from the NBWA," Hacker said in a public statement on the matter. "What else would one expect from a group that may stand to lose some of its franchise on underage drinkers, who consume, according to some studies, as much as 20 percent of all the alcohol downed in the United States, most of that in the form of beer?"

When Rehr wrote Hacker a scathing letter calling the word "thuggish" an insult to NBWA members, "who are small business owners, community activists, parents, religious leaders and philanthropists," Hacker's group did excise the term from its website.

But what really drives Rehr nuts—and gives some credence to the NBWA's neo-prohibitionist paranoia—is that 20 percent statistic. The figure was actually first reported in February 2002 as 25 percent based upon a study released by another NBWA nemesis, the National Center on Addiction and Substance Abuse at Columbia University. The report made front-page headlines around the world and got huge play on CNN—and then was subject to a fierce skin-back the next day by the Associated Press and the *New York Times* and scads of other media outlets that had published it. The *Times* reported that the number, based upon the interpretation of the federal agency that had collected the original data, was closer to 11.4 percent. CASA, for its part, admitted its number was flawed but called the flaw an honest error of statistical interpretation that still didn't diminish what it considered to be an "epidemic" of teen drinking. (Indeed, when I interviewed Hacker about this flap more than a year later, he still maintained that the figure "conceivably could be as high as 20 percent," even if CASA had been forced to restate it as 11.4 percent. He also told me that while Rehr, in person, could be "a gracious and friendly guy," he was clearly "the Attila the Hun of the alcoholic beverage industry.")

Rehr, for his part, believes such statistical errors are intentional and part of CASA's campaign to greatly exaggerate the teen drinking problem to scare the public into injudicious action. Statistically, according to Rehr, underage drinkers are defined as twelve- to twenty-year-olds; by number they constitute 13 percent of the population. For even a 20 percent figure to be correct, you'd have to assume that *every* twelve- to twenty-year-old drinks about 100 drinks a month. "How many twelve- to twenty-year-olds do you know who consume almost 100 alcoholic beverages a month?" Rehr complains. Beyond that, Rehr points to the NBWA's interpolation of federal statistics that show that teenage drinking in the year 2000 was actually *down* 53 percent from 1982 levels; alcohol-related deaths involving teen drivers were *down* 62 percent over the same period.

For all those public dustups, I wondered whether Rehr, who was to give the keynote at this NBWA conference, might be more conciliatory when he took the stage in a cavernous Marriott ballroom to address a crowd that also included a fair number of beer distributors' spouses. The answer was: absolutely not. With huge TV screens flashing oversized pictures of him and a sonorous announcer introducing him as "one of the most powerful lobbyists in Washington," Rehr bounded up to the podium and bit, pitbull-like, right in to his adversaries:

"Thanks to you and your support...we have prevented anti-business voices in Congress from doing harm to our industry and we have enlisted significant support for our positions on key issues. Thanks to the work of beer wholesalers, OSHA is currently drafting *voluntary* ergonomics guidelines to replace the Bill Clinton–era mandatory approach—regulations that would have cost you 30 cents a case. And thankfully, despite cries from some members of Congress and Big Labor, efforts to legislate new guidelines, so far, have not amounted to much....

"I am happy to report that as of today, 224 members of the House of Representatives have heard our message and agreed to co-sponsor Pennsylvania Congressman Phil English's bill rolling back the excise tax on beer to the pre-1991 level. This has been possible because of your unwavering support and involvement— and despite efforts by Mothers Against Drunk Driving and others to double the beer excise tax.

"Although our effort to make death tax repeal permanent wasn't a complete success, we continue to make progress. Last spring, the House passed the permanency bill for the second time. However, while the measure fell short in the Senate, the rules require sixty votes for passage. One thing we might want to do about that is elect four new senators who will help drive a stake through the heart of the death tax once and for all. In fact, if your senator is on this list, you need to help elect someone who will vote to permanently repeal the death tax—and you can do it on November 5."

Later in his speech, Rehr named names:

"A majority of the members in the House and a near majority in the Senate are great friends of NBWA. There are, however, four races which need special attention this year:

"In Missouri, incumbent Senator Jean Carnahan doesn't meet with beer wholesalers. She switched her vote to be against us on the death tax and she enthusiastically supported OSHA's ergonomics regulations. Jim Talent, her opponent, was one of our best friends when he was in the U.S. House.

"South Dakota incumbent Senator Tim Johnson also switched his vote on the death tax as well and believes beer is equated with illegal drugs. His opponent, Congressman John Thune, has been with us 100 percent of the time.

"In Iowa, incumbent Senator Tom Harkin criticized NBWA by name on the floor of the Senate and was the staunchest supporter of the Clinton 30-cents-a-case ergonomics regulations. We need to replace him with Representative Greg Ganske—a physician who believes drinking beer can be part of a healthy lifestyle and who has been a solid supporter of NBWA.

"And finally, my favorite race in Minnesota. Incumbent Senator Paul Wellstone is bad on ergonomics, opposed making death tax repeal permanent, and actually introduced a bill to raise the beer tax 350 percent. We must replace him with former St. Paul mayor Norm Coleman, who, when he ran for city council over a decade and a half ago, received his first political contribution from a beer wholesaler. If every beer wholesaler in these four states, and every beer wholesaler who is not from these states, helps in any way you can, we will determine who controls the U.S. Senate." (Rehr's wish list would come up two victories short; Carnahan was, in fact, defeated; Wellstone died tragically in a plane crash and Coleman beat replacement candidate Walter Mondale. But Johnson beat Thune in a squeaker and Harkin handily maintained his seat.)

Rehr later rallied the troops with an exhortation to defend NBWA principles:

"The beer industry is being challenged as never before.... Those who distrust the concept of personal responsibility are seeking to impose their solutions on all of society, ignoring the rights of the majority and putting your businesses in jeopardy. And they are becoming more shrill, more extreme, and more bold. We all know that many of them are not reasonable people. Reasonable people would talk to us. Reasonable people would work with us. We share the goals of reducing drunk driving, preventing illegal underage drinking, and promoting responsible consumption.

"If we cannot work together toward these common goals, we have no choice but to ratchet up our own efforts.... You operate within a system purged of the evils of pre-Prohibition days. You contribute daily to the well-being of your communities. You offer good jobs to tens of thousands of men and women.

"But we must do more.... Let's not let the neo-prohibitionists take the moral high ground. Let's not give them an opportunity to impose their will on us or the millions who responsibly consume our products. Let's not let them control the language of the debate.

"Consider this: CSPI [the Center for Science in the Public Interest] compares beer to drugs such as cocaine and smack. Listen to these quotes from their issue papers and press releases: 'Alcohol is a drug too.' 'Kids' favorite and most devastating drug is the alcohol in beer.' And, 'Beer, the king of drugs.'

"Unfortunately, earlier this year the White House Office of National Drug Control Policy seemed to have taken the bait. In one of the ads in their campaign to link drugs to terrorism, they recklessly criminalized the consumption of beer. Those of you who were at the joint legislative conference in April will remember the quick action taken by our industry to kill the ad.

"*We* must define the context of this debate. We must be strong, aggressive advocates of beer as part of America's lifestyle. We will give no ground to the neo-prohibitionists."

Rehr ended a couple minutes later to thunderous applause.

Afterward, I ran some of this speech by Frank Coleman, the chief spokesman for DISCUS, the group representing the distilled spirits industry. He laughed and said, "That's David talking to his troops—throwing red meat to the hungry." But then Coleman got serious and added, "David's a great ally to have in any fight—and he's a formidable adversary to stand against."

* * *

Dennis Buettner, meanwhile, wasn't drawing much applause at all.

I caught up with him several times during the four-day NBWA meeting, and it was clear he was getting mostly amused or indifferent reception to his ideas for a beer cable TV network or for his efforts to turn the United States Beer Drinking Team into beer's singular consumer group. (In fact, the Bud people told me later that they'd looked at a number of schemes over the years to launch a beer TV show and never saw a commercial model they thought could work.) Nonetheless, Buettner carried on with the ebullient optimism of the natural salesman he is, and with his wife, Jen, an attractive blonde, helping out with the sales pitches, he maintained a ubiquitous profile, darting here and there to deliver his spiel.

I stayed in e-mail contact with Buettner, and months and months later he told me he'd raised enough money to at least get a Beer TV pilot going. And sure enough, in the spring of 2003, when I visited Sam Calagione at Dogfish Head Craft Brewery during a visit by beer writer Michael Jackson, I ran into a guy named Gary Monterosso wearing a Beer TV T-shirt and lugging a camera. He interviewed Jackson on videotape, and the program did eventually run—on a local Maryland cable TV network. But that was the debut and finale of Beer TV.

As I was putting this book to bed, Buettner admitted that Beer TV hadn't gotten off the ground (though he wasn't willing to permanently give up on the idea and had been experimenting with Beer TV webcasts). He also admitted he was somewhat disappointed that he hadn't gotten a better reception from his NBWA efforts.

"For an industry rife with big-breasted ladies in bikinis and overt sexuality associated with the marketing of their product, we've found Big Beer to be quite conservative," he told me. "They have a great thing going and rely fully on their Chicago and New York advertising and marketing agencies. It seems like they don't move without consulting a focus group."

Still, having beer's fat cats ignore him hadn't discouraged him any. He said the United States Beer Drinking Team had grown to 45,000 members (online sign-up is free), and the website was now peddling USBDT-labeled jackets and merchandise. Buettner was actively seeking a place, and sponsors, for a National Beer Hall of Fame. And the USBDT had just been the subject of a favorable feature in *Stars and Stripes,* the official U.S. armed services newspaper.

Buettner had also concluded that if Beer TV was an idea slightly ahead of its time, Beer Radio was a cheaper-to-launch alternative. And so he'd just contracted with a Maryland radio station to buy time for Beer Radio's inaugural broadcast sometime soon. Indeed, Beer Radio officially debuted in January 2004 and, as of this writing, was still on the air.

Author's note: David Rehr left the NBWA in December 2005 to become president of the National Association of Broadcasters, a trade group representing local and network television and radio broadcasters. Meanwhile, in February 2007, Anheuser-Busch inched into television when it launched Bud-TV, a video-streaming website.

12

The Quest Takes a Southern Lurch

Beer, Elvis, and the Heartbreak Hotel by Way of Woody's

I am for those who believe in loose delights.
—Walt Whitman

I left St. Louis on another cloudless day, intent on hugging the river as much as possible by sticking to Highway 61. But as I pushed on south, I found the going slow, the river towns all too often overrun with mall-sprawl and choking traffic. I gave up after about 100 miles and swerved back onto I-55 headed for Memphis where, in a rare bit of planning, I was going to check into Elvis Presley's Heartbreak Hotel, hoping for an Elvis-and-beer connection.

Nearing the Arkansas border, I saw my first signs for Memphis. (And realized that I'd just blown by Kentucky altogether, seeing as how it has, relative to the other Mississippi River states, just a toehold on the river. Oh, well. It's a state far better known for bourbon and racehorses than beer.) But as I crossed over into Arkansas, I realized I actually knew of a somewhat peculiar place where I might get a fresh beer perspective.

It was That Bookstore in Blytheville, which if you've ever been to Arkansas you know is pronounced *Blyville*, the *th* having been declared at some point too troublesome to include (in the perfectly acceptable way that southerners often truncate speech so that certain words aren't so much work). The owner of the bookstore and the keg that sat in it was Mary Gay Shipley, and she'd actually invited me to do a book signing there once, whereupon I gratefully discovered the keg, which was filled with ice-cold Budweiser. It wasn't so much that I wanted a beer myself (though I certainly took one), but I was hopeful that my audience would want several because it had been my experience, based on events at a literary festival in New Orleans I'd once attended, that beer-drinking book buyers are the most superior book audience an author can have. I did an 11:00 A.M. Sunday morning reading at the Shim-Sham Club on Toulouse Street in the French Quarter and was gratified upon arrival to see that of the fifty or so people in the audience, at least forty of them were drinking beer, Bloody Marys, or Texas Bloody Marys (which involves adulterating perfectly fine beer with tomato juice). So though I felt like a dullard at the podium, swallowing my words, the audience had drunk me clever and considered me not just witty but exceedingly wise. And they had extremely loose wallets. It made me wonder why the book trade hasn't set itself up in more drinking establishments, or why Barnes & Noble doesn't go into the bar business.

Blytheville, as I recalled, stood somewhat distant from the interstate, so I cranked up my cell phone and called the store. Alas, Mary Gay was out, but worse, the keg had been removed for cleaning and refurbishing, thus ruining any hopes I had to hang out with a more literary class of beer drinkers. But Amy, a chatty young woman who was running the store in Mary Gay's absence, did tell me that I shouldn't leave Missouri without visiting Woody's, an extremely famous beer joint in the town of Caruthersville not that far away. The main reason it was famous, Amy said, was that Woody's had a firm policy of not serving beer in bottles because bottles, well, are just too hard on the human head.

I hung up and pulled off the road to consult my map and was happy to learn that Caruthersville, in the so-called Bootheel of Missouri, where a narrow slab of the state digs hard into Arkansas and Tennessee, was in fact just eleven miles east. It sat on the Mississippi equidistant between Cooter, Missouri, and Owl Hoot, Tennessee (not to be confused with Hoot Owl, Arkansas). I made a U-turn and found it without incident.

Caruthersville seemed pleasant enough, a cotton-farming community of modest houses and tree-lined streets with a sign that told me the population was about 7,000. I learned that it had been called Little Prairie until 1811, when one of the most violent earthquakes to ever rock North America (8.0 on the Richter Scale) knocked Little Prairie flat and heaved fire and brimstone out of the ground, causing residents to think the end of the world had come (and for some, it had). Perhaps seeking better luck, Little Prairie rebounded as Caruthersville.

I found Woody's thanks to four kindly men who'd been drinking beer out of brown paper bags in front of a grocery store and volunteered to drive by the place as I followed behind and point it out to me. It was a good thing, too, because Woody's didn't have a discernible sign out front, though, from Amy's description, I might have picked it out anyway. The bar sat in a compact, rectangular, somewhat faded building. It was about one o'clock in the afternoon and I only counted two cars in the parking lot. I wasn't even sure the place was open but I tried the front door and it gave. As I pushed through and my eyes adjusted to the dim light within, I realized that Amy had undersold the place.

The decor—well, the aura might be a better term—made the scruffy Flora-Bama back on the Gulf Coast look like a beer joint out of *Vogue*. The first thing I noticed was a well-worn, cigarette-burned pool table standing in the middle of the floor, surrounded by a vast pile of empty beer cans and peanut shells. I'd say 400 to 500 beer cans might be accurate. Some were crushed. Most were not. Also, every inch of every wall in the place that could be written on had been written on, signed apparently by exuberant patrons. The ceiling was hung with dusty, grimy baseball caps that had once shielded heads from oil changes and chicken coops, and undergarments that looked like they belonged to people who might have been better off keeping them on. I settled in at the bar and was greeted by a lanky man who told me his name was James Ford. I asked him if there was in fact a Woody attached to Woody's. He said there was but that Woody was away at soccer practice.

I perused the beer choices such as I could see them and could tell right away Woody's was a Bud haven. I asked Ford what he served most of. He thought it over and said, "Well, a lot of my customers who don't have much money drink Natural Light. It's cheap, so the fellows who go through a half a case or more a night drink that."

I have to admit I'd never drunk Anheuser-Busch's low-calorie corn lager (it was the company's first light beer offering), so I ordered one. As Ford fetched it, he told me he'd worked at Woody's for a few years and bartended at other places around town. I pointed to the mountain of discarded beer cans and asked whether maybe the cleaning people were on strike.

"Oh, that," he said. "Nah, people just throw their empties under the pool table. When there's too many of them, we sweep them up and take them out."

It did make me wonder how many had to pile up before the too-many limit got triggered, and whether Woody's was worried about its customers tripping over this beer-can minefield or setting off a beer-can slide. That's when I spied a big sign above the bar that seemed to address my concerns: It said, "No Crying!"

I sipped my Natural Light and decided it was a bit sweet and thin for my beer tastes (it seemed like water to a Hophead), though there was nothing particularly terrible about it. And anyway, as I confessed at the very beginning of this book, I don't drink *anybody's* light beer except, as I was doing now, for research purposes. I did wonder, though, what discerning beer people made of Natural Light, so I later went online to BeerAdvocate.com, a popular beer enthusiast site that allows consumers to post beer ratings by brand. Natural Light had gotten ninety-three reviews; of 2,833 beers rated to that point, it ranked 2,829th. Still, it had some fans, like BeerGator2003, who wrote: "It has drinkability...if you chug it. If your wallet's in a pinch and you have to have a beer, this works well. Let me tell you, there's definitely worse out there."

On the other hand, a writer named Hotstuff stated: "This beer, when poured into my glass, had a large white frothy head with small bubbles that fully diminished.... Very little carbonation was observed. There was very little flavor and the mouthfeel was light and watery." As I understand the Beer Geek take on mouthfeel, it's basically a sensory evaluation of the weight or viscosity of a beer, i.e., whether it is light or heavy to the palate. I honestly couldn't argue with Hotstuff's evaluation.

The only other person in Woody's was a retired bartender and short-order cook named Cecil, who said he liked the bar a little better in the daytime since it could get kind of rowdy after dark. He was also drinking Natural Light and going on about a man who'd committed suicide a day or two before by jumping off the Caruthersville Mississippi River bridge. He noted several times that the unfortunate man was from Arkansas, which made me wonder if this happened to other Arkansas people who came to Caruthersville, or if Caruthersville people had a dim view of Arkansas people, or vice versa. I did manage to steer the topic on to the Perfect Beer Joint for a moment. Cecil said he was fond of Woody's, but it wasn't the Perfect Beer Joint because "the Perfect Beer Joint would serve free beer."

Ford, the bartender, offered me another Natural Light, but I declined. I inquired as to the location of the men's room. Ford pointed it out and I went in, for the sole purpose, actually, of discovering what sort of graffiti covered the walls *there*. One thing I'll say: Woody's graffiti writers were prolific and had pretty much left no room for new artistic, poetic, or political statements. And it probably wouldn't shock the reader that the preoccupation of Woody's scribblers was whether certain men were as manly as they claimed, and whether certain women did or did not perform certain carnal acts that, as described, are probably banned in any number of states. I didn't learn anything new, but it did make for five minutes of highly entertaining reading. I was kind of sorry that I couldn't stay around and hang out at Woody's after sunset and watch the beer cans and peanut shells fly. But Elvis was calling.

However, being a dedicated scribe and not wishing to disappoint my readers, I did find a Web account of a night at Woody's. It was a small part of a lengthy journal written by two intrepid modern-day explorers who were navigating the Mississippi by canoe around the time that I visited. One of them, David Groppe, gave me permission to share it:

We ended up at Woody's peanut bar. Woody's had come recommended from the folks at the outdoor shop. They said it was just like a barn party. When you finished a beer, you threw the can on the floor. When you finished some peanuts, you threw your shells on the floor. And when you got drunk enough, you took off your underwear and tied it to the rafters.

We arrived early. The only souls in there were Woody, who wasn't much interested in talking with us, and some guy who kept on referring to us as river rats. We liked the other guy, but we didn't have too much to talk about. All I remember is that he made a crack about people from Michigan being pricks and said that people at the bar down the road "got jiggy." We passed time drinking Stag beers (we were so excited), eating our fair share of peanuts, reading the graffiti, and admiring the overhanging underwear.

Later, the place became quite lively. We joined a table of some college kids.... They skipped the river talk and went directly to sex. One of our conversation mates began talking about their high school English teacher and insisted that she was a lesbian and that all high school English teachers were lesbians. Another took exception to this. His mother was a high school English teacher and she was not a lesbian (so he thought). The tension was broken by the most drunken fellow who revealed to us that he was a "trisexual," meaning that he "would try anything." That conversation didn't last too long. The river rat guy bought us a drink, and we returned the favor. And then we headed back to the canoe.

(Stag, I might add, is another of the relic beers in the Pabst stable.)

* * *

By 3:30 P.M. I'd pulled off the interstate into Memphis and onto Elvis Presley Boulevard in search of Elvis Presley's Heartbreak Hotel. I was assured, when I phoned ahead, that it would be easy to find because it was the only big white hotel in a big parking lot more or less across the street from Graceland, which itself could not be missed because it was the big house with the big white columns, the big lawn, and the big fence around it. Oh, and just look for the swarming tour buses. And besides, the hotel had a sign in big black art deco lettering across its art-deco-inspired facade that said "Heartbreak Hotel," emblazoned with a big red heart stuck on to the word "Hotel." These were fine instructions, and it was as easy to spot as a white alligator in a black-water swamp.

I realize that Memphis is not known particularly as a beer town. Memphis, in fact, is known mainly for three things: barbecue, blues, and Elvis. The first two things go well with beer, but I wondered if Elvis did.

This is why I'd chosen Elvis Presley's Heartbreak Hotel,

which I'd been assured had a bar that served beer. Was there an Elvis-and-beer connection to be made? I was curious, for I had been bedeviled by a question that I had assumed would be simple to answer but for which I had not yet found a convincing result: Did the King himself drink beer, and if so, did he have a favorite?

You'd be surprised at what a controversial notion this actually is among certain of the Elvis People. To explore this, just browse the hundreds of Elvis sites on the Web. Many, many Elvis People insist Elvis didn't drink at all (he was of good evangelical Baptist stock from Tupelo, Mississippi, after all), and when I fired off a beer query by e-mail to a person on an Elvis experts Web site, the answer I got was that this was such an impertinent question it was not deserving of an answer. Opinions on other Web sites insisted he drank sparingly but he didn't really *like* beer or liquor very much. The actress Stella Stevens, in an interview with Fox Movie Channel a few years ago, seemed to be contradicting this Dry Elvis image when she said Elvis swilled rum-and-Cokes on the set of *Girls! Girls! Girls!*, the 1962 movie she made with him. When the Beatles visited Elvis at his Bel Air, California, home in 1965, it was well known that Elvis drank 7-Up while the lads drank Scotch and bourbon.

In fact, after an exhaustive search of Elvis books (okay, true I didn't read them all, seeing as how there are 482 titles, including a hairdo tell-all by Elvis's barber, on Amazon alone), the Web, and substantial newspaper and magazine databases, I could only find *three* skimpy beer references to Elvis. One was a decade-old *Los Angeles Times* profile of a dying Hollywood watering hole called the Formosa Café in which the writer asserted that "this, after all, is the bar where Elvis drank beer" without saying any more about it. A second appeared in a 1992 *Sports Illustrated* account in which Elvis invited Harry Caray, the legendary Chicago Cubs baseball play-by-play announcer of whom Elvis was a fan, to Graceland and, according to the piece, "That night, Harry and Elvis shot the breeze, drank beer, and ate ribs." (Alas, *which* beer wasn't mentioned.) The last was a piece on a pub crawl by a writer for RealBeer.com and included a reference to a Washington, D.C., bar (and, my luck, no longer in business) that had on tap what the bar called "Elvis's Favorite Beer—Schlitz." But, as you can see, none of the above actually *proves* anything. Elvis also, as everybody pretty much knows, served his two-year army hitch in Germany, which is certainly a good place to learn to drink beer if you don't already know how to. But I could find nary a reference to Elvis drinking either subsidized PX beer or fine German lager.

Anyway, it seemed to me, given Elvis's standing in American pop culture, this was a legitimate if not burning question for a wandering beer scribe to pose and if possible resolve. I wondered perhaps if the answer lay among artifacts at Graceland, which I confess I'd never visited but which for the entirely reasonable fee of $16.25 I certainly could and would. I didn't know that much about Graceland, but what I did know made me think highly of it. One was that Elvis bought it for his momma, who promptly put in chicken coops and a vegetable patch even after Elvis had spent a fortune to remodel it, adding, among other accoutrements, a kidney-shaped swimming pool. Another was that before he bought it, Elvis sought the advice of Liberace, which only increased the esteem of both Elvis and Liberace in my eyes.

Now, no, I'm not one of those Elvis People who build shrines to him in their basements. But the King was inarguably an American original with true talent who changed the American music landscape forever. As a child of the 1960s, I can vouch for the fact that Elvis was about the only rock/pop star you could talk to your parents about. My mother adored him, though mostly in his string-heavy ballad-crooning mode. My father, a bluegrass and country music fan who would grow apoplectic when we insisted that the Beatles could actually *sing*, abided conversations about Elvis and would even listen to "All Shook Up" because he knew Elvis to have once been a fine rockabilly and gospel singer. I always liked Elvis's personal style; there was always something homespun and vulnerable beneath that smooth swagger. I thought of him as basically a good hillbilly guy trying his best not to let fame and fortune kill him off. The only thing I held against Elvis is that he let fame and fortune win.

Of course, if it turned out he never drank beer, that would be something else.

I checked into the Heartbreak Hotel, owned, not surprisingly, by Elvis Presley Enterprises and whose motto is "Sleep like the King for a night." (Elvis has made much more money dead than he ever did alive.) Even the check-in was fun when I found out that I could, if I wanted to, stay in one of the four Themed Suites, the two most alluring choices being the Graceland Suite and the Burning Love Suite. The Graceland Suite, according to the literature, "gives guests the sense of living in their own diminutive Graceland Mansion with room designs inspired by Elvis's own living room, dining room, TV room, billiard room and 'jungle' den." The Burning Love Suite, on the other hand, "features a rich, romantic décor (lots of red). It is inspired by Elvis's 1972 hit record 'Burning Love' and his status as a romantic idol." No matter which I chose, I would still get the deluxe continental breakfast, the free HBO, and the free in-house channel running continuous Elvis videos. The other fun thing, the smiling clerk behind the towering purple art deco desk told me, was that I could have one or two room keys but I would have to put down a deposit of $25 per key because, well, those keys, inscribed with "Elvis Presley's Heartbreak Hotel," sure were popular with Elvis Presley's Heartbreak Hotel guests and had a tendency to go home with them—and, in fact, I should feel free to keep my key, which was a popular choice, and they would keep my $25 or $50, uh-huh?

This was a lot to throw at a guy who had just come from Woody's in Caruthersville, Missouri, and who was also being bedazzled by the extremely red welcoming carpet he was standing on, not to mention the purple velour lounge chairs and the white and luxuriously curvy divans sitting invitingly in the lobby nearby. But I thought about the eyebrows that might get raised in the accounting office back in New York if I went for the $469.90 (plus tax!) Burning Love Suite, even though the picture of the super-King-sized bed did indicate it was large enough to accommodate me *and* my rental car, plus I'd never stayed in a room that had a shower with mirrors all the way around it. But I opted for the ordinary $109.95 room and told the smiling clerk that I would take just one key and would return it at the end of my stay, at which point they would return my $25 deposit, right?

"Of course, yes sir. Of course! Of course!" he said. (Let it be noted that the level of politeness at Elvis Presley's Heartbreak Hotel was extremely high.)

I was not disappointed in my room choice, either; though my shower lacked mirrors of any kind, I had very fine pastel walls, very fine movie house carpet, very fine faux art deco furnishings, a lovely checked bedspread, and a very nice picture of Young Elvis above my bed. I turned on the TV and caught a couple of those free videos I had been promised, then went out for a jog past Graceland (though a swim in the hotel's heart-shaped pool was a tempting alternative on a day that was beastly hot).

Around happy hour, I wandered into the bar of the Heartbreak Hotel and found it small and distressingly deserted, which, it being Saturday night, I had not anticipated. So I settled onto a stool, hoping a beer drinker or two would arrive. I ordered a Heineken and struck up a conversation with the smiling and twenty-something waitperson whose name, in an unfathomable lapse, I forgot to scribble down. I think it was Mary.

I asked her the question that I was sure she got all the time: "So, when's the last time Elvis was here?"

She didn't miss a beat. "He comes in on Thursday nights," she said. "He sits right where you're sitting."

I told her of my beer quest and my conundrum of not being able to confirm, with absolute certainty, whether Elvis was a beer man. I wondered what she knew.

She smiled and said, "Have you seen him lately? I won't serve him anything but Bud Light."

About that time some women customers came in looking for frozen drinks. Mary cranked up an amazingly noisy blender and got busy. A bit later a guy appeared, looked around for a place to sit, and settled at the bar a few seats down. He was of medium height, thin, with close-cropped hair and an earring in each ear. I heard him order a beer with a decidedly British accent. A British beer drinker in an Elvis bar portended a good turn of events.

I went over and introduced myself and told him what I was up to. He said his name was Danny Wills and that we could talk about beer but he thought his beer knowledge was "just common." However, he'd love to talk about Elvis.

Wills explained that he was a milkman (yes, Britain still has milk trucks that deliver chilled pint bottles to your doorstep every morning) from the London enclave of Fulham. He described himself as a lifelong Elvis fan and said he was into the third day of his second pilgrimage to Graceland and vicinity. His overriding passion in life was collecting Elvis memorabilia—clothes, music, posters, figurines, beer steins, all Elvis-emblazoned—and he seemed, by description, to be doing a pretty good job of it. "Back home, I've got a spare bedroom upstairs that's pretty much full," Wills said. "Now I'm filling up the garage. After that, I don't know what I'll do with it all."

Since I'd lived in London and while there not detected any Elvis mania (though true, I wasn't looking for any), I asked him if other Brits shared his passion. "Are you kidding?" he said. "Elvis is huge in Britain—huge! In the course of the work I do—I have a lot of elderly customers, pensioners and the like—the number of people who want mementos is huge, just huge! These are people who know they're never going to come over here. Of course, I can't bring back something for everyone—I'd be broke."

Wills said this trip he had two missions, besides visiting Graceland again. One was to fill in the last two songs missing from his otherwise complete Elvis discography of the 542 songs Elvis recorded. The other he'd already accomplished.

"What was it?" I wanted to know.

"You'll never guess what I bought today."

"What?"

"An Elvis suit. You know, the white one. That gives me the full kit. When I was here three years ago, I got the belt."

I recalled Elvis wearing a lot of flamboyant, rhinestone-studded jumpsuits toward the end of his career. I asked Wills why he had picked that one and where he got such a thing.

"I shop at a place on Elvis Presley Boulevard," he said. As for the white suits, they were fairly easy to get and only cost a couple of hundred bucks, which he considered a bargain for such a treasure. He did plan to wear it once he got home, though it would mainly be for display to impress his Elvis-loving mates. "I can tell you exactly where I was when Elvis died," Wills said. "It was August 16, 1977, and I was a long-distance lorry driver on the M1 [the principal freeway looping London] when it came on the BBC."

I couldn't actually remember where I was when the King died, so I steered the conversation to beer.

Wills said, "Oh, when I'm here I only drink Budweiser. I can't take any other American beer, I just can't. I can't, I can't, I can't. I find that Bud is the closest thing to English beer that I can find."

I could only imagine Auggies III and IV being here and saying to the Beer Geeks: "See, we told you so!"

However, in all due deference to Wills's entirely valid Everyman opinion, I couldn't help but ask whether he was aware of the craft beer revolution in America or what his countryman, the beer writer Michael Jackson, had said about it? Wills said he wasn't aware of either but, then again, though he might drink the King of Beers and be fond of it, he was here mostly in search of the King of Rock 'n' Roll. With that, Wills drained his Bud, said good night, and went off for a dinner engagement.

I hung out a while longer at the bar but it seemed to have filled up with a lot of daiquiri-drinking Elvis People, many of whom I overheard say were headed after cocktails to Elvis Presley's Memphis Restaurant downtown. I decided I was giving the King enough of my money already and went off to look for some ribs and beer.

*   *   *

Graceland, which I toured on Sunday morning after a ninety-minute wait in line—a very reasonable wait, I might add, given that 700,000 pilgrims pass its gates each year—was a huge disappointment in my quest to determine whether Elvis drank beer. (It is a mystery that, as of this writing, I still haven't resolved.) There wasn't a beer clue anyplace, which in a way dulled what would have otherwise been my huge appreciation of the Jungle Room, Elvis's white-fur-covered bed, and the video testimonials of various luminous people that Elvis's movies weren't all that bad and Elvis wasn't actually such a bad actor.

But Memphis turned out to be a better than expected beer town, though I didn't find the Perfect Beer Joint there. Still, I found very good beer at several places, notably: the Flying Saucer, with 200 beers on the menu (it's part of a small, Texas-based chain); Gordon Biersch (also part of a large brewpub chain); and Bosco's, another brewpub chain with a nice beer selection. These were all recommended after I wandered on Sunday afternoon into a bar on Beale Street called the Tap Room. One sign outside read: "The Coldest, Cheapest Beer on Beale Street" while another declared the bar held "The World's Largest Antique Beer Can Collection." The beer can collection, I would soon learn, had pretty much been hauled away in a recent makeover of the bar. No matter.

Inside, I found Phillip Morris, a long-haul truck driver just off a twelve-hour road trip from Indianapolis, sipping a Sam Adams and chatting with Lynne Hardin, the Tap Room's welcoming and nicely tattooed waitress. The exchange reminded me of another important social function of the beer joint: to pass on esoteric information of no interest to the larger world but of keen importance to those who seek such knowledge.

"I'm admiring your body art," Morris said to Hardin, "and I was wondering where you got your tattoos? I don't want a real one. But, see, I have this neighbor and I hate the guy—just hate him. So as a lark, I thought I'd get a tattoo with his wife's name on my chest and go out and mow the lawn without my shirt on. You know—just to get a laugh."

Hardin laughed. She said she used a place called the Ram's Shadow in Memphis, but they only did the real thing, not fakes.

"Well, I don't want any body perforations," Morris said.

"Where do you live?" Hardin wanted to know.

"Indianapolis."

Hardin was familiar with Indianapolis. She said, "Well there's a place there that does henna tattoos. They can last a week. I'd wait till I got back there to do it."

Morris, an African-American, wondered whether dark red henna would have enough contrast. "I'm not exactly light-skinned, you know."

Hardin said she thought it would work.

I asked Morris his opinion of the Perfect Beer Joint.

"For a long-haul trucker like me after a hard day?" he said. "Four or five big-screen TVs, a pool table. And it should always have a hospitable female behind the bar open to good conversation."

When Hardin came to inquire about whether Morris needed another beer, he said, "One more, then cut me off the beer, baby." His plan, he told me, was to have another beer, take a long nap in his truck, and then head back to Indianapolis tonight.

Later, outside on Beale Street, I dodged a ferocious thunderstorm by ducking into Elvis Presley's Memphis Restaurant just as the rain started slashing sideways through the air. I chatted briefly with a friendly bartender who was probably two years old when Elvis died. He was of no help on my Elvis-and-beer question, so I went out under the eaves of the restaurant to wait out the storm.

I had no clue as to where I might go next on the River of Beer when I struck up a conversation with Roger Willoughby, a Memphis-area musician and truck driver, who told me he had just come from Tunica, about an hour south, where he'd spent the weekend at "our little Vegas in Mississippi."

Tunica, as I recalled, sat near the river and basically at the top of the famed Mississippi Delta (if you discount purists who say the Delta actually starts in Memphis). No matter: the Delta's fame lay in its hallowed position as a place that had birthed the blues, as an unintended legacy of its historic yet troubled position as the onetime cotton capital of the world. On a rainy day it seemed as good a place as any to head for, so in a lull in the storm I ran for my car, cranked it up, and drove south.

13

Foam Improvement (Or, a Side Trip to See the Grand Wazoo)

Give a man a beer and he'll waste an hour.
Teach a man to brew and he'll waste a lifetime.
—Anonymous

Houston, Tex.—"Here, try this," the man says, offering to pour something from a large dark bottle into my plastic cup.

Well, not just *my* cup. The man has been going around to practically everybody with a cup saying, "Try this! Try this!"

And everybody is trying it and I know I'm expected to try it, too. Here, you're supposed to try everything once. Skirt-Boy told me that as soon as I met him in person.

That's not his real name. His real name is Bev Blackwood and you met him back in the yeast chapter. But a guy named Bev who wears kilts to homebrew club meetings in Houston, Texas, can at the very least expect to get a nickname.

This is a diversion, 300 miles west of the Mississippi, to plumb the depths of homebrew mania.

I am on the semidarkened roof patio of a hotel parking

garage. The air smells faintly of chili and heavily of beer. Doppler sounds of cars float up from a nearby freeway interchange. People are milling about—foraging, actually. Here, mysterious beer, even in its most outlandish interpretation, is the object of all desire.

I hold out my cup, though it has dregs of beer at the bottom—British brown ale to be exact. The man pours and the elixir slides down the sidewall like liquid gold, glinting like a goblin's eye in the poor light. I sniff, as I have now been taught to do, and sinus-clearing vapors X-ray up into recesses I didn't know existed.

I take a small sip. The taste is mellower than the aroma, though it still tracks down my throat like a slug of hot, boozy honey.

Which is what it more or less turns out to be.

"Honey mead," the man says.

Then, grinning and looking around, he lowers his voice, draws closer, and says, "Actually, distilled honey mead."

When I don't immediately react to this because, at the moment, I am still ignorant of the intricacies of mead, not to mention the cascading intricacies of distilled honey mead, the man looks at me with the realization that he has just wasted his prize on an ignoramus.

"I went to Nuremberg," he explains. "There they make mead, then distill it, then dilute it with water. I diluted mine with beer."

I nod.

He looks at me in mild exasperation.

"This is 70 percent distilled mead, 30 percent beer. I added cabernet," he says. "I aged it for a year in a bourbon oak cask. That's why you get all those vanilla tones."

I nod again. He waits for me to say something.

"It's good," I say. "I like it a lot."

I realize how lame it sounds the second it comes out of my mouth.

The man nods as if to say, "Oh, jeez." He goes off with his

bottle, seeking more knowledgeable judgments and more articulate appreciation.

I ask my newly minted acquaintance and mentor Fred Eckhardt, who is standing nearby and also got a splash of this elixir,
to decode this encounter. Fred is a seventy-six-year-old ex-marine
Buddhist who teaches swimming classes to children back in his
native Portland, Oregon. (And yes, the same man who penned
"The Budweiser Menace.") He wrote a book on how to homebrew
lagers in 1969, ten years before homebrewing was re-legalized. His
1989 book, *The Essentials of Beer Style*, has become a kind of
Rosetta stone for homebrewers and those who judge homebrew
competitions. Eckhardt is a soft-spoken, diminutive, roundish
man with blue twinkling eyes and a white mustache and goatee.
Imagine Shakespeare's Puck reborn as a beer mensch.

Fred explains: mead is an ancient beerlike elixir made from
honey, water, and yeast. It's not that hard to make. But throwing cabernet into the mead as you make it is pretty unusual.
Distilling it and diluting it with beer is highly unusual. Putting it
in bourbon casks—also highly unusual.

"It's also not particularly legal to do distilling but you can't
go to these meetings without somebody sidling up to you with
something they've distilled," Fred says. He grins and adds,
"That's why I like these meetings."

He remembers another reason he likes these meetings.
"Homebrewers, you will find, are fearless. They're not afraid to
try anything."

I'm at a homebrewing competition, my first ever, at a Mar-
riott Courtyard off an extremely busy freeway interchange near
Houston's vast Galleria shopping complex. The competition is
called the Dixie Cup and it is sponsored by the Foam Rangers
Homebrew Club, the oldest such club in Texas. The Rangers
have about 100 dues-paying members. This being 2002, it is the
Dixie Cup's nineteenth year and its theme is "The Night of the
Living Fred" in honor of Eckhardt. Fred has never gotten rich

off his beer writings, but he is rich in beer friends. Beer People tend to treat their elder statesmen with great admiration and generosity.

The Dixie Cup is a regional brew-off that this year will attract more than 275 homebrewers, most from Texas, Florida, Mississippi, and Louisiana. That makes it one of the largest regionals in the nation. Brewers will enter 963 beers across a dizzying forty-two styles, including historical beers, meads, and ciders (but not any distilled meads cut with beer; those are just for fun). On the other hand, the Cup, given its proximity to Halloween, has a novelty category that mandates entrants brew up an ultra-strong brew with Halloween candy being one of the required ingredients. The style is called—what else?—Monster Mash.

The Dixie Cup is the last of five stops on a competitive brewing circuit called the Gulf Coast Homebrew Competition. Two of the other stops, to give you an idea of the nature of this, are the C-Cup, sponsored by the Crescent City Homebrewers in New Orleans, and the Lunar Rendezbrew, sponsored by the Bay Area Mashtronauts of Houston (many of whose members do actually work for the National Aeronautics and Space Administration). Puns are never spared, and nothing is sacred to these people save the camaraderie of beer and the unflinching belief that homebrewers make better, more interesting beer than anybody on earth.

This is *not* an exaggeration.

Day 1 of my homebrew competition inaugural has been eventful to say the least. First, I was picked up at the airport by the Grand Wazoo, which is not a thing I can say has happened to me before. His formal name is Jimmy Paige, Grand Wazoo (i.e., president) of the Foam Rangers, and I'd met him earlier by e-mail, seeking his definition of the Perfect Beer Joint. I thought he might come wearing a fez, but he didn't. Instead, he arrived in a Ford F-150 pickup with a bumper sticker that read, "Save the Ales," and wearing khaki shorts and a T-shirt.

Paige is thirty-something, articulate, a big guy with a paunch but not a problematic one. We talked as he motored through traffic. He got turned onto homebrewing by a friend in 1990 while still serving as an officer in the coast guard; his wife bought him his first homebrew equipment back in 1993 "after she got sick and tired of hearing me talk about how much I wanted to brew," he said.

Paige laughed, then added, "Boy, is she sorry. I wouldn't say it's an obsession but it is a pretty serious hobby. Most home-brewers set some pretty high goals. They want to promote beer culture and one way to do that is to be sure somebody isn't turned off by a bad batch of beer." About the only downside Paige could think of to homebrewing was a kind of persistent public igno-rance that "being a homebrewer, you are assumed to be an alco-holic. But I can assure you if you're an alcoholic, you won't stay in homebrewing. There are a lot easier ways to get drunk."

Paige, in real life a marine surveyor, told me that people don't so much get voted Grand Wazoo as they volunteer their way into it. They work hard in the club and make it known that they're fool enough to take on the lead role organizing and presiding over the Dixie Cup, which becomes pretty much a full-time job in the three or four months leading up to the contest. On the other hand, the job really does come with a fez, which I would see Paige don many a time in full Wazoo ceremonial role during the Cup.

Paige tipped me off to the fact that the Dixie Cup was intended to generate some non-beer-related fun as well, and some of that involved plans for Bev Blackwood. I'd had no idea that Black-wood's nickname was Skirt-Boy. Paige told me that Blackwood, a software instructor, had been a single-malt scotch aficionado with a local cable TV program called *The Malt Show* when he'd attended the 2001 version of the Dixie Cup and got hooked on beer judging. He joined the Rangers and quickly made a lot of friends for his brewing skills and for putting out a quirky newslet-ter called *The Brewsletter Urquell*. And then there was the fact that he kept wearing his *Malt Show* kilts to the meetings. This had provided joyful and welcome fodder for the irreverent joshing you might expect to find at the Rangers' monthly meetings, where beer is ever present. Blackwood's fellow Rangers had become so enchanted with his kilts, in fact, that they'd undertaken a stealth write-in campaign to the *Houston Press*, an alternative newspaper that annually publishes a "Best of Houston" list—things like Best Dive Bar, Best Bathrooms, and Best Place for a Last Date. One category was cross-dressing, and the Rangers' campaign had resulted in Blackwood (without him knowing it) receiving a People's Choice Award in the Best Drag Queen category. "I've picked up a pink feather boa, some fishnet stockings, and a bright orange wig, which we plan to present to Bev on the final night," Paige told me. "He has no idea what's coming."

Already in the Grand Wazoo's truck was Randy Mosher (the person who, you may recall, sent me to see Maribeth Raines-Casselman, the yeast diva). Randy is a graphic designer by profession, a beer writer of great skill, a beer historian, and a homebrewer by avocation. He was here as a speaker at the Dixie Cup, for what Randy really is, besides a Beer Geek, is the Willy Wonka of the beer world. He's not content to just make beer. He makes beer (trending toward re-creations of antique and historical beers) with beer machinery that he makes himself. He went to welding school so he could make his own brew kettles and beer gizmos not dreamed up elsewhere. He forages online for things like pressure gauges from cast-off CPR training dummies and high-tech dairy pasteurization sensors with nine different temperature readouts. He buys these things that originally cost $900 or $5,000 for $20 or $140 on eBay and figures out how to mechanize a basement brewery as slick as Anheuser-Busch's. He also has opinions like: "Remember when Tom Wolfe wrote about abstract art and got to the part where the abstractionists had produced a blank canvas? Well, where do you go from there? It's the same with beer. Remember when Miller introduced Clear Beer? You can only go in that direction so long before you hit a wall."

Homebrewers, I was learning, had a complicated relationship

to commercial brewing—even craft brewing. Big Beer was often the object of scorn, but I met a fair number of homebrewers who would clearly have loved to be put in charge of a massive brewery so they could churn out *their* beer on a mass scale. They were more charitable in their view of craft brewers—and why shouldn't they be? By one estimate, probably 85 percent of the nation's craft brewers started out as homebrewers. And, anyway, there was no particular reason to be jealous. I often heard homebrewers lament that once homebrewers went pro they lost their creative edge because, well, they were then required to make beer that they actually had to *sell* to the public.

After the Wazoo got us to the Marriott, which took awhile, Houston traffic being basically equivalent to Los Angeles traffic (but with more American cars), I soon ran into Steve Moore. He, like Blackwood, had been an online buddy for a while, being the guy whose essay had tipped me off to the yeast obsession among homebrewers. (Several Rangers, including Moore, share an online column called "Foam Improvement.") We hadn't been talking long when Steve said, "You wanna go see my Big Rig?"

Now, in contemporary America this is a question a man needs to carefully consider, but I knew, actually, that Steve was talking about his customized homebrew system. This being Texas, only the greenest of rookies are content to brew out of one of those 5-gallon starter kits from the local homebrew shop. A few years back, Steve told me, a Houston Beer Geek who also happened to be a welder got the clever idea of making 15-gallon multivessel, customized homebrew systems, run by a fully computerized console that would automate a lot of the chores that homebrewers face. (The Beer Geek has since moved to Alaska.) Steve bought one, slapping down $3,000 ($2,400 for the brewing apparatuses and $600 extra for the computerized console).

We hopped in his Mazda convertible sports car and, after lunching at a wonderfully run-down diner specializing in succulent ribs called Thelma's Bar-B-Que, bumped along this and that freeway until we got to Steve's house. The Big Rig was in his garage, and it *was* big, though it didn't take up exactly half his garage as I expected it might. And I'm not a homebrewer (a fact that exasperated every homebrewer who found this out, since homebrewers are more missionary than the Mormons), so some of the finer points of the Big Rig were lost on me. But Moore, a thirty-something computer network administrator with close-cropped hair, a dry sense of humor, and an attractive girlfriend a foot taller than he was, ran his hands over the contraption like some men do their bass boats.

At that moment, I totally understood it.

* * *

As noted earlier, homebrewing's signature political moment in America came in 1979, when legislation signed by Jimmy Carter went into effect that finally gave beer brewers the same rights that home winemakers had been accorded after the repeal of Prohibition. The ultimate decision, however, was still left to the states, and five states—Alabama, Kentucky, Mississippi, Oklahoma, and Utah—still prohibit the making of beer at home.

Before legalization, people homebrewed under a system by which authorities in most states generally looked the other way; a smattering of homebrew shops sold ingredients for making beer but they were constrained by law from providing beer-making instructions to their customers. The result: supplies weren't always readily available and were often of dubious quality (corn sugar instead of malt), relegating homebrewing to a fringe, underground hobby indulged in mostly by people whose main interest was making cheap beer. (Even with good ingredients and at today's prices, a pint of high-quality homebrew only costs about 25 cents to make.)

There were exceptions. Fred Eckhardt was brewing out in his native Portland, having discovered a pioneering Canadian company called Wine Art that was attempting to introduce high-quality ingredients and professional methods into home-brewing. Out of Eckhardt's dabbling with Wine Art's ingredients and recipes came his 1969 pioneering tract, *A Treatise on Lager Beer*, which was a primer intended to walk the amateur brewer through the somewhat complicated lagering process. (Lager is much harder to make at home than ale because it requires constant refrigeration.)

In Boulder, Colorado, a guy named Charlie Papazian was also making his mark. In 1976, three years before legalization, he produced a homebrewing guide called *The Joy of Brewing*, which included, among other things, recipes for beers called Goat Scrotum Ale and Toad Spit Stout. In 1984, Papazian published a second primer called *The Complete Joy of Homebrewing*, which became the homebrewer's bible, and followed it up with a sequel in 1991, *The New Complete Joy of Homebrewing*, which has sold 750,000 copies. Papazian in 1978 also founded the American Homebrewers Association (AHA) and launched a homebrew magazine called *Zymurgy* (a term referring to how yeast does the business of fermentation). The homebrewers group is now part of a large enterprise called the Brewers Association, which has hewed to its homebrewing roots while branching out into the promotion of craft breweries.

These days, some two million Americans consider themselves occasional brewers, and 250,000 count themselves as ardent, active hobbyists. They are served by about 300 homebrew clubs like the Foam Rangers (and perhaps another 500 less formal local groups). Some 500 storefront homebrew shops sell supplies, and a less calculable number of enterprises peddle homebrewing equipment and ingredients via mail order or the Internet. The AHA estimates that homebrewing is probably a $25 million annual business in America today.

Competitions like the Dixie Cup have been part of the scene since 1980, and these days they are judged by the standards of a nonprofit group called the Beer Judge Certification Program (BJCP), which defines beer styles and lays out parameters—things such as color, nose, carbonation, malt, and hops profile—that the ideal example of the style should have. (Not unlike, actually, a dog show.) The BJCP, founded in 1985 under the auspices of the AHA but now independent, also certifies homebrew contest judges through an education and testing program. Contests like the Dixie Cup, if they hope to send winners on to national competitions like the Master Championship of Amateur Brewing or the AHA's own National Homebrew Competition, must follow BJCP beer style guidelines; this requires rounding up enough BJCP-certified judges (all of them volunteers) to make sure that at least one BJCP-rated judge sits on the two- to three-person panels that preside over each beer category.

For an outfit like the Rangers, which has forty-two style categories, this is a prodigious organizational effort, given that the judging exams are actually exacting and require far more than just a passing knowledge of things like yeast and fermentation. (They aren't exactly a bar exam, but they are far more formidable than a driver's license test.) On the other hand, Fred Eckhardt told me, "Homebrewers are the most organized people I know. You could turn the government of the country over to homebrewers and they'd do a much better job of things than the government is doing now." At any rate, contest mania, with some 140 competitions all across the U.S., is an entrenched part of the homebrew landscape today. The AHA's National Homebrew Competition in 2007 drew more than 5,000 entries from more than 1,600 homebrewers.

* * *

As for getting the full Dixie Cup experience, it was Bev Blackwood along with Scott Birdwell—a founding Ranger and owner of DeFalco's Home Wine and Beer Supplies, where the club holds its monthly meetings—who told me that I needed to go judge some beer. When I told Birdwell, the nation's first-ever master BJCP-certified judge, that I knew nothing about beer judging, he said it didn't matter: in the preliminary rounds, contests made room for novice judges interested in learning the fine art of beer scoring from the veterans. This is how the system produced future judges. My score would still count toward advancing one or two of the judged beers to the final round of competition, but I would be flanked by one or two judges who knew what they were doing and could rein me in if I got carried away.

Thus it was, on the first day of the two-day Cup, that I found myself being admonished to be on the lookout for *diacetyls* as I sat in one of those nondescript, bunkerlike hotel conference rooms with a bucket full of numbered beers in front of me. When I first got the diacetyl warning I admit I briefly scanned the ceiling above me, the word having sounded somewhat close to *pterodactyl*. But, duh, my immersion in Yeast World jogged my memory and I vaguely recognized it as a Beer Geek term that described some yeasty ester that certain beers threw off.

Luckily, I was in the company of John Donaldson, a geophysicist who worked on oil field seismic projects and was a card-carrying member of the KGB. In this case, it stood for Kuykendahl Gran Brewers, another Texas homebrew club and rival to the Rangers. He had come to the Cup as both an entrant and a judge—perfectly allowable so long as you don't judge in the same style in which your beer is entered. Birdwell had steered me to Donaldson because he was presiding over a common and relatively easy-to-judge style—Bohemian pilsner, which careful readers may recall was the original clear lager perfected in the early 1840s. Pilsner Urquell is a popular commercial rendition of the style, and Donaldson assumed I'd at least sampled it at some point. "That would give you a reference," he told me.

In fact, I'd drunk a fair number of Pilsner Urquells in my beer-consuming career, but I doubted that if one were shoved at me in an unmarked bottle at this very moment I'd be able to name it or necessarily declare it a Bohemian pilsner as opposed to, say, a northern German pilsner, which I'd noticed was another style in the contest. Northern German pilsner was basically a fraternal twin of Bohemian pilsner but slightly drier, Donaldson explained, and was represented by beers such as Bitburger or Holsten Pils. (Holsten I'd tried; Bitburger I couldn't be sure of.)

As to the matter of diacetyl, Donaldson said it was a buttery, even butterscotch flavor that was a by-product of certain yeasts; levels were determined by brewing temperature. Higher temperatures often gave off higher diacetyls, which wasn't usually a good thing. Some brewers, to hold down diacetyl, throw a "diacetyl rest" into their brewing cycle. Donaldson explained this to me in great detail. I nodded as though I understood every word. I understood hardly any of it.

No matter: the real point was that in the beer we were judging, "moderate diacetyl" was acceptable, and moreover, the beer should be "rich with a complex malt and a spicy, floral *Saaz* hop bouquet." As for *Saaz* hops, they were considered to be the world's finest finishing hops; they grew in America these days, but the best of them still came from the Bohemia region of the Czech Republic.

Now, all we had to do was judge the five beers in our flight. Scoring was on a scale from 1 to 50. Donaldson said he'd never given a 50, since "to me, 50 is a utopian idea. There will be a beer like that when we all get to heaven." He considered a score of 40 to be an exceptional beer; on the other hand, he almost never gave a score lower than a 13, "unless the beer's a total stinker." We were expected to back up our scores with pithy written comments defending them. The only tricky thing is that judges are expected to come within a 7-point range of each other; if they don't on the first go-round, the beer in question has to be the subject of instant mediation. "If you give it a 45 and I give it a 14, we'll have to go back and work on it," Donaldson said. "I'll have to come up some and you'll have to go down some. You don't want the brewer, who gets the scorecard, saying, 'What the hell were these freaking idiots thinking?'"

Donaldson was right: being branded a freaking idiot was

something I, Novice Beer Judge, wanted to avoid at any cost. I was already starting to sweat.

We were assigned our own steward to pour the beer, and he was instructed to pour it in such a way that we got moderate head because the head got judged, too, along with the color and aroma. Donaldson then handed me an official style sheet; it said this particular beer ought to be "light gold to deep copper gold, clear, with a dense creamy white head."

"So before you put down your first impressions, always give the beer a visual check. And try to pick out some of those aromas, too," Donaldson admonished me.

As we started to go through the beers, cleansing our palates in between with bites of bread and sips of water, Donaldson told me his route to homebrewing. It was a common story. "Wild obsession, basically," he said. "My dad brewed but I didn't take it up—back then I didn't even like beer but I realize now that's because my exposure was limited to industrial beers. Then a friend later turned me on to homebrewing and, ah, a light bulb went on. For four or five years I was completely consumed by everything about beer. It wasn't good. I was neglecting my work, my family—everything."

Donaldson stopped and laughed and said he'd dialed back his beer mania to a saner level. We then lapsed into the quiet of sipping, musing, and judging.

I held my breath as we got through the first beer. He'd given it a 28; I'd given it a 25. I was secretly elated.

The next beer. I awarded a 27, he gave it a 26. Bingo!

The next beer didn't seem anything like a Bohemian pilsner to me; it was sweet, almost apple-cidery. I said so and boldly gave it a 15.

Donaldson agreed with me completely, saying, "This is more like an apple mead than a pilsner." He scored it more generously but still only a 19.

I was rolling!

We got through the remaining two beers with scores in the low 30s, just a point apart.

Along the way, Donaldson offered running commentary like, "This particular beer is not a bad beer but in character it's more like American light lager than a European pilsner.... This one looks turbulent. My goodness, look at the gas in this beer—it's boiling like the surface of the sun!"

I was relegated to saying prosaic things like "this beer seems flat to me," but at least I was in the scoring ballpark. Maybe I was a Beer Geek in Waiting.

Scott Birdwell came over to see how we were doing, and he even tasted our low-scoring cidery beer, which we had pretty much concluded had been mislabeled and belonged in another category. "Hey, a lambic pilsner," Birdwell declared, inventing a new style completely. (Lambics are sour, wild-fermented Belgian ales.)

"That's nothing," Birdwell added. "I once tasted a Belgian ale made with LifeSavers. It was a very good and very strange beer." (Birdwell later told me he could think of one even stranger beer he'd tried: some guy had made a beer using Beano, the antiflatulence remedy, as a way of producing a low-calorie light beer.)

Birdwell asked me if I was up for more judging. Confident, I said, "Sure."

Which is how I ended up at a judging table with Fred Eckhardt, guru of all homebrew judges, and a Ranger named Sean Lamb. I'd gotten to know Fred a bit by now and liked him a lot. But I wasn't sure I wanted to judge beer with him. I'm a garage-band-level blues guitar player but that doesn't mean I'd want to risk the embarrassment of trying to jam with B. B. King.

Eckhardt, though, made it easy by turning it into a class, but first he offered a short discourse on the value of the homebrewer in the cosmos. "Homebrewers are now the cutting edge of brewing because they are the ones restlessly experimenting," he said. "I'd be willing to bet that there isn't a style of beer made anywhere in the world that some American brewer hasn't made at home. And they are on the cutting edge of beer invention—one of the last styles to be invented, a beer called Bourbon Bock, was invented by a homebrewer."

Then we got to the beer. We were judging a flight of nine beers in a style known as British Mild, a subcategory of brown ales, which are supposed to be, the style sheet said, "medium to dark brown in color with a malty, hopless aroma and a roasty, nutty flavor that could include esters of licorice, plum, raisin, or chocolate." Fred explained: "In England this is the equivalent of light beer. It's very low in alcohol—about 2.5 percent. It's a wonderfully aromatic beer and you can drink a lot of it and still find the subway home. Of course, in England, they don't dare call this a light beer. If they did, people would pour it down the drain."

Eckhardt also gave me a tip about comportment when judging in a group dynamic. "It's bad form to put the beer down and say, 'Oh, shit!' " he said.

We commenced our judging. Nobody commented on beers until after the scoring was revealed.

On the first beer, Sean Lamb asked Fred: "Didn't you find it a little cidery?"

Fred: "Cidery?"

Sean: "Yes, cidery?"

Fred: "No, I found it aggressive."

Sean: "Aggressive?"

Fred: "Well, anyway, I gave it a 40."

Sean: "I gave it a 35. I liked it."

Fred: "I can see you did. You drank it all—what a lush!"

Lamb laughed.

They looked at me. I'd (whew!) given it a 34.

Judging is a deliberate business and we plodded on. Fred interrupted once to ask a peculiar question: "Are you going to listen to the beer?"

I thought he wanted to know whether, in the amalgamation of sniffing, sipping, and gazing at a particular beer, the beer had perhaps revealed some cosmic sense of how it should be scored. But, no, he meant was I going to listen to what each beer sounded like.

"If you listen to enough beer, there are some differences," Eckhardt explained. "Belgian beer is buzz—well, actually more like a lawnmower motor. Some beers that are spoiled sound like a buzz saw. If you listen to Bud, it's got a wonderful sound. In lagers, bubbles will be bigger than they are in ales. They usually produce a fast click. Bud has a slower, noisier click. I don't know what it means but I have fun with it."

We got through four beers and I was feeling exceptionally proud because I had been blissfully in the middle of both Fred and Sean in the scoring, never more than a point or two from one or the other. I could *do* this.

Then beer No. 786 reared its ugly brown little head.

I winced as I heard Eckhardt give it a 39 and Lamb a 37—scores that put it very close to the exceptional category.

I'd given No. 786 a measly 25.

"I didn't like this beer at all," I said.

"What was wrong with it?" Lamb inquired.

"Well, uh, I didn't like the way it looked," I sputtered.

Lamb peered at me. "Well, you know looks only really count for a little."

Silence.

"Hmm, well, flavor-wise, it seemed a little flat," I offered.

More silence.

I tried again. "There's a taste in there I, uh, just can't put my finger on. I, uh—"

More and deeper silence.

I looked at Eckhardt and then at Lamb. "Okay," I said. "I've clearly lost my mind."

This seemed to my fellow judges the smartest thing I'd said all evening.

"Well, 25 still puts it in the 'good' category," Fred said, trying to let me off the hook a little.

We agreed to go on to the other beers and come back to this one, so as to meet the requirement to ratchet all the scores within seven points of each other. I got back on track for the last three beers. And we went back to the disputed No. 786, whereupon, having tasted it yet again, I realized it was really a 32, not a lowly 25. And my brethren judges, who saw no reason to change their scores, smiled upon me charitably.

But I knew this was a blow to my Beer Geek in Waiting aspirations.

The Foam Rangers went on to win the 2002 Dixie Cup, trouncing their nearest opponent by 26 points. Skirt-Boy (aka Bev Blackwood) won first place for the Rangers in the Old Ale category and placed second or third in three others, while the Grand Wazoo (aka Jimmy Paige) placed second in the Old Ale category and second in American Brown Ale. The Rangers took first place in ten separate styles, including the Monster Mash and the Specialty/Experimental/Historical beer category, and thirty-four places altogether. The name of that winning experimental beer was Don't Fuck Me Up with Peace and Barleywine.

14

On the Road Again

The Delta and Beer at the Cross Roads by Way of Clarksdale, Mississippi

Who cares how time advances? I am drinking ale today.
—Edgar Allan Poe

The Mississippi Delta began to assert itself somewhere around Eudora, Mississippi.

Having somehow missed the Highway 61/Old River Road connection out of Memphis, I'd found my way to I-55, and at a town called Hernando, I'd jogged off the interstate and found myself on State Highway 304. It cut through rolling hills that held comely farmland and woods cloaked in thick, forest-green kudzu still slicked in rain and burnished by a late afternoon sun poking through vanishing clouds. I knew I was pushing into the deep, deep South when I saw a hand-lettered sign offering pigs for sale, and another later on advertising competitive barrel racing. (For the uninitiated, this is a sport involving riding horses around tight turns in a course marked with barrels.)

A few miles on, an enormous billboard reared up off the highway. It said, "If God Should Ask Why Should I Let You Into
Heaven, What Would You Say?" I turned on the radio, caught
a gospel station and heard an African-American preacher, in
urgent tones, asking pretty much the same question.

Just west of Eudora, the land gave up all pretense of elevation
and lay down unflinchingly flat as far as the eye could see. Past
a sign designating the Tunica County line, a fallow field of rich,
black gumbo soil stretched out in the mellowing light, a lone tree
the solitary feature of the horizon. Soon, soybean fields, cotton
fields, and a hayfield, the latter forming a golden rectangle in
a sea of green, pressed up to the highway; a tiny farmstead, a
police car pulled up in the front yard, broke the unblemished
fetch of fields. And then some miles hence, as if by signal, a
scrum of gargantuan billboards lurched up out of the landscape
announcing places like Harrah's, Sam's Town, Fitzgerald's, the
Hollywood Casino, and products like Miller Lite, One-Pound-
Steak-and-Egg Breakfasts at $2.99, and an Epic Buffet. If this
seemed incongruous—Las Vegas–style billboard mania in the
middle of endless cotton fields—it was nothing like the impression of the casinos themselves.

As I swung south on Highway 61 and approached Tunica,
there they were, neon megaliths winking in the distance, most
of them clustered together in an arc of shifting light, some
brandishing lasers and spotlights and all set off in a darkening
moat and surrounded by nothing that resembled them—high-
rise aliens amidst the dimming land covered in cotton, and
the sprawling sky holding on to the best light of the day, with
the scattered farms seeming like quaint anachronisms in the
shadows. The impression was of a mirage, but no mirage this.

I headed for the lights and within fifteen minutes I'd arrived,
via Casino Center Drive, in a parking lot that probably could
hold the Rose Bowl crowd. This was the Horseshoe Casino,
which I'd randomly chosen out of what seemed like eight or
nine other possibilities because I was attracted, buglike, to its

turquoise aura and unavoidable rosy pink neon glow. I parked the car and hiked on in.

Though this was a Sunday night in what certainly once passed for the Bible Belt, I needn't have worried about repeating my experience among the elderly teetotalers aboard the *Diamond Jo* casino boat back in Dubuque. The casino—65,000 square feet of it with 2,000 slot machines and a 500-room, fourteen-story hotel attached—was about half full, mostly with slot players, though a saunter through various rooms and anterooms revealed a goodly number of people playing craps and Caribbean stud or some such game. I circled around it, found a bar, and quickly became acquainted with a couple I'll call Richard and Mary. They were dressed in ranch casual—pointy-toed cowboy boots, jeans, and checked shirts (though not matching). They looked to be in their late fifties. They told me they'd lived in the Delta proper until seven years ago, when they moved upriver near West Memphis, Arkansas. Richard had spent most of his adult life as a mechanic; Mary had waited tables and worked briefly in a bank in between raising their kids, who were now grown.

They were drinking Miller Lite and commiserating about how they'd dropped about $100 between them. Richard played video poker; Mary the slots. They'd driven down after church and lunch, church being the reason they were reticent to give me their real names. They explained that they were Baptists of evangelical bent and didn't widely advertise to their Baptist Church friends that they occasionally gambled away their Sunday afternoons over a beer or two.

"There's no harm in it that we can see," Richard told me. "But sometimes it's easier not to have to explain certain things to people."

"Richard," Mary said, "I doubt we're the only gamblin' or beer-drinkin' Christians out there."

He smiled and said, "I know that. But, see, what she's not telling you is that we've got this pastor and, boy, would he let us have it if he knew we were here."

I told them about my quest and said I doubted their pastor, from the sound of it, would ever pick up a book about beer anyway. Richard laughed and said he wanted to make one other religious clarification. "You know Jesus drank wine, and beer's not even mentioned in the Bible one way or the other. That's why we don't see anything wrong with it."

I knew Richard was right on the beer front. The Bible mentions wine many times and has several references to "strong drink" but without clarifying what that might be. Some scholars say there is good circumstantial evidence that strong drink, given the history of barley cultivation in the biblical Middle East, was beer, but nobody knows for sure. Still, any beer-drinking Christian could take comfort from Proverbs 31:6–7: "Give strong drink unto him that is ready to perish, and wine unto those that be of heavy hearts. Let him drink, and forget his poverty and remember his misery no more." (In fairness, Proverbs 20:1 offers this rejoinder: "Wine is a mocker, strong drink is raging: and whosoever is deceived thereby is not wise." On the other hand, this seems to be an appeal to moderate drinking, not a prohibition against alcohol.)

Richard told me that, though they drank Miller Lite most of the time (and Coors regular sometimes), they really weren't big beer drinkers and that since the opening of the first casinos here a decade ago, they pretty much confined their drinking to their trips here. "But as far as beer joints go, you won't find a real beer joint in a casino," Richard said. "People are here gambling, and they might drink. They don't come here to drink thinking they might gamble."

I asked them how the arrival of the casinos had changed things.

"Oh, plenty," Mary said. "This was—what, honey?—the poorest county in the United States before gambling opened up?"

"Something like that," Richard said. "I remember about a dozen years or so ago when people were saying this place was poorer than places in Africa, and they were probably right. You can't say that anymore. I think they've poured, I dunno, tons of money—hundreds of millions—in here, which is a lot for a county that had basically cotton and squat-else before."

I asked if there were any naysayers.

Richard laughed. He said, "I think they [the casinos] are ugly myself, but Mary here thinks they're sharp." Beyond that, he had heard complaints that the casinos had brought crime, traffic, and unwelcome change, and that the good jobs had gone to Memphis people, leaving the locals to scrub floors and change sheets in the hotels. And, this being the Bible Belt, religious pamphleteers sometimes decorated the cars in the parking lot with anti-gambling literature. "But the vast majority of people who remember what Tunica County was like before will tell you they've been a godsend," Richard told me.

"I don't see anything wrong with any of it," Mary said, gesturing around the casino. "This passes for pretty fancy where I grew up."

We talked briefly about what I might find downriver. Mississippi, I knew, wasn't exactly one of the premier beer states. It had no active full-fledged breweries, was one of the few states to still outlaw homebrewing, and was the last state in the union to legalize brewpubs. It had four of them—two in Jackson and two on the Gulf Coast, where the state's other cluster of casinos can be found. It does rank fourteenth in the nation in terms of per capita consumption, at 36.3 gallons per person, but more than 95 percent of the beer it drinks is American Standard lager.

Clarksdale, known as the blues capital of the world and home of the Delta Blues Museum, was maybe forty miles away, Richard and Mary told me. They didn't know of any particular beer joints but suggested I hit Abe's for barbecue. Then they drained their beers and said they had to start driving back. I soon headed out into the neon night myself. As I drove away, billboards told me that unless I lingered a few more days, I would miss not only Joan Rivers but Leon Russell and Edgar Winter, too. I could imagine Leon and Edgar, in their salad days, playing the Delta dives and juke joints that were the pre-casino mainstays here. But Joan? I don't think so.

Before settling into a motel far from the neon glare, I did detour into Old Tunica ten miles south to satisfy myself that a charming Southern town still coexisted with the neo-glitter of the casinos. It had pretty much rolled up and gone to sleep. But it was there.

* * *

As I drove a beeline down Highway 61 the next morning on a misty, overcast Delta day, I realized Richard and Mary had been right about other things, too. I'd checked the *Wall Street Journal*'s archives by laptop and learned that Tunica County had been, by every standard measurement, the poorest county in Mississippi and nearly the poorest in the nation, made poorer still by the restructuring of the cotton industry that by the early 1960s had become totally mechanized, throwing thousands of farm laborers out of work. Civil rights activist Jesse Jackson had visited back in 1985, coming to a wayside of wretched poverty and tumbledown shacks called Sugar Ditch and declaring it "America's Ethiopia." Unemployment was about 20 percent and getting worse.

These days, Sugar Ditch sprouts a low-income housing development, and Tunica County's unemployment rate is about 6.5 percent—a figure representing mostly the hard-core unemployed battling the lingering social and medical dysfunctions of poverty. By one estimate, casino and related construction had pumped $3 billion into the county—perhaps the largest slug of single-purpose private capital ever poured into one locale. The gambling emporiums were producing about $1 billion of taxable revenue a year and had created roughly 15,000 jobs. Even a cranky person who thought the casinos were a neon blight on the pastoral landscape would have a hard time arguing against their economic merits. Scenic poverty is hardly ever scenic to people who live in it. I wondered, as I crossed into Coahoma

County, where Clarksdale is the county seat, whether the casinos were admired as much from a distance.

This stretch of the Great River Road seemed as straight and flat a stretch of road as I'd ever been on, the straightness being a blessing when I overtook a mile-long column of gargantuan double-wide trailers being towed to some destination down the road. My observation of flatness was confirmed by a marker noting that the elevation of the highway between Tunica and Clarksdale deviated only a quarter-inch in the whole stretch. Of course, the road sat on one of the richest loads of compacted alluvial soil found anywhere in the world—topsoil in the area had been measured as deep as 350 *feet* in some parts. Indeed, the topsoil bank found along the river as it winds some 360 snaky miles through Mississippi amounts to one of the biggest natural flowerpots anywhere.

The farther I got from the casinos, the more like Old Mississippi it became. I passed faded churches with faded cemeteries and watched crop dusters fly low overhead, spraying bug and weed killer on vast stands of cotton and soybeans. The other remarkable feature of the countryside was a notable absence. The once ubiquitous shotgun shack, a legacy of the Delta's sharecropping past and a staple of Mississippi's postcard poverty, was simply nowhere to be seen. I wondered whether this might be simply another localized outcome of casino prosperity. But I'd come to learn that the Delta's rural poor, since the 1960s, were being slowly but surely tucked into public housing, rendering the shotgun shack a fading relic of the past.

I'd never been to Clarksdale, but as a minor student of the blues I certainly knew of its vaunted place in American roots music history. It had been the prime stop on the so-called Chitlin Circuit, when itinerant African-American bluesmen in the 1920s and 1930s wandered the Delta from Natchez to Tunica, battered guitars and harmonicas in hand, playing music at turns both wry and mournful—music that tumbled directly from the crucible of poverty, backbreaking work, and racism, and, yes, also from a longing for life, love, and happiness despite all of the above. Every would-be blues player eventually pitched up on Issaquena Avenue in Clarksdale, and the town, long a cotton-trading center, became a music center as well.

Clarksdale proper had produced a stunning number of legendary bluesmen, among them Muddy Waters, John Lee Hooker, Howlin' Wolf, and first-generation blues pioneers like W. C. Handy and Charlie Patton. As famous or infamous as all of them was Robert Johnson, the man who wrote "Hellhound on My Trail" and "Cross Roads Blues" (later commercialized by Eric Clapton and Cream) and who by legend sold his soul to Ole Scratch one night at a dark highway junction in exchange for an uncanny ability to play the blues. Enhancing the legend, perhaps, was Johnson's preoccupation in his lyrics with the devil, sex, and women. The Cross Roads is popularly considered to be the literal intersection of Highway 61 and Highway 49 at Clarksdale (a notion that has many debunkers, who say it is farther south near Cleveland, Mississippi). But folks in Clarksdale will have none of that and have marked the Highway 61/49 junction with a signpost holding three giant blue guitars and "Cross Roads" written on all three sides of a triangle. This bit of touristy kitsch is perhaps forgivable considering that Clarksdale and much of the Delta didn't seriously recognize or attempt to promote its indigenous music until about twenty years ago, and people have been trying to make up for it ever since. (Cynics might say they also discovered there was good tourist money in the blues.) Johnson died penniless in 1938 at the age of twenty-seven after drinking whiskey apparently spiked with poison by a jealous husband and, by one account, crawling around on all fours in a mad rage like the hellhound in his song. The transformation of the blues into a popular art form since then has been as remarkable as the transformation of Tunica County since casinos. A couple of years ago Johnson's estate, inherited by a son he fathered out of wedlock, was valued at $1.2 million—based solely on royalties for his reissued records.

I hit Clarksdale as the sun broke from the clouds and followed signs for downtown for a look around, driving past the Riverside Hotel, a ramshackle building once housing Clarksdale's black hospital and famous for being the place where blues diva Bessie Smith died after a car accident in 1937. The hotel was still open with rooms at $25 a night, no bath included. I was tempted to check in but decided a beer scribe didn't want to be stumbling down dark halls in the middle of the night looking for the john.

Shotgun shacks may have disappeared but pockets of Clarksdale indeed looked impoverished; the lovely if faded old downtown had the feel of a 1950s Southern movie set. There were a few gorgeous, rehabilitated old buildings, one housing a fancy bar owned by actor and Clarksdale native Morgan Freeman, and another holding the Delta Blues Museum, interspersed with lots of lovely but abandoned ones. On first glance, the prosperity of the mighty casinos hadn't made the forty-mile trip here.

I parked in front of an inviting little restaurant called the Delta Amusement Co. & Café and went in seeking a real Southern breakfast and, hopefully, beer knowledge. In my Northern dweller/healthy-food reincarnation, I breakfast solely on fruit smoothies and vitamins. But I come from a long line of bacon-eggs-and-grits eaters on my Arkansas side of the family, and I sometimes crave the stuff. I'd clearly picked the right spot on all accounts—I ordered eggs, bacon, grits, toast, and coffee, all for about $3, and struck up a conversation with the loquacious and plain-speaking Bobby Tarzi, the owner of the place.

When I explained my mission, Tarzi, a Clarksdale native with a pleasing Mississippi accent, looked at me doubtfully. "Hmm, damn," he said. "Monday night in Clarksdale, the beer pickins are gonna be slim. The juke joints around here operate on Friday and Saturday nights, and a lot of places—well, we don't have a lot of places, but some of the other places such as we have—are closed on Monday."

He thought this over for a second, then said, "Hell, come

back here tonight around suppertime. We've got food and Monday Night Football and cards, and people come in and shoot the shit and drink beer. I guess that makes us a beer joint. Why the hell not?"

I thanked Tarzi for his offer and said I'd take him up on it. I told him I'd come from Tunica and wanted, either now or later, to talk to him and others about the casinos. Tarzi said bluntly, "We can talk about it more tonight but it's definitely a mixed bag for us." But he did know of one startling success story: a local guy who had the Bud distributorship and, pre-casinos, essentially stored beer in his garage and delivered it out of the back of his station wagon, so meager was his business. "The casinos moving in were like ten or eleven superstores opening up for this guy. Now, eight out of ten beers sold in this whole area is one of his beers, and with the casinos, that's a helluva lot of beer." Tarzi gave me his name and I called him as soon as I left the restaurant. But an assistant told me, after a couple of conversations, that he wasn't interested in sharing his garage-to-riches story.

I went to lunch at Abe's, as Richard and Mary suggested, and had world-class ribs. Then, undeterred, I went looking for other Delta beer connections and found an interesting if oblique one. It was near Tutwiler, about fifteen miles southeast of Clarksdale, in an overgrown and hard-to-find Baptist church cemetery (the church having long ago fallen down) where blues harmonica legend Aleck Miller, aka Sonny Boy Williamson II, lay buried. The grave, unmarked for years, might have still been impossible to locate except for a stone that had been put up by Williamson's record company a few years back. But the grave has become more than a blues shrine; it also seems to have become something of a popular beer-drinking spot—a development that would have hardly offended Sonny Boy, who, though he went off to England for a spell and did a recording session with British blues imitators the Yardbirds, spent a goodly part of his life in juke joints. (For the record, Sonny Boy didn't think much of the British blues knockoffs, who couldn't keep up with his chord progressions.) Many of the visitors leave behind beer cans (or bottles) or even full beers, plus harmonicas. Grumpy purists clean up the place from time to time (taking the cans and bottles but leaving the harmonicas). Based upon a strictly unscientific survey of the cans I counted in my brief visit, I concluded that most of the beer drinkers attracted to Sonny Boy's grave were Bud people.

I made a couple of more detours before heading back to Clarksdale, driving another ten miles so I could cross the Tallahatchie Bridge made famous by Bobbie Gentry's 1967 number one hit song, "Ode to Billie Joe," her mournful ballad of teenage suicide. The hook of the tune comes from the observation of its storyteller, who furtively spies Billie Joe tossing some mysterious object off the bridge before throwing himself into the muddy, swirling, catfish-rich waters of the Tallahatchie River. Gentry has never said what that object might be. A movie, for which she got a screenwriting credit, portrayed Billie Joe as a put-upon, repressed homosexual (but still didn't say what he threw off the bridge). And even on the Web, which is rife with speculation about almost everything that's ever happened at any time to anybody, real or imaginary, I couldn't find the suggestion that had always occurred to me: that Billie Joe, doing what teenagers have done since the beer can was invented, was tossing his empties into the river so his old man wouldn't find them.

By stopping at a country store for a soft drink, I'd also heard about a place near Clarksdale called Hobson's Plantation, where, if the guy at the store had it right, a person could check into something called the Shack Up Inn. This was said to be a collection of remodeled shotgun shacks that some enterprising entrepreneur had salvaged from nearby fields and operated as a hotel. I drove to Hobson's Plantation and, sure enough, found the shacks, lined up in a kind of gentrified shantytown, but there was no innkeeper about, otherwise I could have no more resisted checking in than I could have resisted checking in to the

Heartbreak Hotel back in Memphis. But it did help confirm my notion that the Delta's shotgun shacks had moved from poverty emblem to tourism kitsch.

I showed up at the Delta Amusement at around 7:30. There were about fifteen, maybe twenty, people there, including Tarzi and a cook. Almost everyone else was engaged in a couple of rambunctious and reasonably high-stakes card games in a side room, which I decided to stay out of, poker player though I sometimes am. Then Tarzi called supper and started laying down big plates of steaks and mashed potatoes and other fixings at tables facing a TV tuned to the football game with the sound turned down; a rock station, at the moment playing Don Henley, provided the audio. The platters were $10, and beer—Bud—was a buck. After the first one, you were expected to fetch the beer out of the cooler yourself and leave your dollar on the counter.

"This ain't Burger King," Tarzi told me as he handed me my food. "At Delta Amusement you *cannot* have it your way."

I liked Tarzi and realized he was one of those Southerners whose style took a little getting used to. He talked loud and peppered his speech with Southern aphorisms and not a few profanities. He offered a running and usually blackly comic commentary on pretty much everything. My Arkansas grandfather would have said that Tarzi was the kind of man who could talk a ham off a hog, and he would've meant it as a compliment. He was busy, too, between hustling the food out to his regulars and the constant stream of telephone calls from people wanting to place bets on a football pool. I dug in to my steak and potatoes, which were tasty, and sipped my Bud.

Before I knew it, the football game was winding down and people were starting to file out; just the structure of the evening, with people absorbed in food, football, or cards, hadn't exactly provided the interview opportunities I was hoping for. Tarzi, sensing this, suggested we could go on a nighttime walkabout of downtown and look for another beer joint. Well, actually, there were only two possibilities, he said, both places nearby. We could see if they were open.

I'd managed to get some basics from Tarzi himself during the football game. He'd bought the place in 1988 after getting tired of being in the wholesale tobacco business. Plus, as a native son, the Delta and Clarksdale were in his blood, and he thought that investing in a business downtown would be the most productive way to join forces with other business and cultural folks who were trying to keep Clarksdale from being totally swept aside by the economic forces of history.

It hadn't been easy since the fall of King Cotton, and he seemed to alternate between cautious optimism and moments of testy defeatism. Blues tourism, and an annual Tennessee Williams Festival honoring the playwright who had also lived here for a while, had helped, but these things mainly brought people to town in big slugs. Generally, Tarzi would order extra beer and food for such events but he never quite knew how much of a splash-over he was going to get from them. As for those casinos back in Tunica, he said, "Hell, they've pretty much killed my card game. As far as I can tell, they're not doing us a damn bit of good."

Out on the darkened streets, Tarzi gave me the lowdown on the straits of downtown. Gesturing, he said, "back in the '50s and '60s, all this street and all down that street was Cotton Row. We had five or six cotton traders downtown. There's one left. And everybody's become an Inc. or Co.—it's all corporate shit now. It wasn't that long ago that a guy with 150 acres could support a family well on cotton. Now, with 1,500 acres you'd be lucky to make it, and only if you get government help."

He went on: "See that three-story building there? That was the Alcazar, a really nice hotel. It's empty now. A doctor just bought the building. This was the movie theater. It's closed, too. You realize that Clarksdale once had *six* bookies in town, and it wasn't all that long ago, either. There was more action here than in Vegas, I'm not lying. Now there's just one. We had six bars down here—now it's a couple."

Tarzi said he couldn't give me an accurate count but he figured about a third of the downtown buildings were now empty. "It's fucked up," he said, "but it's nobody's fault. The world keeps changing and moving on. Sometimes I think that if it weren't for the government money that flows into this town [in the form of agricultural supports, public housing subsidies, and the like], you could take a bulldozer and just push the sumbitch over."

I told him it seemed to me that he'd actually had a pretty lively crowd for a Monday night, given my experience thus far on the River of Beer.

He laughed and said, "It was all right, but c'mon, Ken, there are 20,000 people in this town. You'd think on Monday night a lot more fellas would say, 'Hey, Momma, it's guys' night out. I'm gonna go out and drink a few beers and play some cards and watch some football, and I'll service you properly when I get home.' Hell, I should be doin' better than what I did tonight. It's kinda sad, don't you think?"

I recognized that this little soliloquy could be described by a term that, on the face of it, seems like an oxymoron but is common down South—self-deprecating Southern hyperbole.

Tarzi got distracted by two things: the rain that had started to fall in big splatters and his surprise that at least one of the two other beer joints he had in mind was actually open. It was the bar owned by actor Morgan Freeman called the Ground Zero Blues Club.

Tarzi seemed shocked. "Damn, they're never open on Monday night. Let's go check it out."

On the way in Tarzi allowed that it was gratifying that somebody like Freeman used his Hollywood money to help revivify Clarksdale, saying the local scoop was that the actor had spent a veritable fortune without much chance, short-term, that he'd actually make any money. But maybe that wasn't the point. And as soon as we entered, I knew Ground Zero wasn't exactly a beer joint. It was a spacious and gorgeous watering hole and live music venue slipped into a tastefully restored turn-of-the-century building. And you could get, if you wanted one, a Sam Adams from the bar.

Tarzi didn't hang around long, and I ended up in conversation with a group of beer-drinking locals. In the nicely lazy way things get talked about in the South, especially as the beer flows, the conversation ambled among several vital topics: the notion that Coors Light seemed to be making a real run at Bud, at least in Clarksdale; the temperamental differences between water moccasins and rattlesnakes; and whether there was some truth to the notion that people who often think about snakes see them a lot more often than people who don't. (As a person who'd been an ardent live snake collector back in Louisiana in my youth, I believe snakes can sometimes be conjured. That is, on snake hunts I would often get a feeling I was going to encounter a certain kind of snake, and shortly thereafter I often would.)

I was diverted from these pleasant ruminations by the appearance of an extremely large man at a table over by the door. I noticed a couple of things beyond his size: that he sat in his chair with his head cocked back, as though he might be staring at the ceiling, and that he had a beer in each hand. As I had not encountered any two-fisted drinkers since the short-order cook back in Al Capone's old bar in Dubuque, I decided to go over and investigate.

He told me his name was Jeff. He had thinning hair and a bear's head, a bullfrog-deep voice, and large, protruding eyes that looked like they had been frozen in pleasant surprise. He said he managed a trailer park and that the only beer he would ever consider drinking was Bud, which is what he was indeed clutching now. He had once been a more catholic beer drinker but converted to Bud-only when he learned what Budweiser stood for.

"Do you know what Budweiser stands for?" he asked me.

I was going to answer "King of Beers" or something like that. But he cut me off and said: "Because U Deserve What Every Individual Should Enjoy Regularly."

"Where did you hear that?" I wanted to know.

"Dallas," he said—declining, though I pressed him, to elaborate. "And because of that commitment, I've always drunk it since." (I later checked with the Bud people who say they've heard this slogan but they didn't make it up.)

When I asked Jeff about Clarksdale, he went off on a long discourse about contemporary race relations (better than they used to be), the arrival of gangs in the Delta (there were plenty of them, he assured me), and whether there ought to be slave reparations (there shouldn't be, he said). I steered him back to beer and asked my Perfect Beer Joint question.

Jeff leaned back, looked toward the ceiling in contemplation, and closed his eyes for a long time. Then he said, without opening his eyes: "Loose women. In short-shorts and little tank tops. Pretty women and cold beer."

That's when I knew Jeff was an optimist.

I doubted I was going to get a much better picture of beer culture in the Delta than that. So in a bit I bid Jeff and the Ground Zero good night and headed for my motel.

15

A Detour to the Green, Green Fields of Bud

The sunshine, fresh air filled with the aroma of lupulin, and
pleasant work made the hop-picking time the most enjoyable.
—W. Somerset Maugham

Boundary County, Idaho—It's a hazy morning, the sun leaching lemon light through the gauzy smoke of the forest fires drifting down from Canada next door. But the haze can't diminish the manicured beauty of what Don Kloth sees from a rise off Idaho's Highway 1. Endless rows of hops vines, dappled with cones, stretch toward a horizon framed by the evergreen rises and huckleberry barrens of the distant Selkirk Mountains.

Kloth (rhymes with "tooth") is admiring not just the verdant sweep of hops and their wild surrounds but the symmetry of it all. Contemporary hops fields are staked out in large, interconnecting grids rimmed by tall utility poles supporting sturdy steel cables strung every twenty-eight feet. Flexible wires, the thickness of phone lines, are strung between these cables, serving as guides for rows. Lengths of hemp rope are hand-looped over these guides, pulled taut, and staked down to form simple

Christmas-tree-shaped trellises. The vines (technically called bines) are trained to climb clockwise up these trellises, five or six vines to a rope, to a height of about twenty feet.

There are about 900 plants to an acre, and by this time of the year—August, the traditional harvest month—they fill out thick and lushly green as kudzu, and brim with fragrant hop cones that will soon be plucked, dried, and baled for use.

"Being from a farm myself, the science of getting these poles in a straight line—now that's something," Kloth says, admiring the scene below him. "I don't think we had lasers when we put these in originally."

Kloth has a good reason to be impressed, since he's done the math. This operation, known as Elk Mountain Farm, sprawls across 1,800 acres hard up against the Canadian border at the tip-top of the Idaho Panhandle, making it the largest contiguous hops farm in the world. At 60 poles per acre, that means 108,000 poles lined up arrow-straight—a daunting task in the shifting geometry of interconnecting grids. Of course, if the poles weren't lined up absolutely arrow-straight, Kloth, something of a perfectionist in a company thick with perfectionists, would get them straightened out pretty quickly.

Donald W. Kloth, sixty-two years old as of this writing, grew up on a corn, wheat, and soybean farm near the southern Illinois town of Sparta. He went on to Oklahoma State University to claim the ultimate farm boy credential—a Ph.D. in agricultural economics. He's parlayed that into one of the more unusual jobs in America, which is why I've diverted from my quest to catch up with him in a location far from the Mississippi River. He's the nation's (and perhaps the world's) top beer farmer.

True, nobody grows beer, but plenty of people grow the stuff that goes into it, principally barley, rice, corn, wheat, sugar, and hops. Annually, farmers in nineteen states sell more than $850 million in raw materials to the nation's beer companies, including 4.8 billion pounds of barley malt; 1.8 billion pounds of rice, corn, and other grains; and more than 15 million pounds of hops. Kloth, by way of his corporate position, is both a grower and a buyer of staggering portions of these beer commodities.

His formal title is chairman and chief executive officer of Busch Agricultural Resources Inc. (BARI), the agricultural production and research arm of Anheuser-Busch Cos. BARI was founded in 1981 as part of Anheuser-Busch's quest for manifest beer destiny—a destiny staked to notions of quality defined, in part, by bedrock consistency. All major beer companies have acquisition divisions to manage the purchase and delivery of raw ingredients. But no other beer company in America (or the world) has an operation approaching BARI's ambitions, sweep, and economies of scale.

Kloth wears other corporate hats; he's a senior vice president of parent Anheuser-Busch and once worked directly for Patrick Stokes, Anheuser-Busch's president and chief executive officer. But his main job is to ride herd on BARI and its quality-is-everything mission to research and develop, grow, and/or acquire the vast tonnage of raw ingredients, at a cost of hundreds of millions of dollars a year, that go into Budweiser and Anheuser-Busch's twenty-nine other beer labels.

Kloth is a big guy of mild Midwestern sensibilities and, as might be expected, given his employer, a beer drinker, though lately a carb-and-calorie-minded one fond of Anheuser-Busch's latest light beer offering, Michelob Ultra. He has the measured speech and inquiring temperament of an economist. But his is a high-stakes job, fraught with challenges and perils. Imagine having to manage consistency when you make more than 100 million barrels of beer a year at a dozen separate U.S. breweries and two abroad. Yet if you really want the Bud brewed in Newark to taste the same as the Bud brewed in China or St. Louis, a key element of the quality chain is that you simply can't leave your barley malt, your rice, your corn, and your hops to chance. "The company was growing much larger and we decided we needed to be much more insightful in our quest for quality," Kloth says of the rationale for launching BARI. "The more we've learned from this, the more we wonder why we didn't do it before."

These days, the agricultural unit is a far-flung enterprise, with 1,100 employees in thirty locations scattered over eleven states plus Canada, Germany, Argentina, Uruguay, and China. BARI operates twelve massive barley elevators, half of them in North Dakota, that form the staging areas for the storage and shipment of about 70 million bushels of barley annually. It runs six Midwestern and Western barley contracting offices that oversee the contract growing and purchase of the remainder of the company's barley requirements, plus three seed production facilities that churn out seed stock for its contract farmers. BARI's three malt plants in Wisconsin, Minnesota, and Iowa produce 28 million bushels of malt each year—almost 40 percent of Anheuser-Busch's total requirements. BARI operates two rice mills—one in Jonesboro, Arkansas, and one in Woodland, California—that acquire and process about 375,000 tons of rice annually, a figure that still only accounts for 60 percent of Anheuser-Busch's rice usage. The company is actually the nation's single largest user of rice, consuming 15 percent of *all* domestic rice production.

Beyond that, BARI also funds an ambitious barley research program in Fort Collins, Colorado—in fact, it is the largest private breeder of barley in the U.S. The program's goal is to produce new barley varieties that, when malted, will not only conform to the taste profiles of Anheuser-Busch beers but also be trouble-free to grow, disease-resistant, and prolific. Such research is increasingly important, as Anheuser-Busch needs to feed the malt maws of its two overseas breweries, one in China and one in the United Kingdom, plus seven other foreign breweries where Bud and other products are brewed under license. And this is, after all, a company whose motto is "Budweiser: One World, One Beer," and that once a week flies in beer samples from each of its breweries to St. Louis. There, they must run a taste and aroma gauntlet of picky brewmasters, the pickiest of all being August Busch III, who personally samples each for consistency.

For beer purposes, only two kinds of barley matter: two-row and six-row. Two-row predominates; indeed, almost all European and U.S. brewers use two-row barley exclusively. The notable exceptions: Anheuser-Busch and SABMiller, which use two-row but also copious quantities of six-row barley malt. (The Anheuser-Busch explanation is that, in essence, two-row barley malt produces a smoother, sweeter-tasting beer; six-row a crisper, snappier flavor. Beer Geeks, though, tend to look down at six-row.) Barley research, meanwhile, isn't work for the impatient. "In barley," says Kloth, who joined Anheuser-Busch in 1970 after working as a private sector economist on the Russian grain deals of the previous decade, "you're always working fifteen to twenty years ahead. It takes twelve years to get a simple hybrid cross into production" and "we probably throw away 75 percent of what we test."

Kloth had explained this to me at an early morning breakfast meeting at a Best Western hotel in Bonners Ferry, Idaho, a pleasant town along the scenic meanders of the Kootenai River. We'd gathered there before jumping in SUVs for a twenty-six-mile drive north to the Elk Mountain Farm, which lies near the border town of Porthill, Idaho. In the production scheme of things, the farm, in operation since 1987, is relatively small potatoes—it only provides about 8 percent of Anheuser-Busch's hops needs—and it isn't BARI's only hops farm. It operates a second though smaller one in northern Germany near the town of Huell. But Elk Mountain's stunning location (on a latitude with northern Germany hops-growing regions) and its importance to BARI as a hops experimental station make it one of the jewels in the crown of the BARI empire.

Kloth, who had flown in from St. Louis on the A-B jet in the company of two publicists, had brought along to this meeting Blake Cooper, a Ph.D. plant geneticist who runs BARI's barley research operation in Fort Collins, and Gary J. Wittgenstein,

BARI's director of North American hops operations and manager of the Elk Mountain Farm. The breakfast talk soon turned to hops, but Kloth and Cooper wanted to make sure I understood how central the barley research mission is to Anheuser-Busch. I got the impression, when listening to the depth and passion with which barley was being discussed, that BARI barley people think, talk, and plot barley as much as the Swedes think, talk, and plot sex. It's far from an uninteresting topic, but I'd asked to tour the hops operation during harvest because (a) I was now out of the closet as a Hophead, and (b) if yeast is the mojo of beer and barley malt the soul, hops provide the sex appeal—the perfume, the spice, the heat. I also wanted a look inside the vaunted Anheuser-Busch quality-control machine.

* * *

Elk Mountain is, relatively speaking, a newcomer to the hops scene, and hops, relatively speaking, got to America rather late in beer history. As noted, the Dutch, Germans, and people of the Czech lands were putting hops in their beer by about the eleventh century, though there are records of the Romans introducing them into Britain as a vegetable, and of the Germans using them for medicinal purposes, well before then. Hops are native to North America and the temperate zones of northern Europe and West Central Asia, and they are grown in places as far-flung as Russia, Zimbabwe, Australia, and New Zealand. But they weren't cultivated in America for beer purposes until the early 1600s. Native Americans, however, knew the wild hop plant, *Humulus lupulus*, or wolf of the woods, as both a sedative and a toothache remedy. Of the hemp family, wild hops can still be found along America's temperate river bottoms; the hop's nearest relatives are the nettle, the elm, and, as I'd learned earlier, hemp or *Cannabis sativa*.

By one account, hop roots first came over on the third ship to return to the British Colony at Plymouth Rock, Massachusetts. The first recorded beer-hops garden in America was established in 1629 near the brew houses built by Dutch brewer Adrian Block. By 1648, hops were being grown in Virginia and continued to spread throughout the rest of the colonies. America's first big commercial hops venture was established in New York State in the early 1800s; by 1849, New York was the hops-growing capital of North America, producing more than a million pounds a year—and by 1920 almost 21 million pounds annually. But a blight called downy mildew (and a second called powdery mildew) all but destroyed New York's hops industry in the 1920s (it is just now beginning to make a small comeback), and hops cultivation began to migrate westward toward states with drier climates and reliable sources of irrigation. By 1950, it had largely shifted to California, Washington, Oregon, and Idaho.

As of this writing, the U.S. is the world's second-largest hops producer behind Germany (it actually has led world production in previous years but growers here started cutting back acreage in 2001 because of a worldwide glut). Of the some 36,000 acres of hops cultivated in America nowadays, virtually all are grown in Washington, Oregon, and Idaho, California's hops industry having also been decimated by the mildew scourge in the early 1990s. Hops growing is a small universe; there are only about seventy hops-farming operations in America, many of them family-run ventures. They produced about 58 million pounds of hops in 2006 with a value of about $119 million. By far the most productive region is Washington State's Yakima Valley, with about 77 percent of the total; Oregon was second with 15 percent, and Idaho third with about 8 percent.

The hop is a strangely delicate plant. Once rooted in the right soil under the right conditions, it grows like a weed and can, after being cut back in the winter, rebound and produce cones for up to ten years from the same planting. This is why hops are popular as ornamentals throughout the Northeast, upper Midwest, and Northwest. But the hop plant is picky about where it will take hold and flourish. It likes the loamy terrain of river bottoms, and for the most part it only grows between the 35th and 55th degrees of latitude. It requires long hours of daylight during the growing season but needs a cold, dormant period as well. And history has shown that because hops are so susceptible to the mildew scourges, they can't sustain themselves long-term in climates with even modestly rainy summers. That's why latitudes like the semiarid Yakima Valley and Boundary County, Idaho, with their sixteen-hour summer days, dry weather, and ready sources of irrigation that allow watering of the hops roots without getting the plants wet, have become America's new hops havens.

The other peculiarity of hops—or hops farms, at least—is that they are female bastions; the 1.6 million individual hops plants here at Elk Mountain are all female. In fact, when I asked, in ignorance, whether male plants were kept around the farm for breeding purposes, Don Kloth looked at me as if I'd pronounced Satan's name.

"The last thing you want is a male plant anywhere around here," he said.

The reason: males pollinate females. Pollinated females produce seeds in their cones. Brewers consider seeds worthless; they add bulk to hops while reducing production of lupulins— compounds that contain oils and resins that provide aroma and bite to beer. One male plant could potentially wreck an entire harvest by infesting a crop with worthless, seedy cones. Thus, male hops, if they are kept at all, are locked up securely in closed greenhouses. In fact, continental Europeans so fear the havoc they could bring to cultured hops that they have exterminated male plants in the wild.

Hop cones are actually flowers, and they begin to reach their peak at the end of July, giving growers a short window to harvest them before they become overripe and too fragile to pick. That's why the hops harvest is traditionally a manic effort carried out in three weeks between early August and early September. At Elk Mountain, for example, Gary Wittgenstein aims to get the entire crop in within twenty days or less, working three shifts round-the-clock, seven days a week.

There are probably 100 commercial varieties of hops world-wide though only half of those have wide commercial appeal. New varieties, based upon aggressive hops-breeding research being carried out mainly in the U.S. and Germany, are being invented all the time. As noted earlier, hops fall into two major categories: bittering hops and aroma or finishing hops (also known as noble hops). In the lager-saturated years before America's craft brewing revolution, bittering hops predominated. These days, aroma hops have made a strong comeback, thanks mostly to the demand of craft brewers. The hops grown at Elk Mountain are exclusively aroma hops—in this case Saaz and Hallertau, Saaz of Bohemian origin, Hallertau of German origin. Both are part of the Budweiser recipe though they aren't used in Michelob—all Michelob hops are imported.

* * *

It would be hard to get closer to a hops harvest than I am now, about eighteen feet off the ground in the open air cockpit of a hops combine, a hulking, lumbering, clattering beast moving along at about two miles an hour and towing a top-heavy hops carrier behind it. This machine, one of four like it on the Elk Mountain Farm, costs a quarter of a million dollars and is a BARI-customized hybrid of one type of mechanical harvester used in America's Pacific Northwest hops fields. Until the first mechanical picker came along in 1958, all hops were harvested by hand—a job that through the start of the twentieth century here and abroad was often left to women and children, who flocked into the fields by the thousands.

The combine's job is to cut the vines free from the top of their trellises and strip them of hop cones and leaves, which are then shuttled by conveyor into the hops carrier—a large truck cab saddled with a storage bin so big that it looks like some gigantic Tonka toy ready to tip over. Cones and leaves, once the carrier is full, take a short ride to a processing plant. The vines are passed through and chopped up into mulch that will eventually be returned to the fields. This is all done by an ingenious system of arms, cutters, strippers, and conveyor belts aboard the combine. There is a small amount of hand labor to this: one or two workers with machetes, and wearing chaps, walk ahead of the combine, cutting the vines free from the ground about three feet above the row. (Hops being perennials, this left-behind stalk gives the plants nourishment to feed on and thus a head start for the next year.)

The sensation of riding atop a combine is of being on a noisy amusement park ride with hop chaff flying everywhere and deep hop aromas saturating the air. I love the smell, but one drawback of hops work is that a small number of workers develop severe allergies, including chronic headaches, that prevent them from working anywhere near hops again. And for some reason, hop fields attract legions of stinkbugs, which are nuisances but not predators. Hops succumb to the aforementioned mildews, viruses, aphids, and mites, but neither birds nor animals eat them. I count about twenty stinkbugs up in the cockpit, but they don't raise a stink: the hop smells are too overpowering. The only tricky part to my four-minute ride is the requirement that I duck down every twenty-eight feet to avoid losing my head to the cables that support the field's wire grids. (It's not a hard thing to remember.)

Back on the ground, Gary Wittgenstein, who has run the farm since 1991, catches me up on where the harvest stands. It began on August 12; this is the eighth day, and Wittgenstein hopes to be done in another twelve days, barring some hiccups or an outright disaster. The hiccups usually involve mechanical failure of one or more of the combines or any of the other ninety-nine vehicles deployed to get the crop in. Disaster would be heavy rains that would bog down the combines and carriers in the fields. The Kootenai River runs right through this property, providing the farm's irrigation water, but rain can turn the farm's river bottom soils to mush. Rain, if too heavy, could even pull down trellises. By one estimate, a mere inch of rain falling on Elk Mountain's fully matured and cone-laden vines adds 100 tons of weight to the trellis system. The weather thus far, though, has been flawless.

It's clear that for Wittgenstein—a career Anheuser-Busch employee who worked his way up from office boy by going to accounting school at night—this isn't exactly a job but a calling, and the way he speaks about the farm, he might as well be talking about his own spread. Also a Midwesterner, he's a personable man with a self-deprecating sense of humor who shows flashes of disarming candor. When I ask him how long it takes to learn to drive one of the combines, he laughs and says, "Well, you pretty much learn to drive it in the first five minutes or we yank you right off of there. It's not rocket science—when you've driven through your first row, you're pretty much a pro. But you know how much these things cost. The real skill isn't in driving the machine but it's in the ear—the ability to tell right away from the sound of things that something's about to go wrong."

The farm operates year round, but in July before harvest starts, Elk Mountain runs with only a core of about twenty or thirty employees. That swells to 280 at harvest time, the bulk of them Mexican migrant workers who return year after year to harvest, clean, and process the crops, and then return again in the spring to begin rebuilding the rope trellises. The latter is a particularly labor-intensive and unique job, one usually passed on from generation to generation in migrant families. Called "twiners," these workers stand on tall wooden platforms that put them within arm's reach of the guide wires from which the trellises are strung. Lengths of rope lay at their feet. The platforms are pulled slowly by tractors and, with the tractor in constant motion—"we never stop," Wittgenstein tells me—the workers, with ropes in each hand, loop them over the wires, tie loop knots with half hitches pulled through them, and draw the ropes tight. An average twiner will tie about 13,000 knots a day; by the time all the trellises at Elk Mountain are restrung, they will have looped in place 13,000 *miles* of hemp rope.

"It's something to see," says Wittgenstein. "Every time they pull one rope tight they have to be ready to tie another one. And mind you, they do this one-handed. I can tie the knots but I have to use two hands. Some people can't do it at all. Some people can do it all day. It's really one of the great issues we face out here—in the future, will we be able to find people who can still do this?"

We leave the hops fields for a look at the processing plant, for a short while following one of the truck carriers as it bounces precariously across rows to deliver its load. "It looks like those things will tip over at any moment, but we've never had one do that," says Wittgenstein.

The first stop is a cleaning shed—like the Anheuser-Busch brewery in St. Louis, a model of clattering innovative machinery and impeccable order. Here leaves, stems, and cones are dumped onto a conveyor that, with the help of a series of screens, drums, and dribble belts, separates out the hop cones and eventually lets them drop onto yet another belt for a trip to a vast kiln. There they are raked level to a depth of about three feet.

The kiln is actually a series of large bins with vented floors through which gas-heated air is forced up through the hops. They are dried at an average temperature of 150 degrees F for about nine hours, a process that removes all but about 10 percent of their moisture, then sent to a cooling room for another twelve to twenty-four hours. They are then conveyed to a hydraulic baling device and pressed into rectangular 200-pound blocks, then sewn by workers using stitching machines into cloth bales that measure 20 x 30 x 55 inches. By this time, the cones have flaked into fluffy green-gold particles loosely resembling dried oregano (or marijuana). The bales are then shipped to Anheuser-Busch's breweries, where they are stored at 26 degrees F until they are used.

As we move on to other parts of the farm, Wittgenstein begins to tell me about his goals for this harvest. It looks like a good year; the farm in the past few years has produced somewhere between 1.8 million to 2 million pounds annually. Weather is the main ingredient; cool, 50-degree nights and 80-degree days are optimal, and that's been pretty much the story of the summer so far. Under those conditions, hop bines have been known to grow a foot, even two feet, a day. One barometer of progress is how far the vines have climbed up the trellises by the end of June. By that time they should be close to the top; in fact, "If they're not there by the Fourth of July, we're calling St. Louis and begging for forgiveness," Wittgenstein says.

This year, they made it with time to spare, so he's hoping the harvest will be on the two-million-pound side. But late rains could spoil things.

I ask him whether there's any way to predict the harvest by averaging the number of cones on a vine. He laughs and says, "we drive ourselves nuts every year trying to figure out how many cones are on a bine. We'll know that when they're in the bale."

We spend the rest of the morning looking at Elk Mountain innovations—a test plot of hops being nurtured by a new drip-irrigation system that promises to increase yields while cutting water use. But all along the way, Kloth and Wittgenstein are pointing out other things as well.

"See those clear cuts on the mountains?" Kloth tells me. "They're man-made to create huckleberry habitat to feed the grizzly bears."

Later, when I remark for about the fourth time on the beauty of the farm and its surroundings, Wittgenstein tells me that perhaps the farm's most powerful admirer is his ultimate boss, August Busch III, who comes out to visit at least twice a year. Anheuser-Busch, given its buying power, didn't *have* to be in the hops-farming business. "People say, 'Why do you farm hops?' Well, it's the romance and passion of the industry," says Wittgenstein.

I leave Idaho the next day in a rainstorm, finding myself worrying about those rain-soaked trellises and the extra 100 tons of weight they've taken on. But when I phone back later, I learn the rain was short and Wittgenstein's crews pushed on through it, finishing the harvest a day ahead of schedule.

And Gary Wittgenstein had bagged his two million pounds.

16

A Wrinkle in the Quest
Post-Delta Ruminations on the Beer Goddess Phenomenon

Who does not love beer, wine, women and song
remains a fool his whole life long.
—Carl Worner

Jackson, Miss.—As tempting as it was to stick to the Great River Road and meander through the Delta at the speed of the Mississippi, I'd found myself driving through the countryside in deep thought about the Beer Goddess and her ubiquitous and salutary role in beer retailing. Jeff at Ground Zero had put her into the Perfect Beer Joint mix, as had probably 75 percent of the other people (admittedly mostly males) that I'd posed my Perfect Beer Joint question to. The Grassers back in St. Louis had merely reconfirmed it with their adoring description of Pam at Gladstone's. And then there was Maria back at Paul's in Dubuque.

Having seen the phenomenon in full bloom along the River of Beer, I wondered if I was missing some larger point?

Then it struck me. America being the entrepreneurial hot-house that it is, the phenomenon hadn't simply become spontaneously institutionalized—it had been made into a franchise and applied to high corporate purpose.

So I diverted from the Delta and headed east to a place where it might be possible to see real live modern Beer Goddesses in orchestrated action. I was almost certain, based upon a previous drive through, that I could find, tucked just off the interstate in Jackson, a Hooters restaurant.

My previous Hooters exposure had been limited to a brief visit some years before to a Hooters in Baton Rouge, Louisiana, where on assignment to write a piece about zydeco music I'd killed time drinking a beer while waiting for an interview. Though it was impossible to miss the assemblage of Beer Goddesses back then, I simply hadn't much thought about it. But I realized now—of course—that Hooters was at its heart a beer joint franchise that had made the Beer Goddess the stylized centerpiece of its business plan.

Now, my ruminations on the Beer Goddess are not meant to denigrate the iconic role of the wise and understanding barman in beer joint lore. The Coach and Sam at Cheer's are still important in the beer-joint retailing world. But let's face it: with 84 percent of all beer in the U.S. consumed by men, the basic concept of using women to successfully sell the stuff is pretty solid. I'm also not suggesting that the association of beer and winsome women is anything new. Those beer-loving Sumerians trained women as servers for their taverns, and as noted earlier, beer making and beer selling were largely the province of women through the Middle Ages. For centuries in the West, the prototype of the modern Beer Goddess was known as the barmaid (a term now considered by many to be not just antiquated but sexist). One of her first appearances in literature comes in 1390 in Chaucer's *Canterbury Tales,* when, in a modern rendering of the passage, the Miller describes a randy cleric:

> *There wasn't a beer house or tavern in the whole town*
> *that he didn't visit with his entertainment,*
> *if there was any good-looking barmaid there.*

Prototypical Beer Goddesses also populate Shakespeare's plays, Manet's paintings, and the literature of James Joyce, among many others. And consider this description from a London collection of Victorian essays that sought to capture the lives of those in popular professions of the day. This one was titled "The Barmaid" and, for all its Victorian floridity, lays out very contemporary-sounding insights into the Beer Goddess oeuvre:

> Like the moon she never shines with full lustre till night; then she comes out in all the fascinations of satin and small talk—bestowing, with perfect impartiality, a smile upon one admirer, a tender glance upon another, and a kind word or two upon a third; leaving each in the happy belief that he is himself the fortunate individual upon whom she has secretly bestowed her affections. She carries on a flirtation…and even permits a gentle pressure of the hand when giving you change out of your sovereign. But all this is selon son métier—a mere matter of business with which the heart has nothing to do.

Of course, employment of the Beer Goddess isn't confined to the bar. Beer companies since the dawn of beer advertising have used attractive and often buxom women in ads and commercials. Germanic-looking blondes predominated Art Nouveau beer poster advertisements in the 1890s. In 1935, Blatz Beer, another large beer company felled in the Lager Wars, was still giving away colorful promotional statues of a zaftig blond barmaid kicking up her heels, showing a lot of leg, and toting four frothy pints of Blatz.

In the 1950s, Carling Brewing Co. rolled out one of the most successful advertising campaigns in history with its "Hey, Mabel,

Black Label!" commercials for its Black Label lager. Mabel was a wholesome but sexy blond beer slinger who knew how to make men feel good but didn't threaten women. The spots, and a print campaign, with Mabel played by a succession of comely models, lasted an incredible fifteen years and made Carling, originally a London brewer, a top ten American brewer by 1960. (Carling plummeted downhill in the 1970s. Pabst owns the Black Label rights in America; meanwhile, Coors in 2003 bought Carling Brands' thriving overseas operations from the Belgian brewer Interbrew for $1.7 billion.) Anheuser-Busch's spots of a few years ago featuring the farcical Swedish Bikini Team are but one more contemporary example of the Beer Goddess in advertising, as are the current Miller "catfighting women" commercials in which upwardly nubile young women in bikinis plunge into a swimming pool to fight it out over whether Miller Lite tastes great or is less filling. Still, on the retail front, it seemed to me that Hooters had taken the commercialization of the Beer Goddess to a new high (or low) art, depending on your sensibilities.

I drove into Jackson around the lunch hour, and yes, my memory had served me well, for there was a billboard telling me that Hooters lay just off Exit 100. I took it and spotted the restaurant with its classical diner look and its famous hoot-owl logo—an owl whose huge orange eyes and dilated purple pupils could easily be mistaken for female breasts. This is possible for two reasons: one, "hooters" is indeed both a term for hoot owls and a crude synonym for breasts. The other reason this could be intended is the Hooters credo, which appears on its menus: "Delightfully tacky yet unrefined."

I also had a journalist's working knowledge of Hooters because it had been in the news for about four years running back in the 1990s, when the federal Equal Employment Opportunity Commission first investigated, then sued, the Atlanta-based chain for sex discrimination because it refused to hire men waiters at a Chicago Hooters. Hooters fought back, taking out billboard ads with a large mustachioed guy in a Hooters waitress outfit—owl-emblazoned tank top, orange short-shorts, and flesh-colored stockings—and a caption that said "Washington, Get a Grip!" The EEOC complaint eventually caused so much hooting in the press—one editorial wag suggested that if Hooters fell, men would soon be dancing in the line with the Radio City Music Hall Rockettes—that the red-faced feds dropped the whole thing in 1996. Hooters still gets pilloried about once a year, usually by the National Organization for Women, on the grounds that its uniform and entire concept are demeaning. This is usually rejoined by at least one Hooters Girl (which is what all 15,000 of them nationwide are called) telling some reporter someplace that NOW ought to mind its business, that she adores being a Hooters Girl, and that she can decide for herself whether she is being demeaned. You have to admit it's one of the odder corners of the Culture Wars.

I decided I'd inquire further into the Hooters business model later but for now just wanted to see a Hooters in action. This one was busy, and I declined a table, opting instead for a central counter where there were a few empty stools and a good overview of the place. I sat down and a waitress came forward, bringing a smile and a menu. She leaned forward, put an elbow on the counter, looked deeply into my eyes, and said, "Hello, my name is Selena, and I'll be your girl today."

I looked at Selena and I smiled, too. For though I knew she was just another cog in the Hooters Beer Goddess machinery, it was hard not to appreciate her. She was a tall, statuesque African-American woman in her early twenties with limpid eyes, olive skin, and perfect teeth. She exuded good cheer and good health. And as a bonus she was going to be my girl, which as a professional scribe I knew meant that she was actually going to be my *Girl*. For as I looked around, some of the other seven or eight Hooters Girls working tables were greeting guys (who were 95 percent of the customers) and announcing that they would be their Girls, too. Everybody at Hooters got a smiling and attentive Girl dressed as though she were just heading for the gym for a bout of sweaty aerobics (though Hooters describes the get-ups as cheerleading uniforms).

Now, on one level this seemed like silly, mildly naughty Disneyland shtick. And let's face it: Hooters doesn't fare as well in certain jaded big-city environments where women who frequent bars often dress more provocatively than do Hooters Girls and where the Hooters concept is often considered hopelessly corny. But as a seasoned and somewhat jaded traveler who had been abused by grumpy or aloof help in places a lot fancier than this, I could also see that it was shtick that many travelers and restaurant-goers—well, male travelers and restaurant-goers, at least—might very well appreciate.

I was soon joined at the counter by Billy Nix, an off-duty Greenwood, Mississippi, police officer, who introduced himself when he sat down. Selena announced that she would be his Girl, too, and Nix, who looked to be in his early thirties, seemed as gratified with this development as I had been. As Selena went off to fetch coffee for Nix, he told me that he was delighted by the presence of Hooters in Jackson and tended to drop by whenever he was in town. "It's good clean fun and good service," he said.

Selena came back to take our orders, then went off to wait on other customers. I tried to snatch micro interviews with her as she moved in and out of our orbit while Nix regaled me with stories of his work, which had been made all the more interesting by a crack epidemic that he said had swept lots of small and middling-sized towns in Mississippi.

In between all that, I was able to get the basics from Selena. She told me that Hooters afforded her great tips and flexible hours, and that the people who ran the place were nice, as were her sister Hooters Girls. I asked her what she considered the most important qualification for becoming a Hooters Girl.

"Personality," she said, not missing a beat. Seeing my skepticism, she laughed and said, "No, I mean it. It's important. They're looking for girls who know how to get along with people and to put their customers first. You can't be uptight or grumpy and expect to work here."

But surely, I pressed, there were other qualifications?

"Well, to be hired you have to be able to do the Hula Hoop," she said.

This one stopped me: the Hula Hoop?

"Yes, because now and then we're required to do the Hula Hoop for our customers," she said.

Now, at that moment it was hard not to conjure up Selena, at her Hooters job interview or in the middle of the restaurant, doing the Hula Hoop, and let us be candid enough to admit that it was not an unpleasant image. But as a *Wall Street Journal* editor, I've actually sat in on a few job interviews myself and I was trying to think of any scenario in which I could appropriately ask a woman applicant if she Hula Hooped, much less if she would perform it for me. But I admit that the comparison isn't exactly apples-to-apples, and anyway, I wasn't going to call NOW over this if Selena wasn't.

However, I did find an interesting account by some real-world NOW operatives who had infiltrated a Hooters in Rochester, New York, and filed a report for a 1995 newsletter of the Rochester NOW/WAVE (Women Against a Violent Environment) chapter. After discovering that the Hooters menu was making light of the double entendre that was its name, the two NOW sleuths turned to what they considered sexist sloganeering on the walls before observing some Hula Hooping:

We read them [the slogans] off: "Caution: Blondes Thinking; Hooters Waitresses are Flattery Operated." And there was another one that showed the outline of two breasts, shaped to look like a road caution sign that said "Bumps."

Although we were sure everyone had realized we were feminists who had come to scope the place out, it was soon apparent that no one—except our waitress—was paying any attention to us. All the male customers were like out of *The Exorcist*, with their heads spinning around at 360 degrees.... The only other thing that could be causing them to crane their necks like this had to be the Hooters Girls. In their bright orange short-shorts and halter tops, they were hard to miss.

These men were also watching a curious phenomenon taking place at the entrance to the restaurant. Some of the Hooters Girls were gyrating with Hula Hoops as the onlookers did their onlooking.... We had a good laugh about how all of us—college professors, librarians, neurosurgeons—should be required to Hula Hoop on the job.

Now, I have to say that I did not observe during my Hooters lunch-hour interval any actual Hula Hooping, nor heads spinning round 360 degrees. But did the male customers sometimes look admiringly at the Hooters Girls? You bet. Is that leering or ogling? And if it is, is it harmful? Well, the average male Hooters customer would likely say that men and women have looked at each other admiringly, often harboring pleasant and harmless fantasies, since the dawn of creation. Our feminist sisters see it as appalling when it grows out of a work environment in which women, in their view, are "objectified."

I did ask Selena before I left whether she ever felt harassed by her customers. She said she didn't and that the vast majority of men who came in here understood the rules. She didn't articulate the rules this way but it occurred to me that the Hooters tableau was essentially a live beer commercial in which the customers played a part and were expected to behave as if they were in Cheers, not in some strip joint where you stuck dollar bills in G-strings.

* * *

I later phoned up the Hooters headquarters in Atlanta to get the corporate skinny, talking with Mike McNeil, vice president of marketing. He laid out the bare-bones history: the first Hooters opened as a beach bar in Clearwater, Florida, in 1983, with six transplanted Midwesterners chipping in the $140,000 of start-up capital. Twenty years later, Hooters had expanded to about 350 locations in forty-three states and a dozen foreign locales and was the fastest growing restaurant-bar chain in the nation. It thinks 1,000 restaurants might be possible one day—a projection sure to send shivers up NOW's spine.

Annual revenues had grown to about $750 million a year, and beer sales constituted about 26 percent of that. All Hooters are required to sell Bud, Bud Light, and Miller Lite and then can mix in a few other brews depending upon local preferences. But Hooters is both Budweiser's and Miller's largest collective on-premises account in the U.S., McNeil told me.

The concern is closely held, with the company itself owning about 120 franchises and private investors the rest. It has since expanded into stock car and powerboat racing, a golf tournament, and magazine publishing; in 2003 Hooters started a four-plane commercial airline with Hooters Girls serving as flight attendants. The airline lasted a scant few years but generated enormous publicity for the company.

McNeil told me that Hooters represented the wry, blue-collar, middle-class vision of its six original founders—two painting contractors, a brick mason, a retired service station owner, a liquor salesman, and a real estate broker. They would never claim they invented the connection between beer sales and pretty women; only that they'd noticed that, even in bad financial times, the place that did well was usually the "local roadhouse that had pretty good food, and working behind the bar, was the good-looking daughter or wife of the owner. But we've taken the whole concept to the next level." Hooters, besides dishing up mildly spicy chicken wings, simple seafood, and sandwiches, also considers itself a sports bar, with the requisite wide-screen TVs and sports paraphernalia about. Throwing sports into this mix is pretty much a no-brainer. Finding a good number on the connection of overall beer sales to sports is difficult, since no one tracks things like, for example, beer consumption by recreational weekend warriors. But consider one barometer: beer sales at the nation's ninety-six major league sporting venues, plus horse-racing tracks, accounts for the bulk of the estimated $8 to $9 billion that consumers spend on beer at stand-alone venues and concessions each year. Also consider that 70 percent of Hooters' customers are sports-loving males between the ages of twenty-five and fifty-four.

The Hooters people also say they wish Hooters detractors would pay some attention to the Hooters sense of humor. True, in 1986 it launched the annual Hooters calendar, a glossy, four-color flip album of cheesecake, featuring Hooters Girls in skimpy bikinis. But the months were out of order, and there was a joke on every page, even if many of them were corny Midwestern jokes about people from Iowa or tasteless ones about Tammy Faye Bakker. (Example: "It's not just Jimmy I'm depressed about. Last night, a Peeping Tom threw up on my window.")

On Hooters' official Web site, you can watch a video claiming to be an inside look at Hooters Girls Bootcamp. The whole thing is a parody of its bimbo image: in one scene, a stern drill sergeant stands at a blackboard pointing at chalk drawings of a mug of beer and a chicken wing while Hooters Girls, brows knitted in great seriousness, take notes. McNeil directed me to the company's website to get the official riposte to its feminist critics. It is unabashedly unapologetic:

> Claims that Hooters exploits attractive women are as ridiculous as saying the NFL exploits men who are big and fast. Hooters Girls have the same right to use their natural female sex appeal to earn a living as do super models Cindy Crawford and Naomi Campbell. To Hooters, the women's rights movement is important because it guarantees women have the right to choose their own careers, be it a Supreme Court Justice or Hooters Girl.

Beyond that, McNeil took pains to note that being a Hooters Girl isn't necessarily a dead-end job: Kimberly Rivera, who started as a Hooters waitress, is now the company's vice president of training and human resources. "People have tried to copy us," McNeil said, "but it's one thing to sell the sizzle, it's another to deliver the steak."

* * *

It was only sometime after I talked to McNeil that I learned two things: other people were indeed building franchises based upon the Beer Goddess model, and Hooters itself was, well, sizzling about it. In early 2003, the company sued one rival in U.S. District Court in Orlando for "unfair competition and trade dress infringement."

One interpretation of its claim is that it held a trademark on the Beer Goddess.

"That's it in a nutshell," Crawford Ker, founder and CEO of the sued rival firm, Ker's WingHouse Bar and Grill, told me over the phone when I called him to ask about the suit. "It's ridiculous."

I discovered the lawsuit while trolling a public relations wire service for Hooters press releases. I spotted a release by Ker instead in which he said his company had filed a motion to dismiss the Hooters suit while accusing Hooters of trying to "stifle fair competition in the marketplace" and "maliciously" trying to stomp out his company.

Ker is a former Dallas Cowboys lineman who opened his first WingHouse in Clearwater in 1994 only six miles away from the original Hooters. He said it was his view that Hooters didn't care so much until the company realized that Ker's had grown rapidly to twelve locales—all situated in Hooters territories—and was beginning to rack up big revenues. It had sales of about $19 million in 2003—a drop in the bucket to Hooter's $750 million but extraordinary growth for a company only nine years old.

I went to Ker's website and certainly saw Hooters similarities: Ker's dresses its waitresses in black tank tops, black short-shorts, and flesh-colored stockings not terribly dissimilar to the

Hooters Girl look. His restaurants serve chicken wings and the kind of generic bar food that Hooters serves. But Ker said that his places are much more sports-bar oriented than are Hooters restaurants, with some of them having as many as thirty TV screens. And anyway, in his view, under the Hooters analogy, *Playboy* magazine, by example, could have sued to keep all other competitors out of the market. "Hooters doesn't have a monopoly on attractive women or 'sex appeal,' as they claim in their complaint," Ker said. "Trademark laws protect against unfair competition but not all competition."

I got a copy of the suit that Hooters had filed, and it did in fact say that "the Hooters Girls add an element of female sex appeal that is prevalent in the Hooters restaurants and is *unique* [my emphasis] in the industry." I phoned Hooters, tempted to ask whether this didn't seem like a tempest in a C-cup, but...of course I didn't. And McNeil told me that the real issue wasn't just the Beer Goddess but what Hooters considered the Wing-House's copying of its "decor and atmosphere." In the end, the courts would have none of this and, in June 2006, dismissed Hooters' suit and awarded Ker $1.2 million in legal fees.

Meanwhile, I was left with a final bit of wisdom that I'd gotten from Selena at the Hooters in Jackson. She told me she was glad Hooters only served beer and not hard liquor.

"Otherwise," she said, "who knows what would happen."

The Final Diversion
At Last, Beervana

The greatest stylistic variety of beer available in any country is today to be found in the United States.
—Michael Jackson, The Beer Hunter

Portland, Ore.—How to describe Mary's Club?

A neon sign marks the entrance at the faded end of a downtown block that has no dearth of panhandlers. Inside, it is dark, loud, and cramped, tables scrunched together like a poorly put-together jigsaw puzzle. The air is stale. It is a place, by proclivity and location, clearly perched on the edge between sleaze and camp.

And yet: Beer Geeks would be thrilled to find a wide selection of microbrews at this downtown hotspot. Widmer Hefeweizen is on tap; McMenamins Pale Ale is, too. There are offerings from New Belgium, Full Sail, Deschutes, and Sierra Nevada, among others. In fact, 70 percent of all beer here is craft beer, though you can find Coors, Bud Light, and the anti-globalization crowd's ironical favorite, Pabst Blue Ribbon, on tap.

I ask one Mary's Club entertainer/server about *her* favorite. She has just come from the stage, where she has been dancing (among other maneuvers) to loud salsa music, wearing at the end of her act no more than a smile. She is wearing just slightly more than that now, and her smile has given way to a thoughtful pursing of her lips as she seriously contemplates my question.

"I have to say, I love the Widmer Hefe, but I'm also a big Fat Tire fan," she says.

I ask her what the club sells the most of. She replies, "I'm not sure, really, but I know what we probably sell the least of—Bud Light."

It's not every town where the strippers qualify as Beer Geeks, or where strip clubs are on the front line of the craft brew revolution, or where the patrons of strip clubs seem to be mostly twenty-something *couples* who think the combination of sleaze and craft brew is a swell way to spend an evening.

But then, there's only one Portland—Beervana, to the locals.

This hilly, handsome Pacific Northwest town of about 540,000 is the laid-back nexus of a greater metropolitan area of about 1.5 million people. Sun-drenched in summer, often drizzly and drab by winter, it is hemmed in by vast forests, beribboned by the Willamette and Columbia rivers, and accentuated on its eastern skyline by the snowcapped peak of Mount Hood, a dormant volcano draped with eleven gleaming glaciers. People here seem always to be hiking, biking, jogging, skiing, climbing, windsurfing, and kayaking. Yes, you can find Republicans here, and the usual assemblage of rich and powerful chamber of commerce types. But many Portlanders indulge in progressive politics leaning toward the libertarian side; they think it not the least bit peculiar that there is an anarchist saloon in town, even if anarchism and capitalistic beer retailing wouldn't outwardly seem to be a good mix. Imagine San Francisco's monochrome liberalism cut with a laissez-faire attitude toward life and a slightly cranky edge to its politics. That's Portland.

But what Portlanders are mostly about and interested in is beer—and not "industrial beer," as mass-produced lager is called hereabouts. While craft beer sales account for about 5 percent of all beer consumed in America, in Portland's city limits, craft beer represents 40 percent to 50 percent of the beer sold—a staggering statistical anomaly. In fact, by dint of the density of breweries to population and the beer styles made, Portland can stake a strong claim to being not just the contemporary Beer Capital of America but also the Beer Capital of the World. There are seventy-one microbreweries or brewpubs in Oregon, and twenty-six of them are in the Portland city limits. Milwaukee, the former brewing capital of America, has one remaining big brewery, the SABMiller plant, and about a half-dozen brewpubs. Munich has a half-dozen breweries; Cologne, the other world brewing power, has ten or eleven. All produce many more barrels of beer than does Portland, but they basically make one beer style: lager. Portland's last big lager maker, the Blitz-Weinhard Brewery, went belly-up in 1999, its Henry Weinhard label sold off to SABMiller. Except for the 280 people who lost their jobs, nobody much misses it.

Oh, and yes. There are brewery-hotels here, and it's hard to find a movie house that *doesn't* serve craft brew with the popcorn.

"Portland *was* a lager town, say twenty-five years ago, but now it's a town where as far as beer goes, anything goes. Oregonians in general have a pioneering spirit. We aren't afraid to try all kinds of new beers and our brewers aren't afraid of making every kind of beer possible. Of course, we have the best-educated beer population of any place in America."

I've come, toward the end of my beer travels, seeking the deeper meaning of Beervana, a place that, everywhere I went along the River of Beer, was spoken of as a kind of beer Shangri-la. The speaker trying to elucidate it for me now is Jim Parker, a onetime journalist who, until 1992, wrote about beer, then changed jobs and "moved two and a half feet, to the other side of the bar" and opened a brewpub. He's since worked in breweries and for the American Homebrewers Association. For the past four years, he has been director of the Oregon Brewers Guild, a trade group founded in 1992. The guild represents forty-six Oregon craft brewers, twenty-six suppliers like hops growers and malt makers, and a gaggle of "enthusiast" members known as SNOBs (Supporters of Native Oregon Beers). You see their bumper stickers all over Portland.

Parker is standing under the Brewers Guild tent on a virtually perfect day: a warm, cloudless, deeply blue-skied Friday on the grounds of Tom McCall Waterfront Park, a flat swath of green space flanked by a macadamized bike path that separates the park from the Willamette River. Beer donuts (made with beer-infused batter) are frying in the background. There are hops people about, offering hops candy (and, surreptitiously, home-distilled hops liqueur to a chosen few, I being one of them). The setting is the July 2003 sixteenth annual Oregon Brewers Festival, which the Brewers Guild lends a hand in organizing but whose major driving force is a scrum of energetic volunteer Beer Geeks known as the Oregon Brew Crew. Before it's over, the festival will draw about 80,000 people over three days, and they will drink up almost the entire barrelage of the seventy-two beer makers, most of them from Western states, who have been invited to contribute a single favorite beer here. Twenty other beers, made by in-state brewers, are being dispensed from the Brewers Guild tent.

There are bigger beer festivals elsewhere but none quite as dedicated as this one to the range of beer styles—about twenty-five in all (with multiple, exotic interpretations of each style) are represented among the ninety-two beers that can be sampled. If you've never had an Uzbeki raga ale, a ginseng porter, or a watermelon wheat beer, here's your chance. (Oh, and though this isn't a lager town, there's a rare black lager, called an imperial *Schwarz bier*, on the festival style list. Even Beer Geeks will stoop to lager so long as it's geeked-up lager.)

A more consumer-friendly event you can't find. Entry is free; $3 buys you an official Oregon Brewers Festival plastic mug with a notch one-third up the side. A $3 token gets your mug filled but a $1 token buys you a sample of any beer up to the notch. That makes it easy to sample lots and lots of beers, especially over three days. Some Beer Geeks will go for all ninety-two beers offered, a tricky thing requiring not just artful pacing, but also determining which beers might sell out before the festival ends and getting to them first.

All the beer is draft, and legions of volunteers man the pumps to keep the lines flowing briskly. The kegs are kept in bins fronting a series of huge, open, billowing white tents that provide shade while queuing up and picnic tables for sitting down. You can also take your beer out and sit on the grass and sip it with a view of both the river and Mount Hood. Or, if you're the slightest bit warm, you can take your beer and walk through a mist garden set up at the northern end of the festival grounds.

Too much to drink? No worries. There are squadrons of Alcohol Monitors, staffed by volunteers as friendly as golden retrievers, who will find you a cab or a nice place in the shade to recover your dignity. I saw two guys (the craft-beer-loving homeless, I'm guessing) who seemed to be in a race to see who could get plowed first. The Alcohol Monitors corralled them and politely sent them to the bratwurst stand to get a little something in their stomachs before allowing them to take another sip of beer. (So indignant were they of this deferential treatment that they stalked off; I later saw them drinking Bud Light at a saloon down the street.)

That's the backdrop. To complete the image, imagine thousands of Beer Geeks milling about in the bliss of expectation, as though they had just gained the gates of Paradise. People in line are saying things like "an organic IPA at 75 IBUs? Dude, I've gotta go for that!" A woman sports a T-shirt that says, "Make Beer, Not War." So much beer has been spilled on the lawn and trampled into the turf that the ground exudes a kind of Earth-Mother-Beer aroma. It's strangely *pleasant*. There are bands playing on bandstands and guys walking through the crowds, guitar amplifiers and drum kits strapped to their personages, wailing away at the blues or some interesting interpretation of World Music. Yes, you can get bratwurst with your beer, but there are also gourmet food stands cooking macrobiotic Mexican tortillas and the like.

And get this: about half of the Beer Geeks here are women, another staggering statistical anomaly given that, nationwide, women are only 16 percent of the beer customer base.

Every moment seems to be nirvana in Beervana.

Jim Parker speaks again to remind me, however, that Beervana isn't possible without some dynamic tension. "Here's the deal," he says. "If you don't brew good beer in Oregon, you don't last long. It's Beer Darwinism—survival of the tastiest."

I'm going around gathering other opinions on this matter before tackling a serious job: there will be a beer tasting for the media. The program says we will sample twenty beers and not just any old beers. About half of them would easily fit under the definition of Extreme Beer. We'll have an hour to do it in.

I run into John Forbes, a former marketing man at Bridge-Port Brewing Co., a Portland mainstay and the state's oldest craft brewery. In bicycle clothes, Forbes, a festival regular and onetime festival organizer, has cycled in from the surrounding hills and will soon cycle out again. He says Portland's portal to Beervana is as much a matter of geography as it is of attitude. "We live in an area where we grow a lot of the raw ingredients for good beer—lots of hops and lots of barley. Great Western Malting Co. is just across the river here [in Vancouver, Washington]. Wyeast [the yeast lab] is right here in Oregon, too. And we have really good water." He offers a couple more reasons. First, Portland is an extremely young town demographically, and young people tend to be more experimental with things like beer choice. And second, "There are a lot of cheapskates here. Years ago, since the national beer wasn't any good, people said, 'Hell, we'll make our own.' So homebrewing caught on in a big way, and craft beer always follows."

I run all these theories by Tom Dalldorf, editor and publisher of *Celebrator Beer News*, who is manning a *Celebrator* information desk at the festival. The California-based publication calls itself a "national bimonthly brewspaper." Dalldorf, a cheerful, bearded man who gravitated to beer journalism after starting in the wine import business, says Portland's craft beer anomalies have a lot to do with a kind of positive parochialism. "The beer scene here is very sociable and people here support their own.... One stat I can tell you for certain: Widmer [headquartered in Portland] has more beer taps in the city than does Anheuser-Busch. I've never heard of a craft brewer anywhere else doing that in a city the size of Portland." (Of course, careful readers will recall that those shrewd people at A-B have a minority stake in Widmer.)

Dalldorf says the long existence of a high-quality wine industry in Oregon clearly paved the way for the craft brew movement here. Portland's earliest microbrewery was founded in 1980 by a vintner; the brewery didn't last but the enthusiasm Portlanders showed for homegrown beer was unmistakable. In 1984, two more vintners, Dick and Nancy Ponzi, launched BridgePort, which thrives today (in 1995 the Ponzis sold BridgePort to the Gambrinus Co., San Antonio, Texas, one of the nation's top beer import concerns).

In 1985, Dalldorf adds, the Oregon legislature adopted one of the nation's first laws enabling brewpubs, under the argument that serving beer on the premises of a brewery wasn't any different than vineyards serving wine to consumers in tasting rooms. Small brewers got another lift in 1999 when the legislature passed a bill allowing those who made 500 barrels of beer or less per year—in essence brewpubs—to distribute their own beer, bypassing wholesalers, who often gave scant place on their trucks to the beers of small breweries. (The 500-barrel limit has recently been raised to 1,000.) It hasn't hurt either, says Dalldorf, that Oregon's beer excise taxes are relatively low (though there was an effort, beat back at the last minute, to raise them in 2003; in fact, the anti-tax people were out in force at the festival).

Roaming the festival is the ubiquitous Fred Eckhardt—it's his hometown after all. He's such a Portland craft beer fixture and hero that Hair of the Dog Brewing Co. in town has named its ultra-strong bottle-conditioned ale (11 percent ABV) Fred. Eckhardt, when I catch up with him, has just come off a sermon inveighing against the neo-prohibitionists, specifically religionists who not only are teetotalers themselves but would make everybody else so.

"What's wrong with these people?" he asks. "Don't they know that Martin Luther himself was 'fortified' when he pinned his theses to the church house door? He wasn't 'fortified' on water, I can tell you that." (It's a pretty safe bet that Luther, a good German, was a beer drinker.)

Eckhardt stops to gather a little more steam, then says, "A big part of our problem in society is that we've developed a just-say-no-to-*everything* policy....In the old days, young people learned to drink responsibly by drinking with their elders. Now, they can't do that anymore....If you give an eighteen-year-old an IPA, he'll probably take a sip and spit it out. But if he drinks in the company of his elders, he would learn something about it, and he might eventually come to appreciate it."

Eckhardt then seamlessly switches to the subject at hand: whither Portland's distinctive position in the beer universe. "Portland people understand what beer is and what beer isn't," he tells me. "They know it's not yellow industrial pre-piss....It's not just something you go and get drunk on on Saturday night....Beer is seasonal....It can be strong, dark, roasty, light....There are fifty to one hundred ways of brewing it."

Eckhardt thinks beer's complexities are what make it attractive to Portlanders and Oregonians in general, who perhaps lead the rest of the U.S. in beer knowledge. He credits this to the fact that most of the early beer writers like himself hailed from out West, where the craft beer revolution began, and where craft beer still probably gets more press exposure than in other regions. "An educated clientele is a big part of it, honestly.... Every time you get an article in the newspaper it helps. Look what the wine writers have done: they've educated people about wine. When the newspapers everywhere start paying as much attention to good beer as they do good wine, we'll sell a lot more good beer everywhere."

Portland, Eckhardt wants to point out, may be wildly anomalous, but it's hardly the only craft brew haven. The greater Seattle area, Colorado, Northern California, Vermont, and upstate New York all show promise of how it might be possible to end the lager domination of American beer, he says.

Later I talk to Lisa Morrison, another beer journalist who writes a column under the pseudonym the Beer Goddess. She moved to the city with her husband about fifteen years ago after visiting on vacation and falling in love with the place. She's of the opinion that Portland has somehow gained so much critical craft beer mass that nowadays beer passion is passed on by osmosis. "If you've lived in Portland more than two years and you don't know anything about craft beer, you're not listening. *Everybody* in Portland knows what an IPA is. You can sit down at a table in the company of strangers and you can start talking about IBUs and *everybody* knows what you're talking about."

* * *

I find myself in a scrum of ostensible Beer Geeks—the beer press—but everybody in this scrum doesn't necessarily know an IBU from an IPA. One or two people don't seem to know anything. We've gathered for the start of the aforementioned press tour and the twenty beers that await our sampling. Behind me is a man who's asked, more than once: "All these breweries, surely they're not independent? Who owns them all? Anheuser-Busch?"

Later somebody will ask, apropos of nothing: "Are there hops in Budweiser?" (And, no, this was not a facetious Beer Geek asking the question.)

It takes me awhile to realize that there are posers in the bunch—not that anybody cares. They won't be the first people ever trying to scam free beer. It's an otherwise legitimate gathering of beer scribes; two have come all the way from Germany, one from Britain, most of the rest from the Pacific Northwest.

Pretty soon our Official Beer Geek shows up. He's a smiling, mildly earnest man named Noel Blake, a festival volunteer. We know he's our Official Beer Geek because, shuffling through the press handouts we got earlier, we see he's the author of a two-page handout titled "Beer Geek Speak."

Examples:

"First, the two most used words: malty and hoppy."

"Hoppy refers to the contribution of (surprise!) hops!"

"Another frequent taste word is estery.... Fruity is the most common ester that people notice."

"OG, or Original Gravity, tells you how much malt sugar the beer started with.... The higher this number, the stronger the finished beer will be.... FG, or Final Gravity, tells you how thick the beer you drink is."

To really get down and geeky, Blake recommends we "compare the IBUs to the OG and FG. Chop the 1.0 off the OG rating and compare what's left to the IBU."

(Warning: Don't try this sober.)

There are twenty or twenty-five people assembled. We've all been issued official mugs. Blake gathers us around him and lays out the beer plan. We'll start with lighter beers first, then segue into the really heavy ones; first stop will be a beer called Hogwart's Kölsch. "If you find you're reaching your limit, just hold your mug down so they won't pour anything into it. But you really should try a little of all of them."

Behind me somebody says, "Don't worry about *that*, Noel."

We reach the Kölsch tap and everyone gets a pretty good squirt of it. I do the math based upon what seems like a reasonable estimate of what was poured in each mug—about three ounces. So: 20 beers x 3 ounces = 60 ounces of beer. That's five-sixths of a six-pack. And a few people, I notice, are taking whole mugfuls.

It's a little after 11:00 A.M.

The Hogwart's is made by the Port Halling Brewing Co.* of Gresham, Oregon. I sniff, sip, and scribble a note—"tasty." I'm not, I realize, improving in my beer vocabulary. Blake informs us that "This beer goes back 500 years.... The brewer is a fanatic about using herbs and spices in beer.... This is very healthy beer" because it's full of things like "lavender, grains of paradise, marsh rosemary, chamomile, and mugwort."

"What are we tasting here, Noel?" somebody asks. "The mugwort?"

Blake says he thinks it's the lavender that's coming through.

"What's mugwort taste like anyway?" somebody else asks.

Blake doesn't hear this question. Nobody else has an answer.

We blast through a Belgian ale and a couple of Belgian wit beers, which are beers made with unmalted wheat and, in one case, coriander, orange peel, and spices. ("The orange peel gives you a taste in the back of your mouth," Blake tells us.) I've sampled wit beers before and have decided they are an acquired taste. Both of these make me pucker. At least I'm not alone because somebody asks, "Is this a sour beer?"

Blake says, "Well, it's not like a red ale. The Belgian reds are very sour."

Our fifth beer turns out to be geeked-up lager called Hopfen-kopf—a made-up word that could be translated as Hophead. It's made by the Portland representative of BJ's Restaurant and Brewery, the big brewpub chain, and the literature on the beer raises the question: "What would an IPA have been like if Germany, rather than England, had colonized America?"

Blake tells us he hasn't tried this beer yet and he can't resist a pun when he introduces it: "When in Portland, don't worry, be hoppy!" (After only four beer samples, this draws huge laughs.)

---

* Port Halling Brewing has since gone out of business.

We all get a squirt and, being a Hophead, I love it dearly. For the first time I break my one- or two-sips-per-beer rule.

Blake takes a sip and says, "I'm very impressed....I think the cleanness of the lager ferment helps bring out the hops....This should give you something to talk about if you want to talk about hoppy lagers."

We linger on this beer. Many other people take more than one or two sips. Before we leave the tap, Blake says, "Anybody else want more Hopfenkopf? I think I'll have another splash." (I have another splash, too.)

Around Beer 9, we run into King Gambrinus, the patron saint of beer. In real life his name is Art Larrance. He not only co-founded Portland's fourth microbrewery, the Portland Brewing Co., but he is also the brain behind the brewers festival, which drew 15,000 people in its first year. He's dressed in full king kit and with full king makeup. He's lugging a beer, of course, but he waves to us royally with his free hand. A few people bow, as though they're doing the wave at a football game. A few people, apparently active in the anti-beer-tax movement, shout out, "No more beer taxes! No more beer taxes." The King assures us he's the last guy in the world who would ever raise beer taxes.

Beer 9 is by Stone Brewing Co. of San Marcos, California. It's called Ruination IPA; it's 7.7 percent alcohol by volume and measures a whopping 100 IBUs on the hops meter. ("Think of IBUs as the temperature of a beer," Blake admonishes us.)

"Dang," says the official description of Ruination, "this beer has more hops than a sackful of bunnies!"

"Drink a lot of this beer and you'll think you've had a shot of novocaine," says Blake. "You'll also get brewer's droop."

We inquire as to what that might be.

"Hops contain herbal estrogen," he explains. This causes some brewers to become...chesty. (A Beer Geek later informs me that brewer's droop also refers to that malady known in modern terms as erectile dysfunction.)

At Beer 14, we reach the earlier alluded-to imperial *Schwarz bier*. We are forty-eight minutes into the tour and running behind. In fact, some people have lagged behind. One person has dropped back and is now lounging on the lawn. The Alcohol Monitors have come by, checking us out but keeping a friendly distance. They wave. We wave back.

The imperial *Schwarz bier* is by Rogue Brewery, Newport, Oregon. It's name is Skullsplitter. It's 9.2 percent ABV. Those still bothering to read the descriptions learn that Skullsplitter is a "towering product" of the brewer's "fertile beermagination. Amarillo dry hops give a tangerine citrus nose that is enveloped by a burnt toffee aroma."

At Beer 14, it's kind of hard to resist a beer named Skullsplitter. My tasting notes say, "Wow!"

Second sip: "Yikes!"

I notice the two German journalists in animated discussion (in German). I ask one of them what he thinks of the beer.

"Many of the American beers overdo it on the hops. But this is *zehr* interesting!" he tells me. "Very interesting!"

He goes for a second helping of Skullsplitter—a mugful.

At Beer 17, we run out of time; some people have run out of steam. We've lost about a third of our number. One of the Germans is listing badly. Beer 17, named Domaine Dupage, is brewed by Two Brothers Brewing Co., Warrenville, Illinois. It's a French country ale also known as a *biere de garde*. Blake tells us it's the "indigenous beer style of France" and that it should be "kind of nutty, with just a hint of chocolate."

I think the novocaine that Blake warned us about in the Ruination IPA is starting to kick in. I can't really taste the nuts or the chocolate.

Blake sips his *biere de garde* and says, "Well, I think we are coming away with lots of talking points."

Somebody says, "Hip hip hooray for Noel!"

Somebody else says, "Three cheers for Noel!"

Soon people are chanting, "Noel, Noel, Noel!"

About the third time it comes out, "Nool, Nool, Nool!"

* * *

On Saturday, I take a break from the festival to go looking for beer and dogs.

No, not beer and hot dogs.

This is Portland, remember?

I arrive, after a short drive from downtown, at the Lucky Labrador Brewing Co. in the city's tie-dyed Hawthorne neighborhood, a mixed commercial-residential enclave in southeast Portland known for, among other things, a profusion of fruit storage facilities. The Lucky Lab, as the brewpub is called, sits off a busy commercial strip in a cavernous, blocky building holding a former sheet-metal warehouse.

Inside, though, it's the spacious and airy place you'd expect an artfully converted warehouse to be—skylights in the ceiling, a well-trod wood floor, exposed beams in the ceiling. The furnishings are kind of utilitarian-communal, which befits a place where the Portland Socialist Club holds its meetings. There's a long bar to my left and scads of picnic tables scattered cafeteria-like elsewhere. I make a stop at the bar to check out the beer list before heading out to the patio, where I understand most of the Lab's action is.

I notice a sign above the bar that says, "Beer: Not Just a Breakfast Drink." I also notice I have several dog-named beer choices—Superdog and Black Lab Stout among them. (I also see, on a menu on the bar before me, that Miller Lite is the "guest tap.")

This being my first visit, I feel obligated to order a dog-named beer. I ask for a pint of Black Lab, my Hophead leanings having been satiated at the press tasting the day before.

I head out to the patio to check out Beervana's premier beer-and-dog scene, for the Lab not only offers tasty beer and cheap food; you can bring your mutt along for company while you sit and sip. It's late afternoon—maybe 4:30-ish. The crowd is a bit thin but I look around and see at least a half-dozen Beer People/dog combos. Most seem to be couples or groups of friends enjoying a late lunch, dogs lounging under their tables or at their feet. I spy a lone diner with a big dog sitting at a table in the back and head that way.

Her name is Jeannie Wood, and her dog is Calvin, a tall, rangy black mutt of imposing but unclear bloodline. Jeannie is finishing off a bowl of bento, an inexpensive Japanese rice dish that's a Lucky Lab staple, while waiting on a cell phone call from her boyfriend. She happily invites me to have a chat about the Lab. Calvin comes over to sniff me. He accepts a pat on the head and decides I'm okay. (Which is a good thing, considering Calvin's size.)

Jeannie is twenty-six. She works in a title insurance company and when she isn't working is a rabid outdoorswoman, partial to camping and white-water rafting. Calvin goes on these trips and on one recent one, she tells me, spent the entire time in the water, swimming behind the raft. "He was one tired dog, but he really loves the water." That's pretty much how she describes Calvin: tireless and cheerful. She said she got him as a stray when a friend found him but her friend's father wouldn't let him keep him.

She's been coming to the Lucky Lab for the past five years; she's a committed stout drinker and waxes eloquent on the style and why she likes malty, dark beers. She wonders, as a beer-drinking dog owner, why somebody in Portland didn't think of starting a place like the Lab before. (The Lab, it turns out, has been open since 1994.) She says she particularly enjoys Dogtoberfest, an Oktoberfest takeoff at which the main event is a dog wash, attended by celebrity dog-washers, to raise money for a local animal-emergency treatment hospital.

The everyday ambience, however, is what draws her back time after time. "It's fun to come and hang out. It's mostly dog owners, pretty relaxed. People who don't like dogs or don't want to be bothered with them can always sit inside."

She has one other observation: "A lot of wealthy people come here. I don't know why, but they always sit over there," she says, pointing to a cluster of tables.

Most of the dogs that are here now are, like Calvin, on their leashes, including a dog named Dexter that has appeared at the table next to us. Dexter is a boxer that can do high-fives. His owners, John and Victoria Berry, recently moved to Portland by way of Chicago and Alaska. This is their first time at the Lab; they'd been out cavorting with Dexter at a Portland dog park (there are several in town) when somebody suggested a place where they could have their beer and their dog, too.

"It's fun," Victoria says. "We would definitely come back here with Dexter."

After a nice chat, the Berrys leave and Jeannie Wood, who has now made plans to meet her boyfriend, asks me if I'd look after Calvin while she goes inside to pay her bill. (The French, of course, would let you take your dog inside.) I'm delighted. For about five minutes I'll have my own dog; Calvin and I can have a real chance to bond.

After Jeannie disappears, I notice another dog, unleashed, heading our way. It's an irresistibly cute yellow Labrador puppy and it comes over, tail wagging frantically. I check out Calvin to make sure he's okay with this and see he's wagging his tail, too.

I'm holding my beer mug in my left hand. I switch it over to my right hand (the same hand holding Calvin's leash) and settle the mug on my knee. I bend down to give the Lab a pat on the head and get in a pretty good one before the pup goes scrabbling off to its owner.

That's when I notice Calvin's got his nose pretty deep into my mug and has gotten a pretty good snort of Black Lab Stout.

I'm tempted to say "bad dog," but, hey, I realize (a) I was negligent and (b) Calvin's just being a dog. So instead, looking around to make sure that no one is pointing a dog abuse finger at me, I say, "Why, Calvin, I hope you enjoyed that."

Then Calvin and I enjoy another few minutes of beer-bonded

silence until Jeannie comes back. I'm too embarrassed to tell her what happened though she probably would've been fine with it. She takes Calvin's leash, thanks me for watching him, and bids me a cheerful good-bye.

Calvin looks back at me and I know that look—he's a dog in Beervana.

18

Quest's End

On the Road to New Orleans: Contemplating Rock & Sake, Darryl and Sheila

What's drinking? A mere pause from thinking.
—Lord Byron

As I crossed the Mississippi River bridge, New Orleans lay sprawled and steaming in the flat, hot light of a late Louisiana afternoon. The river below was the color of dark mustard and moved as though it were a lethargic snake prodded reluctantly into motion. A tug pushing a string of barges upriver carved a white, frothy ribbon through the current, and in the distance a cargo ship did a slow, awkward pirouette, attempting a toe-point downstream toward the Gulf of Mexico just a few more bends in the river away. The air smelled heavy with rain.

In most places, summer reliably loosens its grip in September. In New Orleans, which, after all, sits in a swamp, summer cloaks the city like damp mosquito netting until sometime in October—often, late October—when a cool front finally has the guts to come and rip the stultifying veil away. Yet its rain-drenched, mosquito-plagued, equatorial summers aside, I love New Orleans.

I grew up sixty miles to the southwest in a little place called Bayou Black near the Cajunized town of Houma, which once proclaimed itself the "Oyster Capital of the World." And for years New Orleans seemed as close as I might ever come to places like New York or San Francisco. It was my Big City. It was where as a kid you arrived, after an impossibly slow car ride along a winding, turtle-backed highway through swamps and sugarcane fields, and across a high, scarily narrow bridge called the Huey P. Long, to find high-rise buildings on the Mississippi and streetcars clanging down boulevards and gorgeous Victorian row houses, emblems of wealth and mystery, along oak-lined avenues; where a zoo sat (and still sits) on a broad green lawn under ancient oaks; where an amusement park that surely rivaled Coney Island stood on a vast lake that looked like the ocean to me; where you could sit at a sidewalk café and dunk sweet *beignets* in café au lait—the French Quarter, with its bricked streets and exotic smells, seething and alive all around you.

It was where when I turned eighteen, then the legal drinking age, I came with friends to Bourbon Street to gape at what seemed so forbidden and sophisticated; to sit in darkened, smoke-filled clubs where bartenders in bow ties, with an unerring eye for rustics like us, emptied our wallets collecting for mandatory, overpriced Singapore Slings while women who seemed like apparitions of desire danced in ways that our Catholic mothers never warned us about. We would then, though usually broke, slip into some jazz club, hoping the crowds would shield us from the dreaded Two-Drink Minimum, and listen to music that we knew was superior to all other music and that we ourselves listened to in a superior way. For we knew jazz belonged to Louisiana and to New Orleans and thus to us. And though we were from the country, we were natives; and we were not, at least, from Iowa.

I have now seen New York and San Francisco, Sydney and Cape Town, London and Paris, and yet New Orleans endures as my favorite city, hardly the most handsome, definitely not the most cultured, incurably not the most progressive. Still, I love the wet mystery of it, the feral seediness of it, the laconically joyful way it continues to shrug at most of the conventions that the homogenized ramparts of America live by. New Orleans always seems more Latin and European than American to me. It is like a dissolute but beloved old uncle—sometimes drunk, often outrageous, at turns maddeningly irresponsible, but always hilariously interesting and passionately moved by the verities: food, music, love, sex, and booze.

God is everywhere here: in the city's monuments to old-world Catholicism, like St. Louis Cathedral; in its moldering cemeteries; and in its lawn shrines to the Virgin Mary; and sin is everywhere, too.

But as to the subject at hand—beer—New Orleans, I have to admit, is, at best, only an average beer town.

Since the days of that gifted rumrunner Jean Lafitte, New Orleans has always been more bourbon than beer, but that doesn't mean, if you count wretched excess, that it doesn't have its own brand of beer culture. New York is the city that never sleeps, and the world has a surplus of cities on the move, cities that work, cities that see the clear arc of the future and pose themselves accordingly. Thank God New Orleans will never be one of those.

New Orleans is the city that never stops drinking (and, I could add, eating).

At the moment, though, I was temporarily *leaving* New Orleans, saving what I could find of its beer culture for tomorrow. For New Orleans is not the last habitable ground on the Mississippi River. If you cross over the Mississippi's West Bank and find Highway 23 off the clutter of the West Bank Expressway, you can drive another seventy-five miles to a place called Venice. It is the southernmost town reachable by road in Plaquemines Parish, a low-lying, hurricane-susceptible peninsula hemmed in by the river and its levee on one side and sprawling marshes and bayous on the others. The Mississippi, just below Venice, divides into three channels, the largest known as Southwest Pass, before finally surrendering to the Gulf. In between New Orleans and Venice are other hamlets with names like Jesuit Bend, Happy Jack, Empire, and Port Sulphur, all attesting to the area's history, aspirations, and position as a corridor for chemical and offshore oil production. Though I had spent much time in New Orleans in my youth, I had only ventured down to Venice once and remembered it vaguely as a place drowsy in the summer heat, the air abuzz with mosquitoes, where shrimp trawlers and charter fishing boats and giant oil field crew boats bobbed together in the silty-salt estuary of the Mississippi. Given the three-odd decades that had passed, and the propensity of sleepy places to wake up one day covered in 7-Elevens and strip malls, I had no idea what I might find.

But I knew two things about Venice. One: it had been named by an optimist, for you would never mistake the burg of about 500 residents scattered up and down the highway for the storied Italian city of the same name. Two: as one of those bayou communities serving as a staging hub for the beer-loving Cajuns and Texans who make up the bulk of the Oil Patch workforce, Venice would definitely have a beer joint or two. In fact, I'd learned from an Oil Patch buddy in Houston with knowledge of Venice watering holes that some of them had reputations as rough-and-tumble places. So I decided to bring along some company, a boyhood friend by the name of Jack Anderson.

Jack now lived and worked in the West Bank town of Harvey but had grown up down where I had in Houma. We'd played baseball together; slung hamburgers at a greasy spoon together; gotten in and out of a few scrapes together. I'd dated his sister Jill in high school, and there was a year or two when our mothers were confused as to our actual living arrangements, since we moved and dined like nomads between households. We'd also taken up surfing together, though you won't find South Louisiana one of the stops in the classic surfing documentary *The Endless Summer.* (Jack, wiry, trim, and fit past fifty, still surfs.) But one fall a hurricane named Betsy had rearranged the sandbars at a low-lying barrier island on the Gulf called Grand Isle, and thereafter, if the winds and tide were right, you could get a decent two- or three-foot break. Thus we became South Louisiana surfing pioneers, even forming the South Louisiana Surfing Association, which held at least one surfing competition before dissolving into lethargy and anarchy, surfer dudes being about as organizationally inclined as cats.

What forged our kinship as much as anything was our mutual tenuous hold to the very bottom rungs of the lower middle class. We were always broke, possibly because slinging burgers paid so poorly, possibly because what it paid we spent on surfing gear, beer, girls, and gas to get to and from the beach every weekend. We drove two of the most scrofulous cars that ever existed, mine a rattletrap VW Beetle with a convertible top so ragged that I carried an umbrella in the car to protect my passengers from rain when the top was *up.* Jack drove a hulking white gas-guzzling Dodge station wagon, a kind of Li'l Abner land yacht whose rust-to-body ratio was perilously close to disintegration. I have a searingly clear memory of a Saturday drive to our surfing hotspot, our boards strapped jauntily to the top of Jack's wagon, and hearing a strange plopping noise coming from Jack's right front tire. I watched in amazement as an entire layer of the tire simply fell off—peeled away and tumbled bobbity into the roadside bushes like some road-struck rabbit. I waited for the blowout that never came. We made it all the way to the beach and back, a seventy-five-minute drive each way, on that tire, its sidewall bristling threads like Paul Bunyan's razor stubble.

Thanks to Alamo, we had a far better car this time, and we left the West Bank after Jack got off work, where he crunches numbers for an oil field supply concern, and drove, all tires behaving, some ninety minutes in the dark to the end of the road. Jack had heard there was a bar called the Cypress Cove

Marina there. After stumbling around, passing a coast guard station and sprawling oystershell-covered parking lots, where oil crews parked cars before hopping on boats for the Gulf, we found it. Alas, it was essentially a sports fisherman's bar and there were hardly any sports fishermen around, and those that were sipped Bud Light and talked quietly over a Top 40 jukebox. In fairness, the Cypress Cove seemed a pleasant enough place, and it was, as far as I could gather, the very last bar you could drive to on the Mississippi River. But by this time on the River of Beer, I'd raised the bar for the Perfect Beer Joint quite high, and I was eager to avoid covering ground that seemed already too familiar. So we didn't linger.

Based upon observations of neon signs, we'd certainly noticed other prospects on the drive down. We found one of them around a sharp curve in the road not too far up from the Cypress Cove. Dry ground is at a premium in this part of the world, with the marsh edging right up to the highway's shoulder in some places. It did here, and the bar sat, looking mildly forlorn, in what looked like a giant, grassy mud puddle. The building was architecturally uninteresting, but the neon sign outside was odd. It said: "Rock & Sake."

I assumed the Sake in question was in fact the word for Japanese rice wine, but why? I was having a hard time imagining how a sake bar had gotten plunked down into the marsh this far into the Bud Light–and–Gumbo Belt.

We parked the car and literally waded through a stretch of ankle-high water smelling of salt marsh, tiptoeing so as not to ruin our shoes, and bounded up short steps to a porch covered in Astroturf. By that time, ravenous mosquitoes had sprung from the marsh and were dive-bombing us with kamikaze zeal. We slapped them away with equal dexterity, having gotten lots of practice at doing this in our youth, and pushed through the front door.

Inside, we were greeted by what I can only describe as a multimedia and multicultural experience. A wide-screen TV broadcast videos of attractive Asian women acting very attractive and very sultry; meanwhile the sound system was blasting out a kind of salsa/hip-hop hybrid, and though it seemed very energizing, it was being played at a decibel level about that of a 747 at takeoff. Though it was tempting to run back out into the mosquitoes, we pushed toward an empty table, of which there were perhaps fifteen or twenty. Indeed, we noticed that, except for one other customer and three desultory Asian waitresses who had not yet seen us come in (and certainly had not heard us), the joint was empty.

We looked around and the decor and music reminded me of a food term I'd heard out in San Francisco when, in one of those trends that whirl through the restaurant world, Collision Cooking was popular. This was, by way of example, taking say, chicken lo mein and merging it with, say, chicken cacciatore to produce a dish that neither Asians nor Italians wanted to eat but that San Francisco yuppies couldn't get enough of. In this case, Bud Light posters blended in with vaguely Oriental flourishes like Japanese lanterns and things that seemed somehow Tiki.

I already knew there was no sake on the menu.

Eventually, we got the attention of one of the waitresses and she came over to take our order. She was young and looked bored and sleepy. Getting her attention didn't coincide with the lowering of the volume of the jukebox, however, so it took what seemed like several minutes of very loud talking, intricate lip-syncing, and gesticulating with arms to get across the somewhat complicated point that we wanted two Budweisers. They came, and they were, I have to say, really cold.

Meanwhile, the music switched to something on the romantic side, sung, however, at the previous volume and in a language that I couldn't understand. And those Asian women were still cavorting attractively on the videos. I wondered if we had stumbled upon some exotic rendering of the Beer Goddess, though not a single beer flickered across the screen. Eventually, unable to even talk to each other over the music, we decided Rock & Sake was a mystery perhaps best left unraveled. It no doubt had aspirations, but being the Perfect Beer Joint I don't think was one of them.

Up the road a bit, we found a gaggle of pickup trucks and cars pressed into the parking lot of a place called The Den. We went in and at least there was life. The bar was about two-thirds full and a jukebox was playing, at reasonable volume, a favored local style known as swamp pop. It was clearly a workingman's bar; there were guys in jumpsuits of a kind that mechanics wear on offshore oil rigs and a few in headgear hereabouts called "welders' caps"—essentially ball caps cut from wild floral prints and popular with the off-duty welding set. The Bud Light was flowing.

I noticed a cluster of guys off to my right that I figured to be engineering types—one wore chinos and another even had a pocket protector tucked into a white shirt. They were laughing and carrying on, the first animated people we'd seen all night. So I ambled over to see if I could post my Perfect Beer Joint question and was brusquely told by one of them—a paunchy guy with a fleshy red face who talked with a Texas accent—to get lost. The River of Beer had, so far, been a remarkably hospitable place, and for all I knew, these guys (whom I'd clearly mistaken for cordial drunks) might have actually been engaged in some deep moral problem-solving. I retreated to find more congenial company.

That's when I spotted, with a nudge of Jack's elbow, a sight that was certainly more pleasant than the grouches I'd just left. There were two women working the crowd in their underwear, holding large rolls of red tickets of a kind that get you on the Ferris wheel at the county fair.

Well, actually, it wasn't *their* underwear, after all.

A friendly guy standing next to us by the name of Mike Russo, who later told us he was an Oil Patch consultant, explained that this was The Den's weekly lingerie show and that it probably accounted for a goodly part of the crowd here tonight. He was going to explain how a lingerie show worked when the women actually appeared before us and introduced themselves.

"Hi, guys!" said one of them. She then told us her name was Denise and, in case we hadn't noticed, "I'm wearing a body stocking."

"This is Sandy," she said of her friend.

Sandy smiled and said, "Hi, guys!" too, but she didn't say what she was wearing. We could tell it wasn't much.

"Have you ever been to a lingerie show?" Denise asked me.

I said I had not, which was not exactly true. As I'd waited for Jack at the West Bank Holiday Inn that I'd checked into, I'd peered into the bar there to check out the beer scene and saw a woman walking around in her underwear there. But I hadn't thought that much of it. Rules governing a wide spectrum of social behavior are relaxed in South Louisiana. For example, it's the only place that I know of that has a chain of successful drive-through convenience stores called Daiquiris-to-Go, where you can, without leaving your car, load up on a quart of the rum-laced frozen concoctions. (The law technically prohibits drivers from drinking the daiquiris bought there—and was only changed in 2004 to prevent passengers from imbibing.)

Anyway, I didn't want to deprive Denise of the pleasure of explaining how a lingerie show at The Den worked.

"We sell raffle tickets—$5, $10, $20," she said. "At the end of the night, they draw the numbers, and you can either win nothing, a drink, or lingerie."

"Ah," I said. "It sounds like fun, but I don't wear lingerie."

Denise smiled at me and said, "Silly, you're not supposed to wear it. You're supposed to let it fall to the floor and kick it aside."

To which Sandy said, "Like this!"

Whereupon, in a remarkable move, Sandy shrugged about one-third of the way out of the almost-nothing garment she was wearing, and then deftly feigned how, having stepped out of it, she would kick it aside.

This rendered us temporarily speechless and eventually had the hugely desirous effect (for Sandy and Denise) of having Jack,

Mike, and me pony up exorbitant sums for raffle tickets, since the money went to a really good cause (Sandy and Denise).

Unlike the grouches, Sandy and Denise seemed intrigued by my quest to find the Perfect Beer Joint and were on the verge of giving me all of their particulars, hoping they might be included in the book, when they realized there was something they needed to tell me.

"One of us is a Bud Girl," one of them said—meaning she went around, wearing quite a bit more clothes than she had on now, promoting Budweiser at various events. "And as Bud Girls, we're not supposed to do lingerie shows. They don't like it. We're supposed to be, you know, good, wholesome, all-American types."

I took a quick poll of Jack and Mike, and we all agreed that Denise and Sandy seemed like good, wholesome, all-American types to us; that this seemed merely another perfectly valid interpretation of the Beer Goddess model; and that we had not been harmed by our encounter, except perhaps for mild and fleeting arrhythmias brought on by Sandy's feint.

Denise and Sandy then moved on and I noticed that they were greeted quite a bit more warmly by the grouches than they'd greeted me. I noticed, in fact, that the grouches spent lavishly on raffle tickets as well.

Jack and I hung around till they pulled the raffle tickets, and alas, we won neither drink nor lingerie.

And happily, neither did the grouches.*

* * *

Around nine the next morning, I strolled through the French Quarter looking for morning beer life, aware that a goodly

---

* The Rock & Sake was destroyed by Hurricane Katrina in August 2005, and The Den was badly damaged. The Dixie Brewery was also put out of business for a while, but the brand reemerged in fall 2007.

number of bars in and around the Quarter stay open round-the-clock. When I said earlier that New Orleans was only an average beer town, I meant, of course, in beer choice, not volume. I've never seen a reliable estimate, but I'd hazard to say that more beer is consumed in New Orleans during that annual quasi-religious beer bash known as Mardi Gras than Detroit drinks all summer. Think of two million people in the streets and spilling out of bars, pretty much all of them clutching giant plastic cups of lager, and you get the idea.

As a brewing city, though, New Orleans is a C-minus. The city was once home to a large Falstaff plant and a midsized regional lager maker named Jax, but both died in the Lager Wars in the 1970s. It supports one remaining regional lager maker, a quirky brand named Dixie that has been in business since 1907 and revivified itself a few years back by introducing a few new beers, notably one called Blackened Voodoo, a rare dark lager, that has turned into a popular local seller. North, across Lake Pontchartrain, a microbrewer called Abita Brewing Co. sprang up in the piney woodlands in 1986 and has since outgrown the microbrew label to produce more than 35,000 barrels of beer annually out of a stunning, state-of-the-art, automated brewery that I would amble over to tour. Abita makes some wonderfully interesting beers—one called Turbodog, a dark brown ale, and another called Purple Haze, which is an American wheat beer made with a pinch of raspberry puree. Both Abita and Dixie do very well in the South Louisiana–Mississippi Gulf Coast market. But except for them and a handful of brewpubs and craft beer tap bars, the beer scene here—indeed, in all of Louisiana—is pretty much just another extension of the Bud Belt. On the other hand, face it: the long, hot, sultry summers here make it prime American Standard lager territory.

In fact, this day was starting out as a good lager day. It was clear and hot, the sun slanting through a light mist and casting sharp shadows across the Quarter's narrow streets and alleys as it climbed high up over the river. Yet I'd found surprisingly little beer action: of two twenty-four-hour sports bars I'd peeked into, one was open but empty save for a bartender drying beer glasses, and in the second, three men clustered at the bar, and two of them had their heads down on the counter. Just outside that bar, a Budweiser truck was groaning through a tight turn; a sticker on its rear bumper read, "Drink Responsibly."

After about a half-hour stroll, I realized the coffee shops were a lot busier than the beer joints. New Orleans, so far, wasn't living down to its reputation.

I had slightly better luck when I wandered into a friendly, open-to-the-street pub named Good Friends at St. Ann and Dauphine streets. There I settled in at an L-shaped counter and found a barman named Tyler, agreeable but exhausted near the end of his graveyard shift that had begun at midnight. I ordered a virgin Bloody Mary and asked Tyler what he could tell me about New Orleans beer culture. He said he wasn't much of a beer drinker and Good Friends wasn't primarily a beer bar, and besides, it had been incorrigibly slow as of late. "Do you know how much I made last night? Twelve lousy bucks," Tyler said. "I'm burnt out. I think I need to get another job."

I'd noticed a couple of men bellied up to the other leg of the bar when I came in. As I was explaining my beer quest to Tyler, I realized one of them, an older man with chin stubble and a smoker's pallor and wearing a jaunty straw hat, was trying to ask me a question. I had to get him to repeat it twice before I finally understood.

"Ah, okay," I said, as I found myself repeating the question back to him. "You want to know if I'm one of the drag queens in town this week?"

Good Friends was never going to be a candidate for the Perfect Beer Joint. But this was the most surprising question I'd been asked so far on the River of Beer.

Now, it is true I'd gone into training for Beer Year, as I called my book assignment, and that even past fifty, I sometimes flatter myself by thinking that I still have a swimmer's build. But I would've thought my mustache made me a poor candidate for a drag queen. Still, I had the good manners to understand that the question perhaps contained a kernel of flattery. So I laughed and said I wasn't. And I knew then, of course, that Good Friends was a gay bar. Alas, it was mostly empty and, as Tyler had explained, didn't sell that much beer.

About that time, another of the customers, drinking some exotic concoction about the color of the Mississippi, came over and introduced himself as Gary. Gary *was* a beer drinker and gave me a pretty thorough rundown on what he considered to be New Orleans' best places for beer—the Abby nearby on Decatur Street; Cooter Brown's in the city's Garden District; D.B.A. over near the city's Warehouse District. (D.B.A., as you may recall, has a sister bar in Manhattan.)

I asked him if he happened to know which bar ranked as the oldest in New Orleans, thinking perhaps it might be a fun morning beer stop.

"I think it's Lafitte's Blacksmith Shop," he said.

I thanked Gary for all of his suggestions, left poor Tyler a sizable tip, and struck out for Lafitte's Blacksmith Shop, which Gary said was nearby.

I found it at the corner of Bourbon and St. Phillip streets in a lovely faded stucco building that literature inside told me had been built sometime before 1772 and was one of the few remaining examples of original French period architecture left in New Orleans (most such buildings had been devastated by fires in 1778 and 1794). Lore had it that Jean Lafitte and his brother Pierre had once owned the building and used it as a front for their privateer enterprises. Lafitte escaped prison by helping Andrew Jackson rout the British in the Battle of New Orleans and, after receiving a presidential pardon, drifted off into the deep Louisiana mists, a figure of enduring mystery and legend here. People are still looking for his buried treasure.

I loved the feel of the bar. But it was inhabited by a sole tourist from Nebraska, who had come in mostly to beat the gathering heat while sipping a soft drink. A friendly waitress confirmed that, of all New Orleans bars, it was the one inhabiting the oldest building. But it mostly did a brisk nighttime business, selling a lot of that popular indigenous concoction called the Hurricane to tourists.

There was a bit of the morning left and I walked out into the bright light of Bourbon Street and made a left, heading in the direction of Canal Street, New Orleans' major north–south commercial artery, off of which I'd parked my rental car. Bars in the French Quarter are as ubiquitous as mosquitoes outside the Rock & Sake, and I knew most would have opened by 11:00 A.M. I still might find a gathering of beer-enamored poets willing to share the meaning of life and beer with me and thus give me something to write about.

That's when I ran into Darryl and Sheila.

I noticed Darryl first—he was the one with khaki shorts, a faded New Orleans Saints T-shirt, flip-flops, and a large white plastic beer cup balanced on his head.

He was walking slowly, as though the cup were full (which it turned out to be).

Sheila, in matching khaki shorts and what looked to be a baseball jersey, was walking alongside. They were a handsome couple, in their late twenties, I'd guess, all the more striking because Darryl was at least a foot taller than she was. They were in the middle of the street until a garbage truck came around a corner and herded them to the sidewalk. Darryl took his time so as to not jostle his beer.

I caught up with them and introduced myself, telling them in short form what I was up to. They gave me their names and from their accents I guessed they were probably locals. Sheila said they'd recently gotten engaged and hadn't quite yet stopped celebrating.

Darryl stopped walking and looked at me out of the corner of his eye and said, "Damn, man, that's some job you got. You need an assistant?"

I laughed and told him I'd had lots of offers for assistants along the River of Beer.

I asked Darryl what was with the beer on his head.

"Oh, that. Well, it's a bet I got with Sheila here. See, I gotta make it all the way to Canal without spillin' the beer. If I do, well, I get a present. If I don't, I don't get anything."

I looked ahead and saw the street wasn't all that crowded yet.

"You probably have a good chance," I said, "if you take it easy. What's the present?"

At this, Darryl started laughing. Upon laughing, he put his hands to his stomach so that his laughter would not upset his rigidly upright body attitude and thus his beer.

Sheila put a hand on his arm and said, "Dar-ryl, don't you drop that beer now. You'll be sorry if you do!"

That's all it took.

Darryl bent over double with laughter and the beer did a somersault off his head and splashed into a wet half-moon on the sidewalk. The cup clattered into the street. I got, not for the first time during my trip, beer on my sneakers.

Darryl and Sheila were now down on the sidewalk, clutching each other in hysterical laughter.

"Aw, man," Darryl said when he had recovered. "That's not right."

Sheila looked at me and said, "If Darryl had made it all the way, he would've been a happy guy."

"Really happy," Darryl said, smiling sheepishly.

"Really, really happy," Sheila replied.

"C'mon," Darryl said. "One more chance, Sheila. Just one more chance."

Sheila thought this over for a second, then nodded. "Okay, but if you don't make it, you're taking me to Biloxi on the weekend."

Darryl said he would, absolutely.

They got up off the sidewalk and dusted themselves off. I followed them up Bourbon Street until Darryl came to one of those stalls where you can buy giant draft beers for $3 or a smaller one for a buck. (By my actual count, there would be sixteen walk-up beer stations between the start of Darryl's quest and Canal.) He came out with the beer and he balanced it on his head.

Darryl had close-cropped hair and a fairly large head, which helped. But I also now realized there was a good chance that Darryl and Sheila had been part of the beer-for-breakfast crowd I'd looked for so far in vain. He didn't exactly walk with the sure gait of those women I'd seen in Africa carrying jars of drinking water on their heads.

I decided to drop back quite a bit, not wanting to take a beer bath and not wanting to be responsible for distracting Darryl into failure.

I needn't have worried. Sheila distracted him plenty, and Darryl didn't make it more than a block when the second beer tumbled off. But Sheila was very liberal in her interpretation of last chances, and on about his fourth beer, Darryl gained the finish line.

At the fabled intersection of Canal and Bourbon, he gingerly took the beer from his head and chugged most of it down. He gave the cup to Sheila. She finished it off but with slightly more delicacy than Darryl had shown. He took the cup from her and tossed it into the air and then he grabbed Sheila up and they went around and around, her legs trailing. I feared for a moment that they would go crashing to the street or into someone else and this would end badly.

But it didn't. Instead Darryl put Sheila down and raised his arms in triumph. And then they locked arms and, looking up and down Canal Street, made a dash to the streetcar median, where Darryl briefly flew out of one of his flip-flops. This was the subject of more hysterical laughter of a kind that most people, after a few beers, would indulgently recognize. I thought they'd forgotten about me, but once Darryl recovered his shoe, they turned and, scanning to find me on the sidewalk, waved an energetic good-bye.

I waved back and watched them dash the rest of the way across Canal.

For a moment I considered running them down so that I could ask them about their beer preferences and their favorite beer bars, not to mention their full names and ages and what they did for a living.

But, nah. Darryl and Sheila were in love and beer-buzzed on a sunny day in a fabled and feral city, and they were running off with exuberance to settle a hilarious wager. Whether they had arrived at this happy state drinking Bud or Abita seemed totally immaterial.

I would go on to sample some very nice beer at the bars that Gary back at Good Friends had recommended, and I stumbled onto a few of my own. The Crescent City Brewhouse on Decatur Street—the French Quarter's only brewpub—served up a righteous German lager made to Old Country standards; indeed, I would pass part of a lovely afternoon sipping handmade beers with Wolf Koehler, the brewpub's owner who is also a sixth-generation brewer. And I was able to find a surprisingly large selection of craft beer at D.B.A., which doubles as a lively roots-music venue in the nearby Marigny District. Still, as a beer scene, New Orleans is never going to be Portland. But Darryl and Sheila proved part of my thesis. I wouldn't find the Perfect Beer Joint here, and New Orleans may be, in the end, only an average beer town. But the whole place serves as a hothouse for the free-form beer joint; as my morning encounter on Bourbon Street proved, a beer joint could just spring up here, anywhere at any time.

Though at Quest's End, I still had one bit of beer business to attend to a bit farther down the road.

Epilogue
Pa and Pabst

I left New Orleans and drove for an hour, over roads much improved in the decades since I'd first made the trip, to my old stomping grounds in and around Houma. Including side excursions, I'd covered about 2,600 miles along the Mississippi in my quest to find the Perfect Beer Joint.

Had I found it?

Not exactly. The Casino in La Crosse, where a homeless man slept out of harm's way, where happy lesbians danced to Diana Krall, where the beer was fabulous, and where Clay Holman had regaled me with stories of a bar-hopping Amish man, had come close. And I'd been charmed by most of the places I'd visited and the people I met along the River of Beer. Thoreau, I concluded, had it right when he said, "The tavern will compare favorably with the church." Or to put it in a modern context: the TV tavern Cheers is alive and well across America, where the beer joint does in fact function as a place of community and comfort; a place where people ordinary and extraordinary gather around Ben Franklin's benighted elixir, taking solace in friendship, camaraderie, and beer.

This is exactly the kind of thing that I'd have loved to discuss with my dad, under whose watchful eye I'd sampled my first brew as a kid. But he never got to know that I'd cadged a book contract to explore the River of Beer. Otherwise, he'd have thrown his head back and had a good laugh, for the idea that his beer-loving son would get a sabbatical to roam the country, steeping himself in all things beer, would have both pleased and befuddled him. I could easily imagine him lapsing into one of his Arkansas aphorisms and declaring, "I'll swan, Ken. What were those people up there in New York thinking?" (Sometimes I wondered the same thing.)

Pa was in good health but died suddenly, in July of 2000, felled by a heatstroke as he pushed his lawnmower through his overgrown suburban yard on one of the hottest days of the year. My mother had passed away five years earlier but Pa was doing all right. He had few expenses, a pension from the Post Office, a bit of stock he'd accumulated during a seven-year detour into retailing with Sears, Roebuck & Co., and a small monthly disability check from his World War II combat service with the Marines. He had a routine and family nearby, friends and company enough to keep him going. He could've paid some kid ten bucks to mow his grass, but Pa was a stubborn guy. He was seventy-nine, an old marine determined to look after himself, and cutting the grass was a duty to his independence. The heatstroke killed him quick, which is how he'd have wanted to go.

Pa left a will and small estate, most of it tied up in his stocks and the little tract house he and my mother had lived in when we moved from the country out on Bayou Black the year after I finished high school. Even settling little estates can drag on, what with listless real estate markets and the endless red tape of stock transfers. So we'd finally tidied up the last bit of his business and distributed his small legacy to kids and grandkids about the time I finished my journey down the Mississippi.

One of the virtues of Pa doing all right was that he always had beer in the refrigerator (what he called the "icebox"). It was cheap beer, trending to Old Milwaukee and Pabst, but it was usually plentiful and always nice and cold. And part of his legacy, discovered on the day he died, were four cans of Pabst stuffed way back in a corner of his much-cluttered icebox. My brother, Pershing, had put them aside and kept them refrigerated all this time, awaiting a day when he, our three other brothers, and I, all of us with families and busy lives, could get together and drink them in celebration of Dad's life.

So it was that we finally found ourselves on a sunny day in a boat, speeding through the lovely, wild estuary south of Houma, going fishing at Dad's favorite saltwater spot after launching at an end-of-the-road hamlet called Pointe-aux-Chenes. The watery world beyond Pointe-aux-Chenes is a place of meandering bayous; brackish, marshy bays; deep holes; and mudflats. It's a place we'd come, for as long as I could remember, to chase redfish, flounder, and speckled trout. It was one of the places where Pa taught us not only the art of fishing but a great deal about the wild wetlands around us. And he was never so comfortable as he was out here—rod and reel in one hand, beer in the other—offering fishing advice, a running commentary on the unfolding day, or telling stories of glorious trips past.

On this day, we stopped at each of Dad's favorite fishing holes. And at the last one, with the sun high on the water and pelicans flapping in the distance, we broke out Pa's four Pabsts. We recognized we were pushing the outer limits of lager life, but each beer opened with the "koosh!" of a beer still kicking. We poured them into five red plastic cups we'd brought along and offered a toast—"Rest you, Pa, and thanks for everything."

And then we quaffed our beers, which tasted perfectly fine, and went about doing what Pa would've done. We fished our way back, picking up a fish here and there. We drank a few more beers we'd brought along.

It wasn't the best fishing day; it wasn't the worst. It didn't matter. For we knew Pa was right when he said, as he often did, that the fishing, in a way, wasn't really what it was all about. It was about being out under the open sky in the wild places you loved in the company of family or friends who shared that love.

And who, Pa would hasten to add, also shared their beer.

A Brief Glossary

Acetaldehyde—A kind of green-apple aroma given off as a by-product of fermentation; Budweiser is considered by many to have a mild acetaldehyde bite.

Adjuncts—Barley substitutes, such as rice or corn, used to make lighter-bodied beer; they also lower brewing costs.

Alcohol by volume (ABV)—The volume of alcohol in the total volume of beer, expressed as a percentage. The higher the number, the stronger the beer.

Amber—A generic term generally applied to reddish ales, though it can apply to some lagers.

American Standard lager—The most common beer style in the U.S., epitomized by Budweiser; a pale to deep golden lager light in body, mild in hops, and high in carbonation.

Barley—A cereal grain and the backbone of beer; sprouted then dried and roasted, it turns into barley malt, the source of sugars for yeast to turn into alcohol. The extent of roasting determines beer's color. (See **malt** and **mash**)

Barley wine—Ale made at near the strength of wine, i.e., a very strong ale.

Barrel—The standard measurement of beer shipments in the U.S.; a barrel equals 31.5 U.S. gallons. (See **keg**)

Beer yeast—Microscopic, potato-shaped fungi of the genus *Saccharomyces* that, when added to wort, convert sugars into alcohol and carbon dioxide through the process of fermentation. (See **wort**)

Biere de garde—An earthy-tasting French country ale typically brewed in spring and drunk in summer.

Bitter—A term designating a broad British style of well-hopped ale.

Bock—Of German origin, a strong, usually dark lager.

Bottle-/cask-conditioned beer—Beer, usually ale, to which live yeast is added after bottling or casking to increase alcohol and/or carbonation levels.

Brewpub—A combination bar and restaurant where beer is brewed on the premises, usually with annual production of 1,000 barrels or less. The first U.S. brewpub opened in Yakima, Washington, in 1982.

British mild—Lightly hopped, malty, low-alcohol ale. Now rare, it was once the British workingman's session beer.

Brown ale—A nutty, malty style associated with the English city of Newcastle, though there are southern English variants.

Clone-purify—The process of isolating a single cell of a pure beer yeast strain and culturing it into amounts significant enough for brewing.

Congeners—Any of a vast number of organic alcohols, sulfur, and other compounds produced during fermentation and accounting for distinctive characteristics—from earthy barnyard aromas to flavors approximating things such as green apples, bananas, and vanilla—in beer and other alcoholic beverages. (See **esters**)

Craft beer/craft brewing—Beer made by a loose alliance of microbreweries, brewpubs, and moderate-sized regional brewers dedicated to repopulating America's beer landscape with thousands of new beer choices. (See **microbrewery** and **brewpub**)

Diacetyl—A fermentation by-product responsible for a common buttery or butterscotch flavor in beer.

Esters—Chemical flavor compounds, by-products of fermentation, that account for the fruity, earthy, or spicy notes often found in beer. (See **congeners**)

Extreme Beer Movement—A movement of craft brewers dedicated to pushing the boundaries of brewing by developing esoteric, ultra-strong, and/or aged beers, or replications of ancient or historical beers. (See **craft beer/craft brewing**)

Framboise—A Belgian style ale; a fruited lambic to which raspberries have been added. (See **lambic**)

Gravity (original and final)—The density of fermentable sugars relative to water in a brewing mixture; original gravity measures the alcohol potential for a beer; final gravity measures the sugars left behind after fermentation.

Gueuze (geuze)—A lambic that undergoes secondary fermentation in the bottle. (See **lambic**)

Gruits—Ales dating from medieval times and brewed with herbs instead of hops; or, the mix of herbs used to make such beers.

Hefeweizen (hefe weizen)—A German wheat beer with a signature clovelike taste and aroma. American hefeweizen often lacks these characteristics.

Hops—A vine-growing plant common to dry, temperate latitudes; it produces flower cones that when added to beer provide bitterness and aroma, while acting as a preservative.

India Pale Ale (IPA)—Originally a nineteenth-century British style of strong ale, super-hopped as a preservative to withstand the long voyage from Britain to its colony in India. Nowadays, a style particularly popular with American craft brewers and known for its signature extra-hoppy taste.

International Bittering Unit (IBU)—A measurement of the level of hops compounds in beer.

Keg—One-half barrel, or 15.5 U.S. gallons. (See **barrel**)

Kölsch—A German ale known for its lagerlike qualities, including pale color; clean, crisp taste; and light body.

Lambic—A sour Belgian wheat ale fermented with naturally occurring wild yeast and other microflora—i.e., beneficial bacteria. (See **gueuze**)

Light beer—In America, a reduced-calorie lager; in Canada and Australia, a low-alcohol lager.

Malt—Germinated, kilned barley that forms the backbone of beer and gives it its color.

Märzen—A German-style, reddish, medium-strength lager, traditionally brewed in the spring and aged until fall.

Mash—A porridge produced by mixing malt with water and gently heating it. (See **wort**)

Mash tun—a large vessel, often copper, where the mash is processed.

Microbrewery—A brewery producing 15,000 barrels or less beer per year.

Mouthfeel—A term describing the relative heft of a beer—thin or viscous—on the palate.

Pale ale—A British style, whose color is closer to an amber or a golden lager than traditional brown or dark ales, such as porters and stouts. (See **porter** and **stout**)

Pilsner (pilsener, pils)—The "golden lager," of which Pilsner Urquell is the original example.

Porter—Of London origin, a medium-bodied, medium-dark ale that has virtually disappeared in Britain but is a style much in favor with certain U.S. craft brewers. (See **stout**)

Schwarz bier—A dark, strong lager of German origin.

Stout—A dark, often black, ale with a rich, roasty flavor, typified by brands such as Mackeson or Guinness. Variations include oatmeal stout, in which oatmeal is mixed with malt in the brewing process; and imperial stout (sometimes called Russian Imperial Stout), an extra-strong ale that the British exported with great success to czarist Russia starting in the nineteenth century.

Tripel—Of Belgian and Dutch origin, a term that designates the strongest beer in the house or of a particular brewery.

Wit beer (white beer)—A Belgian-style ale, often spiced with coriander, that is brewed with unmalted wheat and known for its cloudy appearance and slightly citrusy taste.

Wort—A sweet, amber liquid, rich in fermentable sugars, extracted from mash. (See **mash**)

Zymurgy—The study and science of how yeast do the work of fermentation.

Notes on Sources

The author acknowledges that for the purposes of this book he has used, with considerable literary license, the term "beer joint" throughout and applied it to establishments that may more usually refer to themselves as bars, saloons, taverns, pubs, diners, and roadhouses.

Interview methods: In all cases, I identified myself as a *Wall Street Journal* reporter writing a book about beer. My preference was to use the first and last name of all interview subjects included in this book. In a few cases, I've used only first names, either because of the informality of the setting, the nature of the encounter, or because the subjects only proffered a first name.

As the reader will see, the author made full use of that marvelous new research tool called the Internet, which puts vast stores of knowledge previously stuffed into libraries and newspaper and magazine morgues at a writer's fingertips. As a *Wall Street Journal* reporter, I also had access to the huge Dow Jones–Reuters searchable electronic database known as Factiva.

Introduction: Why Beer, Why Me?

Statistics on the size and contribution of the U.S. beer industry to the nation's economy come primarily from two sources: "Beer

Serves America," a 2003 report published jointly by the Beer Institute of Washington, D.C., and the National Beer Wholesalers Association (NBWA) of Alexandria, Virginia, and the 2003 edition of "Beer Is Volume with Profit: Comprehensive Facts on the U.S. Beer Industry," published by SABMiller Brewing Co. of Milwaukee. (I draw some updated statistics from the 2006 versions of these reports.) Where possible, I checked such figures with independent sources and against statistics published in a variety of independent publications, including the *Wall Street Journal*. The $144 billion figure for the GNP of beer is taken from the "Beer Serves America" report and is a product of statistical modeling.

Comparative country GDP comes from the U.S. State Department Country Commercial Guides; gross state product comparisons come from the U.S. Department of Commerce's Bureau of Economic Analysis, "Gross State Products, 1991–2000."

"Beer Is Volume with Profit," edited by Joan Zitzke, sales communications manager of SABMiller, also provides the lion's share of the demographic, sales, and per capita beer consumption statistics in this section and other chapters. In interviews with beer experts, this report was repeatedly cited as among the best, most comprehensive, and clearest sources of beer statistical information in the country.

Most historical information for this section comes from the Beer Institute's online report, "Beer Facts." The introduction and rise of lager in America is referenced in numerous sources, including "A Short History of Beer in America" by Gregg Smith for the Brewer's Association of America (BAA), a Durham, North Carolina, trade group; "The History of Pale Lager" at www.mrbeer.com, a seller of homebrewing kits and equipment; a July 2002 cover story by Max Rudin in *American Heritage* magazine called "Beer and America"; "The Birth of Lager" by Michael Jackson on his www.beerhunter.com Web site; "The Rise of the Beer Barons," a 1999 article by Carl H. Miller in *All About Beer* magazine; and "The Rise of Lager Beer" chapter in the seminal 1909 book *American Beer: Glimpses of Its History, and Descriptions of Its Manufacture* by G. Thomann of the United States Brewers' Association. (The book is reprinted in full at http://brewery.org, an Internet site for homebrewing enthusiasts.) I also drew from these sources for Chapter 5, my abridged history of America's River of Beer and the forces that shaped it.

Statistics on craft beer market share come from the Brewers Association, another craft beer trade group, in Boulder, Colorado.

Chapter 1: Anatomy of a Beer Spill

There are no notes on sources for Chapter 1; it is based completely on original research and reporting.

Chapter 2: The Quest Begins

Statistics on dry counties in America are courtesy of the Distilled Spirits Council of the United Sates in Washington, D.C. Statistics on the Mississippi River are taken from a report, "Educational Facts About the Mississippi," by the Mississippi River Parkway Commission, Minneapolis, Minnesota. A passage on the history of the beer joint in America was drawn from numerous sources, notably a "History of American Beer" timeline by BeerAdvocate.com and the Beer Institute's "Beer Facts" report. The Tun Tavern's place in U.S. Marine Corps history is a ubiquitously known bit of beer history; you can find interesting details on the history link at Tun. Tavern.com (the Philadelphia tavern, by the way, is still in operation).

For information on the sea change in U.S. beer-buying patterns, I relied heavily on the SABMiller report, "Beer Is Volume with Profit." Contemporary and historical information about Stillwater, Minnesota, comes from the town's official website and from a companion website, www.stillwatertraveler.com.

Chapter 3: A Diversion to Consider the Beer Cure

For the brief segment on the history of craft brewing in America, I supplemented original sources with BeerAdvocate's "History of American Beer" timeline; the 2002 Institute for Brewing Studies "Craft Beer Industry Statistics"; and an Association of Brewers synopsis called "History of Craft Brewing." That, and other historical and contemporary information on craft brewing, can be found at the Brewers Association website, www.Beertown.org.

Statistics on the number of people in America who drink some form of alcohol come from the federal government's "2002 Survey of Drug Use and Health." Statistics on total U.S. alcohol consumption are drawn from a variety of sources, among them a 2003 National Institutes of Health report by its Office of Research on Women's Health titled, "Alcohol: A Women's Health Issue."

Chapter 4: On the Road Again

Information on the cobbling together of the Great River Road and the historical anecdotes come largely from the Great River Road link of the Mississippi River Parkway Commission's website.

I supplemented information gleaned from interviews on Winona, Minnesota, with material from visitwinona.com, the official Web site of the Winona Convention and Visitors Bureau. Population, historical, and other information on La Crosse, Wisconsin, was likewise supplemented with materials from www.explorelacrosse.com, that city's official convention and visitors bureau website. Among the most useful sites for historical information on the game of lacrosse is www.e-lacrosse.com, an online lacrosse magazine.

For a passage on the past and recent history of Pabst Brewing Co., I relied on information from a phone interview with Pabst chief executive officer Brian Kovalchuk and a number of stories in the *Wall Street Journal*'s archives. The number and names of the Pabst labels brewed comes from the Pabst official website, www.pabst.com. The most recent revenue data on Pabst comes from a December 2003 report by *Hoover's Company Profiles*, a closely held business information concern. Pabst's appeal as a "hipster" beer was a thread I picked up from a number of disparate interviews along the River of Beer. In doing background research, I found it first mentioned in an *Atlanta Constitution* article in 1999; it has since been written about by, among other publications, the *Washington Post* and the *New York Times Magazine*.

Chapter 5: The Plymouth Rock Beer Detour

This chapter drew upon original reporting and a multiplicity of sources, a number of them already enumerated in the notes on Chapter 2 regarding the rise and dominance of lager in the U.S. and world beer markets. Also, the previously referenced BAA treatise, "A Short History of Beer in America," and Max Rudin's "Beer in America" piece in *American Heritage* magazine both provided excellent overviews for a scribe looking to get a handle on beer history. I also drew from several helpful historical timelines: "History of American Beer/Beer 101" at BeerAdvocate .com; "A Chronology of the American Brewing Industry" at BeerHistory.com and reprinted from the book *American Breweries II* by Dale P. Van Wieren; "A Concise Timeline of Beer History" by Linda Raley at BeerBooks.com.

I got supplemental information on the Pilgrims' landing and beer deprivation in the New World by reading parts of William Bradford's *History of Plymouth Plantation* published in 1650.

A very good synopsis of the Sauer-Braidwood argument can be read online by clicking the library links section at www.brewing techniques.com.

The Odai Hussein beer find is based upon an April 2003 Associated Press account filed during the invasion of Iraq.

A full account of the Ninkasi beer experiment by Fritz Maytag and Solomon Katz can be found in the July/August 1991 edition of the journal *Archaeology*.

A good overview on the discovery of ancient Egyptian beer recipes and the efforts of Scottish & Newcastle to brew the Tutankhamen Ale is an article by Robert Protz called "Brew Like an Egyptian." It can be found in the online archives of *Ale Street News* at www.alestreet news.com.

Some details on the King Midas brewing project I gleaned from Dr. McGovern during an interview at Dogfish Head Craft Brewery. For a fuller account, I recommend "Re-creating King Midas's Golden Elixir" by Gregg Glaser in the July 2002 edition of *Modern Brewery Age*.

The narrative chronology of beer from the eighth century through Victorian times drew upon many of the aforementioned timelines and overviews, plus the G. Thomann book *American Beer*. Other sources include *The Secret Life of Beer*, a 1995 book by Alan D. Eames; *Beer in America: The Early Years, 1587–1840*, published in 1998 by Gregg Smith; and *American Breweries II*, published in 1995 by Dale P. Van Wieren. The Finnish Kalevala, replete with its beer references, can be found online in full at finlit.fi/kalevala.

Vassar College hasn't forgotten its founder. Matthew Vassar's contributions to his namesake college, and the nature of their origins, can be found on the Vassar website at www.vassar.edu.

Other sources for the passage on the rise of lager and the lager barons are referenced above and in the notes on the introduction.

An excellent overview of Prohibition and the causes that led to it, plus Richard P. Hobson's broadside against beer and alcohol, can be read in full on the "Clash of Cultures" link on the Ohio State University History Department's Web site at http://history.osu.edu.

Chapter 6: The Quest Continues

Basic demographic and historical information on Prairie du Chien, Wisconsin, comes from its official Web site, www.villageprofile .com/wisconsin/prairieduchien; information on Buffalo Bill's appearance and the Great Railroad Excursion was gleaned from, among other sources, the history link of www.prairieduchien.org.

To supplement my reporting done on visits to Dubuque, Iowa's, visitors center and the National Mississippi River Museum, I consulted the official city website, www.dubuquechamber.com. Al Capone's ownership of the Julien Inn is still widely known in Dubuque and is referenced on the hotel's website, www.julieninn .com. There are numerous accounts of Capone's brewing days in Chicago and his connection to Sieben's, including good ones at crimelibrary.com and alcaponemuseum.com.

As of this writing, a recipe for Capone's Prohibition Lager ostensibly made at the Sieben Brewery in 1924 could be found at www.characterevents.com/caponebeer.html.

Per capita beer consumption figures and rankings for Iowa, Wisconsin, and New Hampshire come from the 2003 SAB-Miller report, "Beer Is Volume with Profit."

Chapter 7: A Side Trip Deep into the Lair of Extreme Beer

Figures on the estimated current number of craft breweries and brewpubs in the U.S. are based on surveys by the Brewers' Association of America and the Association of Brewers. The estimate that the craft brew movement has put perhaps 10,000 individual new beers on the market is an educated guess based on an assumption that each of the 1,500 craft breweries and brewpubs today offers an average of six to eight beers.

Chapter 8: Back on the River of Beer

Data on flood mitigation efforts in Louisa County, Iowa, comes from the U.S. Army Corps of Engineers and online reports by the Iowa Emergency Management Division.

Supplemental statistics on the Latter-day Saints Temple at Nauvoo, Illinois, are taken from the church's media website at www.lds.org. To refresh my previous reporting on the Mormon church for the *Wall Street Journal*, I brushed up on some historical facts by reading the official church history on the Latter-day Saints Web site and perusing an excellent online synopsis done by the Public Broadcasting Service in tandem with a 1999 PBS documentary on Joseph Smith called *American Prophet*. Details can be found at www.pbs.org/american prophet.

Mark Twain quotes: Twain's description of Hannibal appeared in his book *Life on the Mississippi* published in 1883. His beer escapades in San Francisco are taken from the seminal Alfred Bigelow Paine book *Mark Twain: a Biography*, published in 1924. His commentary on the New York/Hoboken beer scene came from a collection of letters he penned to a San Francisco newspaper in 1867. It can be found at www.twainquotes.com.

Chapter 9: We Divert West to Sleuth Amongst the Yeast Rustlers

Beyond numerous interviews with beer yeast experts, this chapter relied on a multiplicity of sources: White Labs' "Beginning Yeast Basics" at whitelabs.com; Wyeast's Laboratories' "Yeast Education Info" at www.wyeast.com; BeerAdvocate.com's "Yeast Guide"; RealBeer.com's "Yeast Information and Technical Info"; a *Science Week* article titled "Eilhardt Mitscherlich and the Nature of Crystals" published in 2000; HomeBrewDigest's 1995 online article by Dave Draper called "Culturing Yeast and Using Slants," which can be found at http://hbd.org; the "Beer Judge Certification Exam Yeast Study Guide" at www.bjcp.org; and the Pasteur Institute's online biography of its namesake, Louis Pasteur.

For an excellent survey on the yeast genome project, see the Web site at www.yeastgenome.org (and particularly the link

"Yeast Information for the Non-Specialist"). Information on the Comprehensive Yeast Genome Database can be found at http://mips.gsf.de/genre/proj/yeast/index.jsp, a site maintained by the Munich Information Center for Protein Sequences. I also relied on a helpful short summary of the yeast genome work published by the National Health Museum in 1996 titled "Complete DNA Sequence of Yeast."

Estimates on the number of homebrewers and sales figures for the value of homebrewing in America come from the Association of Brewers.

Chapter 10: Questing Onward

Anheuser-Busch is a publicly traded company; sales, revenue, and market share figures come from official company financial reports. Other corporate details in this chapter come from the company's annual report and other reports posted on its website at www.anheuserbusch.com. Statistics concerning Anheuser-Busch's foreign sales and operations come directly from a 2006 report by its Anheuser-Busch International Inc. unit.

The controversies involving the "100% Share of Mind" program and the battle between Anheuser-Busch and Jim Koch and his Boston Beer Co. over labeling are now stuff of lore in the beer industry, and I rarely had an interview with craft brewers in which both didn't come up. The issue was covered extensively by both the beer trade press and the daily press at the time. To flesh out my background knowledge on the subject, I went back and read numerous archived accounts in, among other publications, the *Wall Street Journal*, *Barron's*, the *Boston Globe*, *Beverage World*, *Adweek*, *All About Beer* magazine, *BrandWeek*, *Celebrator Beer News*, and *Modern Brewery Age*.

Likewise, the continuing legal battle over the use of the Budweiser name in Europe has been covered exhaustively by both the trade and the popular press, including numerous accounts in the *Wall Street Journal*.

I supplemented the annotated history on the founding of Anheuser-Busch provided by my tour guide with details from the history sections of the Anheuser-Busch website. Some technical details regarding the brewery were provided upon request by the Anheuser-Busch press office.

Details of the Soulard neighborhood and its history not gleaned from interviews come from the official city of St. Louis website at http://stlouis.missouri.org/soulard.

Chapter 11: Prowling Among the Beer Suits

Figures on the beer industry's contributions to the U.S. economy come from the previously cited 2003 "Beer Serves America" report published jointly by the Beer Institute and the NBWA and from the Beer Institute's 2002–2003 annual report called "State of the Industry: Industry Growth Accelerates." (Updated figures were from the 2006 reports.)

The NBWA was named the eighth most influential lobby group in America by a May 2001 *Fortune* magazine ranking of the "Washington Power 25."

Rehr's first broadside at MADD over its putative collusion with the liquor industry came in a September 2002 interview with *Modern Brewery Age*, a beer trade magazine. The NBWA's clash with the National Academy of Sciences and George Hacker over the NAS underage drinking report was widely reported in the press; one detailed account appeared in an issue of *Modern Brewery Age*.

Chapter 12: The Quest Takes a Southern Lurch

Details about the 1911 Little Prairie earthquake were taken from the U.S. Geological Survey "Earthquake Hazards Program" website www.usgs.org; supplemental historical information on Caruthersville comes from the Cape Rock Gazetteer at www.caperock.com.

Basic biographical information on Elvis Presley and basic information on touring Graceland and the number of tourists it draws each year comes from www.Elvis.com, the official Presley website.

Chapter 13: Foam Improvement

I interviewed extensively on the rise of homebrewing in America. To fill in the background, I read a number of articles on the subject; a good overview piece is "American Homebrewers: Setting the Pace" by Stan Hieronymus in the archives at www.realbeer .com. Other good resources are the Association of Brewers website at www.beertown.org and the Beer Judge Certification Program at www.bjcp.org.

Chapter 14: On the Road Again

Figures on the impact of casino gambling in Tunica County, Mississippi, come from a variety of sources, including "Tunica Facts," an online Tunica, Mississippi, information guide at www.tunica-ms.com; a 1999 report called "The Effects of Casino Gaming on Tunica County, Mississippi" by James Thomas Snyder of the Social Science Research Center at Mississippi State University; an April 1999 report by the Associated Press; and a July 1999 report by the *Memphis Commercial Appeal*.

Mississippi's beer consumption and ranking information come from the SABMiller report "Beer Is Volume with Profit."

Information on the Mississippi Delta's soil bank is taken from the Delta Blues Museum history link at www.deltablues museum.org; the site also proved a highly useful refresher on the history of the Delta blues and the major figures who created the blues and nurtured its development. At least a portion of the biographical information on the blues artists mentioned in this chapter also comes from the thirty-one profiles on the site. I bolstered interviews about Clarksdale and its history with information gleaned from www.clarksdaletourism.com; another extremely useful site about the Delta and the blues was www.blueshighway.org.

A good source of information on blues legend Robert Johnson, his influence on blues and rock, and a lawsuit over his estate can be found at www.deltahaze.com (a link on the site will let you read in full the Mississippi Supreme Court decision on the matter).

As of this writing, you could hear a clip of Bobbie Gentry singing "Ode to Billie Joe" on the Mississippi Writers and Musicians Project link on the Starkville Mississippi High School website at www.shs.starkville.k12.ms.us.

Chapter 15: A Detour to the Green, Green Fields of Bud

Statistics on the operations of Busch Agricultural Resources Inc. not gleaned from interviews with Anheuser-Busch employees are taken from a 2001 profile on the unit published by Anheuser-Busch. Information on its international beer operations comes from the previously mentioned 2003 report by its Anheuser-Busch International subsidiary.

I interviewed extensively on the history of hops and hops growing in America. I also found valuable production information on the Hops Growers of America website, www.usahops.org, and good overall information, including valuable insights into history, at www.hopunion.com—the website of Hop Union, a private consortium of hops growers headquartered in Washington State. I also drew from an excellent survey article called "Hops: a Brief History" first published in 1990 in the magazine *Zymurgy*, the journal of the American Homebrewers Association.

Chapter 16: A Wrinkle in the Quest

The 1849 essay "The Barmaid" by Albert Smith can be found in full on the website for Victorian London enthusiasts at www.victorianlondon.org. For the section about Beer Goddesses in advertising, I drew on a number of sources, including a fine 2002 overview, with details about the Carling Black Label campaign, by Carl H. Miller in *All About Beer* magazine. (A reprint appears at www.beerhistory.com.) A private website, www .heymabelblacklabel.com, touting itself as an "unofficial Carling Black Label tribute page," also offered interesting details.

The Hooters/EEOC lawsuit generated literally hundreds of stories, including some in the *Wall Street Journal*, which I read to refresh myself on the background. A signed editorial suggesting an EEOC victory in the case would lead to males dancing in the Radio City Rockettes line appeared in the November 18, 1995, edition of the *Atlanta Journal-Constitution*. A full account of the NOW/WAVE sleuthing mission at Hooters can be found at the Rochester chapter of NOW's website, www.rochesternow.org.

Chapter 17: The Final Diversion

The estimate that 40 percent to 50 percent of beer sold within Portland's city limits is craft beer is just that—an estimate—based upon conversations with Portland-area craft brewers, beer enthusiasts, and beer journalists who regularly cover the beer scene there. Many of those believe that number could actually be higher.

Chapter 18: Quest's End

Though Dixie Brewing Co. gets only brief mention in this chapter, the beer is a sentimental favorite of mine. A nice profile of the company, its history, and contemporary marketing efforts appeared in the November 27, 2000, edition of *Modern Brewery Age*.

You can find a more detailed description of Lafitte's Blacksmith Shop and the pirate's association with it on a New Orleans tourism website called atneworleans.com. An interesting overview of Lafitte's life in Louisiana can be found in the archives of www.crimelibrary.com.

A Brief Glossary

The author acknowledges that the following sources and people were invaluable in the formulation of this glossary: beeradvocate .com; beerchurch.com; Michael Jackson's beerhunter.com; Julie Bradford at *All About Beer* magazine; and Sam Calagione at Dogfish Head Craft Brewery.

Acknowledgments

Foremost, to my esteemed *Wall Street Journal* colleague Alix Freedman, who, during a books brainstorming session, first suggested there might be a book in beer and then suggested I might be the person to do it; to Steve Adler, a *Journal* deputy managing editor and head of our books unit, who encouraged me to pursue a proposal and then smoothed the way with various powers that be to make reporting and writing of the book possible; to Bill Rosen and later Fred Hills at Simon & Schuster/Free Press, who worked with me to refine my thinking into the book that *Travels with Barley* would become, and to Fred, especially, for his patience and sage advice all along the way and for his thoughtful, helpful editing of the manuscript; to Paul Stieger, the *Journal*'s managing editor, for his unflagging support of the *Journal*'s books effort in general and my project in particular; and to Rose Ellen D'Angelo and Daniel Nasaw of the WSJ books group, who kept me in the loop during Beer Year (which turned into Beer Year and a Half) and did innumerable favors, small and large, that helped keep the book and me on track. And none of this would have been possible without the wise counsel and eagle eyes of my agents, Tim Seldes of Russell & Volkening and Joe Regal, now of Regal Literary.

Though I am both a writer and an editor, the advice and encouragement of other writers and editors was indispensable in this case. To my pal and former colleague Tony Horwitz, among the masters of literary nonfiction, who convinced me that this book should, at its core, be a journey; and to those who read all or parts of this and gave me invaluable feedback (and who, not to mention, caught my errors, inconsistencies, dangling participles, misplaced modifiers, and typos): Aya Goto of the Words and Music Festival in New Orleans, and my *WSJ* colleagues Steve Adler, Carrie Dolan, Jeffrey Grocott (who is not just a gifted scribe but also a committed Beer Geek), and Elizabeth Seay.

The River of Beer turned out to be an extraordinarily hospitable place. This book required the cooperation and indulgence of scores of people that I met and interviewed across the country. Though I owe them all, a few deserve special attention: Sam Calagione at Dogfish Head Craft Brewery, who abided numerous intrusions into his life and business in my exploration of Extreme Beer, and who generously and promptly answered my incessant technical questions; Daniel Bradford, president of the Brewers' Association of America, who early on indulged incessant e-mail and phone queries; ditto for Jim Koch at Boston Beer Co.; and ditto for Carlos Ramirez at Anheuser-Busch Cos. Jim Massey in Dubuque became a friend overnight and has patiently answered many follow-up queries; Bev Blackwood of the Foam Rangers Homebrew Club in Houston obliged a blizzard of inquiries and helped shape my thinking on key chapters; I'm also indebted to Bev's confederates Jimmy Paige, Steve Moore, and Scott Birdwell—better ambassadors of Beer Geekdom you will not find. I also got great cooperation (and knowledge) from America's chief beer sage Fred Eckhardt in Portland, Oregon. I also owe a special thanks to the inestimable Fritz Maytag of Anchor Brewing Co. in San Francisco, whose candor was invaluable and whose lucid and passionate explication of the marvelous mysteries of beer yeast convinced me that a chapter on yeast was indeed a worthy pursuit. That chapter was ultimately possible because Randy Mosher in Chicago put me in touch with Maribeth Raines-Casselman in California, and Maribeth cleared a goodly chunk of time from her busy schedule to talk yeast with me. I also owe a special reporting debt to SABMiller Brewing Co. Its annual report, "Beer Is Volume with Profit," is as good a compendium of U.S. beer sales statistics and demographics as exists, and many of those stats were invaluable to this enterprise.

The reporting of this book was as much fun as perhaps a writer ought to have. But an entire summer and fall spent locked in an attic office writing, writing, writing, with only the demons of deadline for company, didn't necessarily make me a cheerful or accessible guy. Thus, I'd also like to thank my wife, Lisa, and daughters, Becca and Sara, for their patience, understanding, and encouragement during the long slog to the finish line.

Finally, though I traveled widely in my quest to find the Perfect Beer Joint, I would be remiss in not mentioning the beer joint where I spent a fair amount of pleasurable time plotting the reporting and writing of this book with colleagues (the Cranks, in particular) over a salutary pint or two of Fuller's ESB. So to Foxhounds, an elevator ride and a half-block walk from the office; its genial staff, notably Joe, Joseph, Jessie, Fiona, Mary, and Eddy, simply confirm my reportorial observations that the community of beer is a vibrant and hospitable feature all across the American landscape.

Index

About the Author

Ken Wells, a career journalist and part-time novelist, grew up in a beer-drinking family on the banks of Bayou Black deep in Louisiana's Cajun Delta. He began his writing career as a nineteen-year-old college dropout covering car wrecks and gator sightings for the *Houma Courier*. He left the bayous in 1975 for the University of Missouri School of Journalism, where he earned a master's degree and went on to a feature writing job at the *Miami Herald*. In 1982, his final year at the *Herald*, he was a finalist for the Pulitzer Prize for a series on how a vast flood control system built for powerful agribusiness interests was helping to decimate the Florida Everglades.

Wells joined the *Wall Street Journal* that same year and served stints in its San Francisco and London bureaus before moving to New York in 1993 as a features editor and writer for Page One. He's covered stories as disparate as polygamy in Utah, the Exxon *Valdez* oil spill, South Africa's transition to a multiracial democracy, and the first Persian Gulf War. As a Page One editor, he supervised a small team of reporters who wrote exclusively for the front page on issues such as race, immigration, and the environment. Since the end of Beer Year, Wells has traded in his editor's post on Page One to lend a hand helping to run the *Journal*'s book publishing enterprise.

In his spare time, Wells drinks beer, fishes when he can, dabbles in songwriting, and writes fiction. He is the author of three well-received novels of the Cajun bayous, *Meely LaBauve*, *Junior's Leg*, and *Logan's Storm*. He is also the editor of two anthologies from Wall Street Journal Books, *Floating off the Page: The Best Stories from the* Wall Street Journal's *"Middle Column"* and *Herd on the Street: Animal Stories from the* Wall Street Journal. Wells works in Manhattan and lives with his family under some very large oak trees on the far outskirts of town. You can visit him in his bayou milieu at www.bayoubro.com.